Second Edition

MASTERING EXCEL
A PROBLEM-SOLVING APPROACH

Second Edition

MASTERING EXCEL
A PROBLEM-SOLVING APPROACH

James Gips
Boston College

WILEY

John Wiley & Sons, Inc.

Cover: *Hans Holbein the Younger, Portrait of Erasmus of Rotterdam. Louvre, Paris. Réunion des Musées Nationaux.*

ACQUISITIONS EDITOR	Beth Lang Golub
EDITORIAL ASSISTANT	Lorraina Raccuia
MARKETING MANAGER	Gitti Lindner
SENIOR PRODUCTION EDITOR	Petrina Kulek-Ford
DESIGNER DIRECTOR	Maddy Lesure

This book was set in Times New Roman by James Gips and printed and bound by Malloy Inc. The cover was printed by Brady Palmer Printing Company.

This book is printed on acid free paper. ∞

ISBN   0-471-20323-8

Printed in the United States of America

10 9 8 7 6 5 4 3 2 1

To Amy and Jonathan

PREFACE

Excel is both useful and fun. Millions of people have purchased Excel to run on their personal computers, and many of them use the program every day to solve all kinds of problems. Excel is fun to learn and fun to use. The program is rich and well-designed and has many capabilities. There is a real sense of satisfaction in mastering the fundamentals of the program and then in mastering more and more of its features. As you become increasingly capable with Excel, you can use the program to solve a wider variety of problems and increasingly difficult problems.

The purpose of this book is to help you master Excel.

The book has grown out of my teaching thousands of people to use the computer over the past twenty-five years, both in universities and in industry. I love teaching. I love seeing people walk in knowing little or nothing about the subject and perhaps being a bit fearful, then watching the lights turn on in their minds as they become increasingly capable, and then seeing them leave brimming with confidence in their newly gained abilities.

Over the years I have been fortunate to teach people to use Excel and similar programs many times. I believe I have learned from this process and have been able to refine my presentations—to see what works and what doesn't, to see where people have problems and where they gain valuable insights and skills. I hope this is reflected in this book.

My general approach to teaching Excel is to explain and demonstrate the program at the mouse click and keystroke level, but also at the conceptual level. I like to show how a capability of Excel can be used to solve a problem, and along the way make sure that people understand the basic concept involved. But then, after an hour of listening and watching and asking, it is important for people to try to use that aspect of the program on their own to solve increasingly challenging problems.

This book is structured the same way. In the body of each chapter, we discuss new capabilities of Excel and use them to solve problems. We cover the mouse clicks and keystrokes involved and the concepts that underlie them. We look at the pitfalls and some of the unexpected applications, and I try to answer the questions that I think might arise. At the end of each chapter is a set of exercises. Some of the exercises take you step by step through the mechanics of using Excel. Some of the exercises are paper and pencil exercises that help you ensure that you understand the ideas in the chapter. Some of the exercises simply present you with a problem that can be solved using the capabilities and features just covered. This is where the real learning and integration take place. It is in the exercises, in the problem solving, that the real mastery of Excel develops. An old proverb says, "I hear and I forget, I see and I remember, I do and I understand."

There are versions of Excel for almost all popular machines and operating systems. This Second Edition of *Mastering Excel: A Problem-Solving Approach* is based on Excel XP. The versions of Excel are all quite similar. I hope this book will serve you well whichever computer and operating system you are using.

The book is the successor to *Mastering Lotus 1-2-3: A Problem-Solving Approach*. The books have benefited from the suggestions of many reviewers. I would like to thank Rob Abraham of University of Northern Iowa, Gary Armstrong of Shippensburg University, Chris Clark of British Columbia Institute of Technology, Jim Davies of DeAnza College, Robert P. DeSieno of Skidmore College, Wallace J. Growney of Susquehanna University, Priscilla McGill of Rogue Community College, Farrokh Mamaghani of St. John Fisher College, Marilyn Meyer of Fresno City College, John W. Miller of Pennsylvania College of Technology, Roger Alan Pick of University of Missouri at Kansas City, Jack H. Ryder of Kean College of New Jersey, Pandu Tadikamalla of University of Pittsburgh, James Teng of University of Pittsburgh, and Jane Thorsen of Alma College for their helpful and insightful reviews. (The affiliations are those at the time of review.)

Thanks to Dave Malcolm of British Columbia Institute of Technology for his very helpful suggestions.

Thanks to Harvey Deitel, who during the many lunches we enjoyed when he was a colleague at Boston College greatly encouraged the writing of these books.

Thanks to Michael McFarland, S.J., Howard Straubing, Peter Kugel, Peter Olivieri, Bill Ames, Meghan Jenkins, and Brian Vassallo for allowing me to use exercises they developed. Thanks to other colleagues, students, and seminar participants at Boston College, Harvard University, Arthur D. Little, McGraw-Hill, Chase Manhattan Bank, and Standard & Poor's, where I have taught various parts of this material in courses and seminars.

Thanks to Amy Gips, who took a course that used this book and offered suggestions for improvement, to Kathy Gips for her suggestions for exercises, to Jon Gips for his help with proofreading the first edition, and to Joan and Bill Gips for their encouragement.

Thanks to Beth Golub, Lorraina Raccuia, Maddy Lesure, Petrina Kulek-Ford, Gitti Lindner, and all of the other fine people at John Wiley & Sons, Inc. for their efforts.

I welcome your comments, ideas, and suggestions. The easiest way to reach me is by email at james.gips@bc.edu. Please write!

A brief note about the cover. The cover shows a portrait of Erasmus that was painted by Hans Holbein the Younger in 1523 and is on display in the Louvre Museum in Paris. Erasmus (1466?-1536) was a Dutch priest and scholar. He is said to have been the last person to have mastered all of human knowledge, to know all that was known at his time. All of human knowledge! If Erasmus could master all of human knowledge, surely we can master Excel.

Let's get started!

James Gips

CONTENTS

CHAPTER 1

INTRODUCTION

OBJECTIVES

In this chapter you will learn:

- The major uses of Excel
- The origin of electronic spreadsheets

WHAT IS EXCEL?

Excel is a best-selling computer program published by Microsoft Corporation of Redmond, Washington. The program has been put to a wide variety of uses.

The most important and most common use of the program is as an **electronic spreadsheet**. In an electronic spreadsheet program, the main memory of the computer is divided into rows and columns. The computer is used to perform mainly numeric computations. An example of the use of Excel as an electronic spreadsheet is shown in Figure 1-1. Here, one enters in the Net Sales and different Operating Expenses for each of the quarters. The computer calculates the Year To Date totals in column F, the Total Operating Expenses figures in row 16 and the Operating Income figures in row 18.

Another important use of Excel is for creating **business graphics**. In business graphics the computer draws bar charts, line charts, pie charts, and other types of charts used in business. Excel draws these charts based on numbers in the spreadsheet. For example, the chart in Figure 1-2 was drawn by Excel from the numbers shown in the worksheet in Figure 1-1.

A third use of Excel is for **data management**. In data management the computer is used to deal with large amounts of information. An example is the worksheet in Figure 1-3, which shows the homes for sale in a town.

	A	B	C	D	E	F
1						
2			INCOME STATEMENT			
3			Widgets Unlimited			
4						
5			Q1	Q2	Q3	Q4	YTD
6						
7	Net Sales	$65,400	$68,900	$58,600	$73,445	$266,345
8						
9	Operating Expenses					
10	Payroll	9,120	10,667	10,230	11,878	41,895
11	Utilities	2,133	2,471	2,490	1,751	8,845
12	Rent	1,900	1,900	1,900	1,900	7,600
13	Ads	2,040	2,584	2,176	3,468	10,268
14	COG Sold	24,924	26,014	21,882	30,041	102,861
15						
16	Tot Op Exp	40,117	43,636	38,678	49,038	171,469
17						
18	Operating Income	$25,283	$25,264	$19,922	$24,407	$94,876

Figure 1-1. A typical Excel spreadsheet.

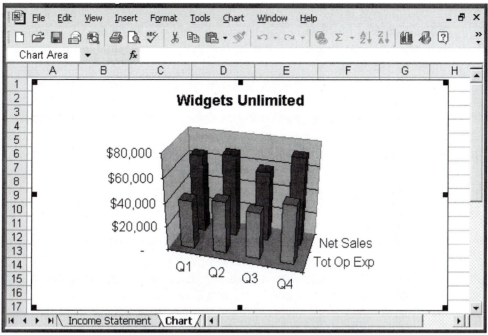

Figure 1-2. A chart drawn from the values in the worksheet in Figure 1-1.

File	Edit	View	Insert	Format	Tools	Data	Window	Help			

D11 ▼ *fx* 0.3

	A	B	C	D	E	F	G
1							
2			CURRENT LISTINGS				
3							
4	ADDRESS	BDRMS	BATHS	LOT	HEAT	AGE	COST
5	12 Elm Street	5	3	0.4	Gas	48	$290,000
6	46 Hearthstone Road	5	2	1.2	Oil	3	$345,000
7	690 Rice Avenue	3	1	0.6	Oil	25	$109,500
8	90 Bay Road	2	1	0.25	Oil	33	$78,400
9	455 Nathan Street	2	1	0.3	Elec	16	$51,300
10	18 Garden Street	2	1	0.4	Elec	12	$62,700
11	203 Somerset Avenue	4	2	0.3	Gas	98	$159,500
12	34 Farley Place	7	4	2.3	Oil	52	$560,000
13	26 Lantern Lane	3	1	0.3	Solar	9	$104,300
14	11 Panama Street	3	1	0.5	Gas	38	$87,900
15	155 Auburn Blvd.	5	2	1.0	Oil	5	$269,600
16	132 Jamaica Way	4	2	0.3	Gas	67	$149,500
17	315 Fremont Avenue	3	1	0.4	Nuclear	8	$432,800
18	1322 Bellevue Road	6	3	0.3	Elec	56	$233,500
19	5 Pond Street	4	3	1.5	Oil	2	$275,400

Listings / Clients / Sheet3 / Sheet4 / Sheet5 /

Figure 1-3. Part of a real estate database in Excel.

In the real estate worksheet, each row corresponds to a different home for sale. Excel could be instructed to find all the homes with more than 3 bedrooms that have oil heat. Or, the program could be instructed to rearrange the rows so they are in order by the price.

The most common use of Excel is as an electronic spreadsheet. While we certainly cover how to use Excel to create charts and to manage data, we will spend most of our time on the many uses of Excel as an electronic spreadsheet program for solving a wide variety of problems.

A LITTLE HISTORY

In the bad old days of computers, before the advent of personal computers and electronic spreadsheets, people who wanted to use the computer to solve some numerical or financial problem usually had to write a special-purpose computer program in a language like BASIC or Fortran. It is much easier to create a spreadsheet in Excel to solve a problem than it is to write a computer program. A problem that requires 1 hour to solve using a spreadsheet program like Excel might require 10 hours or more to solve by writing a program.

The idea of an electronic spreadsheet was invented by Dan Bricklin when he was an MBA student at the Harvard Business School.

> Sitting there in the spring of 1978, I came up with the idea of the electronic spreadsheet. With all those other classmates to contend with the professor, there's lots of time for daydreaming, especially if you sit in the front row and the professor looks out above you. I invariably made simple addition mistakes in my homework. I wanted to do what the professor did on his blackboard: he would erase one number and Louis in the back of the room would give him all the calculations that he had done all night to recalculate everything. I wanted to keep the calculations and just erase one number on my paper and have everything recalculated. (Dan Bricklin, "VisiCalc and Software Arts: Genesis to Exodus," *The Computer Museum Report*, Summer 1986, p. 8.)

Dan Bricklin and a friend, Bob Frankston, wrote the first electronic spreadsheet program, for the Apple II, and called it VisiCalc ("Visible Calculator"). VisiCalc was published by a small company, Personal Software, in 1979. VisiCalc became wildly popular, the best-selling computer software of its day. Personal Software changed its name to VisiCorp and brought out related software, including VisiPlot and VisiTrend, which were written by Mitch Kapor.

Mitch Kapor became a product manager for the company, but then left to form a company called Lotus Development. Lotus brought out the program 1-2-3 for the IBM PC in 1983. The developers of VisiCalc thought that the Apple III, the ill-fated successor to the very popular Apple II, was the computer of the future and targeted their advanced version of VisiCalc for the Apple III. Bricklin and Frankston also became involved in a messy lawsuit with VisiCorp. Lotus concentrated on the IBM Personal Computer from the beginning. Lotus 1-2-3 became the best-selling applications program of its time. Later, Lotus bought out the rights to VisiCalc, which is published no more.

The arch rival of Lotus Development in the personal computer software market was Microsoft Corporation. Microsoft was best known for developing MS-DOS, the original Disk Operating System of the IBM Personal Computer and compatibles. Lotus 1-2-3 was the most popular spreadsheet program for DOS machines. Microsoft introduced a spreadsheet program called Multiplan to compete with Lotus 1-2-3. Multiplan evolved into Excel. When Microsoft switched over from DOS to Windows, Lotus was slow to update 1-2-3. Microsoft took advantage of the situation to make Excel the most popular spreadsheet program for the Windows market. With the introduction of new versions of Windows, the dominance of Excel accelerated. Lotus Development was bought out by IBM in 1995. Microsoft Excel has captured the vast majority of the spreadsheet market. Microsoft brings out new versions of Excel every year or two.

Excel is the third spreadsheet program to dominate the market. VisiCalc dominated the Apple II market. Lotus 1-2-3 dominated the MS-DOS market. Excel dominates the Windows and Macintosh markets.

All spreadsheet programs are reasonably similar. All are elaborations on Dan Bricklin's original idea. Once you learn Excel it is straightforward to learn to use any spreadsheet program.

WHAT IS MICROSOFT OFFICE?

Microsoft Office is a **suite** of programs brought out by Microsoft and sold together as one package. The Microsoft Office package includes Excel, Microsoft Word (a word-processing program), Microsoft PowerPoint (a presentation program), Microsoft Outlook (an email and calendar program), and perhaps Microsoft Access (a database program) and Microsoft FrontPage (a website development program), depending on which edition of Office you purchase. The exact combinations in the packages vary over time. (See www.microsoft.com/office.) The idea is that the programs work together as a coordinated unit so that it is easy to create a spreadsheet in Excel, use it in a report created in Word and in a presentation created in PowerPoint.

WHY LEARN TO USE EXCEL?

Excel is widely used for many problems. Many of its most devoted users work with financial and accounting problems, including budgets, cash flow projections, sales reports, balance sheets, and expense accounts.

Some of these applications tabulate past results. For example, we were budgeted to spend so much in each of these different categories. So far this year we have spent this much in each of these areas. How much is left in our budget?

Other applications look to the future. We hope to sell so many copies of this proposed product at such and such a price. Our expenses for the product are expected to be so much. How much money will we earn? What if certain expenses are 25% more than expected, how will this affect our profits? What if we sell only so many copies? What if we lower our price and increase our advertising budget? This is known as using Excel to perform "**What if**" analysis. "What if" analysis is an area where spreadsheet programs excel. Indeed, if you look back at the quote from Dan Bricklin, the inventor of electronic spreadsheets, "What if" analysis is the specific type of application for which electronic spreadsheets were developed.

As the years have gone by, computers have become more and more powerful in their hardware so they support more and more powerful software. With each new version of Excel new features are added. Excel has become a powerful tool for statistical analysis, for operations research, for management science, for engineering and scientific calculations. Excel is used for non-numerical problems as well. It is used for alphabetizing lists, for drawing charts, and for looking at databases. Excel is used in marketing research, in sales analysis, and in human resource management.

A good working knowledge of Excel is a requirement for many professional positions. Many a student has obtained a good summer job just on the basis of expertise with Excel.

Learning Excel is an important skill you will be able to use for the rest of your life. I hope you soon will see why.

CHAPTER 2

CREATING SIMPLE WORKSHEETS

OBJECTIVES

In this chapter you will learn how to:

- Enter information into an Excel worksheet
- Move to different cells of the worksheet
- Correct typing errors
- Create and evaluate formulas
- Create simple worksheets
- Save your work on the disk
- Print your work

THE BASIC IDEA

A simple Excel **worksheet** is shown in Figure 2-1. This worksheet was set up to give price quotes for potential customers. There are three products: widgets, grommits, and connectors. Widgets cost $1.19 each. Grommits cost $2.49 each. Connectors cost $0.69 each. A 6% sales tax is added to each order.

In Excel, the complete document or file you are working on is called a **workbook**. Each workbook contains various worksheets. Think of the workbook as being the electronic equivalent of a three-ring binder and the worksheets as being electronic sheets of paper.

Each worksheet is divided into **columns** and **rows**. The columns have letter names (A, B, C, ...). The rows have numbers for names (1, 2, 3, ...). The intersection of each row and column is called a **cell**. Each cell has a name. Cell E7 is in column E and row 7. That is, the name of each cell is the letter name of its column followed by the number name of its row.

Each cell can be **blank** or it can contain **text**, a **number**, or a **formula**. Text can be a word or phrase. Cells F4 and B7 in the worksheet in Figure 2-1 contain text. Cells D6 and E7 contain numbers.

The key to electronic spreadsheets is the formulas. Cells in column F in the worksheet in Figure 2-1 contain formulas.

The formula in cell F6 is

	A	B	C	D	E	F	G	H	I
1									
2		Price Quote							
3					Unit				
4		Product		Quantity	Price	Total			
5									
6		Widgets		100	$1.19	$119.00			
7		Grommits		50	$2.49	$124.50			
8		Connectors		200	$0.69	$138.00			
9									
10		Amount Before Tax				$381.50			
11									
12		Sales Tax				$22.89			
13									
14		Total Amount				$404.39			
15									

Figure 2-1. A simple worksheet for giving price quotes.

$$=D6*E6$$

The initial equal sign indicates that this is a formula. In Excel, the asterisk means multiplication. This formula tells Excel that the number displayed in cell F6 is the number in cell D6 multiplied by the number in cell E6. The formula has been typed into the cell, but the computer normally displays the result of evaluating the formula in the cell. That is, the computer displays 119.00, the result of the multiplication, in the cell.

The formulas in the worksheet are shown in Figure 2-2. Here the actual formulas are displayed in the cells, rather than the values that result from calculating the formulas. The formula in cell F7 is

$$=D7*E7$$

so the value in cell F7 is the result of multiplying the number in D7 times the number in E7. Similarly, the formula in cell F8 is

$$=D8*E8$$

Cell F10 contains the total for the order before sales tax. This value is calculated by

	A	B	C	D	E	F	G
1							
2		Price Quote					
3					Unit		
4		Product		Quantity	Price	Total	
5							
6		Widgets		100	1.19	=D6*E6	
7		Grommits		50	2.49	=D7*E7	
8		Connectors		200	0.69	=D8*E8	
9							
10		Amount Before Tax				=F6+F7+F8	
11							
12		Sales Tax				=F10*6%	
13							
14		Total Amount				=F10+F12	
15							

Figure 2-2. The Price Quote worksheet with the underlying formulas displayed rather than the values that result from evaluating the formulas

the computer by adding the values in F6, F7, and F8. The formula is

$$=F6+F7+F8$$

The Sales Tax is 6% of the Amount Before Tax. The formula for the sales tax in cell F12 is

$$=F10*6\%$$

Finally, the Total Amount is the sum of the Amount Before Tax and the Sales Tax. This formula, in cell F14, is

$$=F10+F12$$

SO WHAT?

Here we have a lot of money for a computer and the Excel software. Plus we have to take the time to learn to use the computer and Excel. Wouldn't it just be easier and faster to do this by hand? You could do the same "worksheet" with paper and pencil. For $10 you could buy a calculator to do the arithmetic. Why bother with a computer?

In using a computer the benefit usually is not in the first time you perform some action. The benefit is in the repetition, especially in the ability to make changes. The major benefit of using a word-processing program is in the ability to make changes or revisions without retyping the entire manuscript. Similarly, the payoff of an Excel worksheet is in the third or the tenth or the hundredth time you use the worksheet.

What happens with our price quote worksheet? The potential customer says, "Oh, no. I don't want 50 grommits. I want 150 grommits." If you are using paper and pencil, you must erase the numbers in F7, F10, F12, and F14 and then recalculate the new amounts. The next person you speak with has new quantities to order. You would have to do the calculations all over again for that person's order. If you give out hundreds of price quotes each day, you would have to redo the calculations hundreds of times.

Watch what happens on the computer. We change the number in cell D7 from 50 to 150. The formulas in cells F7, F10, F12, and F14 are recalculated automatically by the computer and the results of these calculations appear automatically in the cells. (See Figure 2-3.) Similarly, we change the price for widgets from $1.19 to $0.98 by changing the number in cell E6 from $1.19 to $0.98. As soon as we make the change, the formulas in cells F6, F10, F12, and F14 would be recalculated automatically by Excel.

	A	B	C	D	E	F	G	H	I
1									
2		Price Quote							
3					Unit				
4		Product		Quantity	Price	Total			
5									
6		Widgets		100	$1.19	$119.00			
7		Grommits		150	$2.49	$373.50			
8		Connectors		200	$0.69	$138.00			
9									
10		Amount Before Tax				$630.50			
11									
12		Sales Tax				$37.83			
13									
14		Total Amount				$668.33			
15									

Cell reference: D7 = 150

Sheets: Sheet1 / Sheet2 / Sheet3

Figure 2-3. When we change the number in D7 from 50 to 150, the formulas in F7, F10, F12, and F14 automatically are recalculated.

The key to Excel is in the automatic recalculation of the formulas. Text, numbers, and formulas are entered into the worksheet. Whenever any number is changed, the relevant formulas are recalculated by the computer automatically. The speed of the computer allows the recalculation to be done almost instantaneously.

An Excel worksheet has been described as an electronic piece of paper with a built-in pencil, eraser, and calculator. You enter the labels, numbers, and formulas into the worksheet. The computer performs all of the calculations automatically. Change one cell and the computer automatically recalculates the formulas.

As we proceed you will learn how to create larger and more complicated worksheets, involving thousands of calculations. Excel also provides us with a straightforward way of organizing and solving complicated problems.

Now we will take a look at the process of actually using Excel on the computer.

GETTING STARTED WITH EXCEL

Excel

We start up Excel just as we would any other program, by double clicking on the Excel icon on the desktop or by finding *Microsoft Excel* under *Programs* in the Windows *Start* menu. This copies Excel from the disk into the primary memory of the computer. The computer begins to run the program. The initial screen displayed depends somewhat on what was specified by recent users.

Figure 2-4. When you start up Excel you might see the Task Pane to the right of the worksheet.

Sometimes when you start up Excel, you see the New Workbook Task Pane as in Figure 2-4. Task Panes give you the opportunity to select common tasks. To hide the Task Pane click the "X" button at the top right of the Task Pane. You can restore the Task Pane by selecting *Task Pane* in the *View* pull-down menu.

From hereon we will keep the Task Pane closed. A new blank workbook is shown in Figure 2-5. The various elements of the Excel window are indicated in the figure.

Working our way down from the top, we see the **Title bar**. The Title bar tells us we are working in Excel and gives us the name of the active workbook. The current workbook we are working on is called "Book1". When we save the workbook on the disk we will give it a more descriptive name.

Below the Title Bar is the **Menu bar**. The Menu bar contains **pull-down menus**. The pull-down menus allow us to issue various commands to Excel to perform different functions. For example, to save the current workbook on the disk we could select the *File* pull-down menu and then select *Save* within the menu.

Below the Menu bar is a **toolbar**. A toolbar contains various buttons that are an alternative way to issue common commands to Excel. For example, the third tool button in from the left in the toolbar in Figure 2-5 shows a picture of a disk. This is the **Save button**. Clicking on this button is the same as selecting *Save* from the *File* pull-down menu.

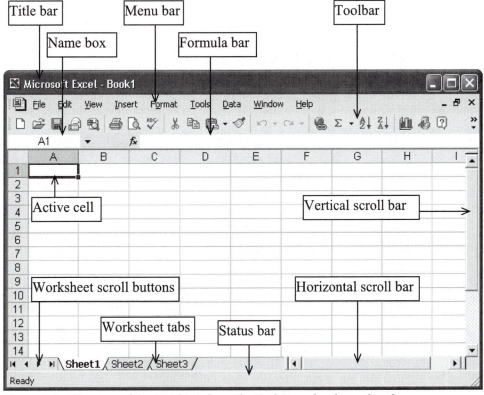

Figure 2-5. Elements of the Excel window. The Task Pane has been closed.

The toolbar that is shown in Figure 2-5 is called the **Standard toolbar**. Over a dozen different toolbars are available in Excel. As many toolbars can be visible as you would like. You control which toolbars are displayed on your screen by selecting *Toolbars...* in the *View* pull-down menu.

More than one toolbar can be visible. When you start up Excel there might be no toolbars showing. There might be one toolbar showing. There might be two or more toolbars showing. You can control which toolbars are visible on your screen by selecting *Toolbars...* in the *View* pull-down menu.

Below the toolbar is the **Name box** and **Formula bar**. The Name box tells you which cell is active right now. Note that in Figure 2-5 the Name box contains "A1" and that cell A1 has a black box around it. If you start typing, the information will go into cell A1. Cell A1 is the **active cell**. The information that you type will appear in the Formula bar, which shows you the contents of the current active cell.

Below the Name box and Formula bar is the current worksheet itself. We start out with all of the cells in the worksheet being blank.

Below the worksheet are the **Worksheet scroll buttons** and the **Worksheet tabs**. The sheet tab in bold with a white background is "Sheet1". This is the name of the currently active worksheet. We are working on Sheet1. A workbook contains multiple worksheets. If we want to work on Sheet2, we would click on the sheet tab that says "Sheet2". We will discuss using the Worksheet scroll buttons and creating workbooks with multiple worksheets in Chapter 8.

At the bottom of the screen is the **Status bar**. The Status bar usually indicates the current status of the program. If the status bar says Ready or Enter then the program is ready for us to issue commands or enter information. The Status bar also indicates the status of various keys on the keyboard. For example Caps indicates the Caps Lock is on. Many people hide the Status bar when they are working in Excel to allow more room for the worksheet itself. To hide or show the Status bar, select *Status Bar* in the *View* pull-down menu. The Status bar and Title bar are not shown in most figures in this book.

CHANGING WHICH CELL IS ACTIVE

When we start up Excel, cell A1 is the active cell. Cell A1 is the cell in the top left of the worksheet. If we want to enter information into cell A1, we simply type the information and then press the Enter key.

If we want to enter information into another cell, we need to change it to the active cell. There are two basic ways to do this. First, we can use the mouse to point to the new cell and then click the (left) button. Alternatively, we can use the **arrow keys** on the keyboard to move the active cell in any direction.

What happens if the cursor is in the bottom row on the screen, for example in row 14 in the worksheet in Figure 2-5, and you press the down arrow? The active cell moves to row 15. The screen displays rows 2 through 15. Row 1 moves off the top of the screen. This is called **scrolling**.

THE SIZE OF THE WORKSHEET

The screen actually is a window onto a much larger worksheet. When you start up Excel you might see 12 columns (A through L) and perhaps 25 rows (1 through 25). The exact number of columns and rows will depend on the version of Excel you are using, the size of your monitor, the size of your window, what toolbars are displayed, and other factors. Each Excel XP worksheet contains 256 columns and 65,536 rows! The columns are named A through Z and then AA through AZ and then BA through BZ and so on until IV. The rows are named 1 through 65536. Some quick calculations show that in order to display all of the cells in the worksheet at the same size they usually appear would require a screen 20 feet wide and 1500 feet high! Your computer screen would need to be as high as the tallest building in the world to display the entire worksheet!

CHANGING THE PORTION OF THE WORKSHEET IN THE SCREEN

The screen is best thought of as a window that displays a small portion of the entire worksheet. You can change the portion of the worksheet that is displayed in the screen in several ways. You can use the **vertical scroll bar** to the right of the worksheet and the **horizontal scroll bar** at the bottom right of the worksheet, for example by clicking on the arrows on the screen or by moving the slider. You can use the arrow keys on the keyboard to move the active cell on the screen, thereby forcing the worksheet to scroll. To move the active cell to any cell in the worksheet, you can just type the address of the cell in the Name box at the top left of the screen (see Figure 2-5) and press the Enter key.

ENTERING INFORMATION INTO CELLS

Suppose we want to enter the Price Quote worksheet in Figure 2-1 into the computer. We start with a blank worksheet, move the cursor to cell B2, and type the text Price Quote. Notice that the text appears both in the cell and in the formula bar at the top of the screen (Figure 2-6). Notice also that buttons with a red X and a green check mark appear to the left of the formula bar when you begin typing.

Figure 2-6. Entering text into a cell.

Once we have typed in Price Quote we either press the Enter key on the keyboard or click on the **Enter button** (the green check mark). The text is "entered" into the cell.

We move the active cell down to cell B4 using the down arrow or by clicking on B4. Type the word Product, and so on.

How does Excel know which cells contain formulas and which contain text or numbers? The program looks at the first keystroke, at the first character that we type into a cell. If the first character in a cell is an equal sign (=) then the cell contains a formula. If the first entry in the cell is just about any other character then the cell does not contain a formula. If the cell contains a formula, Excel displays the result of evaluating that formula in the cell.

This is an important point, a common source of error. Begin each formula with an equal sign. If you begin a cell entry with a letter or a space, rather than an equal sign, the cell actually will contain text rather than a formula to be evaluated. If you type C7*D7 into a cell the computer will take this to be the text C7*D7 rather than a formula because it begins with a C, a letter. The computer will not evaluate the formula. Rather it simply will display C7*D7 in the cell as text.

CORRECTING TYPING ERRORS

It is common to make typing errors. The best way to correct a typing error depends on when the error is discovered.

If you realize that you have made a mistake before what you have typed has been entered into the cell, then you can correct the error by pressing the **Backspace key**. The Backspace key is located on the top right of the typewriter portion of the keyboard and often is indicated with a long left arrow. The Backspace key erases the most recently typed character.

You can instruct Excel to ignore all your current typing into the cell and return the cell to its previous contents (perhaps, blank) by clicking on the **Cancel button**, the button with a red X that appears between the Name box and the Formula bar. Pressing the **Esc key** ("Escape" key) is equivalent to pressing the Cancel button.

Again, if you click on the Enter button, to the right of the Cancel button, the text will be accepted and entered into the cell.

If you realize that you have made a mistake in text or a formula or a number that already has been entered into a cell, simply make the cell active and correct the entry either in the Formula bar or in the entry in the cell itself.

To erase an existing entry in a cell, make the cell active and then press the **Delete key** or **Del key** on the keyboard or select *Clear* in the *Edit* pull-down menu.

It is a common mistake to try to erase a cell by typing a space in the cell. It looks as if the cell is erased but really the cell contains text, namely a space. This can have subtle but unfortunate consequences.

UNDO AND REDO

Have you ever done or said something and wished immediately that you could undo it or take it back? Excel provides that opportunity.

 The button with an arrow that curves counterclockwise is the **Undo button**. Clicking on this button will cause the most recent action taken to be undone. This could be a cell entry or a command issued through a tool button or pull-down menu. You can click on the Undo button several times to undo several of the most recent actions.

An alternative to clicking on the Undo button is to select *Undo* in the *Edit* pull-down menu.

 If you undo an action and are sorry, you can press the **Redo button** and Excel will redo the action.

SIMPLE FORMULAS

The key part of Excel is the formulas. As discussed previously, formulas begin with an equal sign.

Examples of formulas include

$$= 3+4*5$$

$$= C4 / 5 + 7$$

$$= (D3+G5) * (H7 - (5+D6) / 8)$$

Formulas can contain numbers, cell addresses (like C4 or H7), arithmetic operators, and parentheses.

The arithmetic operators include

+	addition
-	negation or subtraction
*	multiplication
/	division
%	percent (placed after a value, as in 25%)
^	exponentiation

The minus sign can be used in two ways, as the negation of a single value (-3) and as the subtraction of one number from another (6-4).

The percent operator causes the number to the left of the percent sign to be divided by 100.

The exponentiation operator raises a number to a power. For example, 2^3 means 2^3, which is 8. As another example, 64^0.5 means $64^{0.5}$. This calculates the square root of 64, which is 8.

EVALUATING FORMULAS

What would be the result of evaluating the formula =3+4*5? Is it 35? Is it 23? The correct answer depends on whether the computer performs the addition first or the multiplication first, on the **order of precedence** of the arithmetic operators. Generally, multiplication is done before addition. Thus, the value of the formula =3+4*5 would be 23. If we want the addition to be performed first, we would type =(3+4)*5. The parentheses tell the computer to perform the operation inside, in this case the addition, first. The value of =(3+4)*5 would be 35.

What would be the value of the formula =6-5-1? Is it 0? Is it 2? The correct answer depends on which subtraction the computer performs first. That is, it depends on whether =6-5-1 is the same as =(6-5)-1 or whether it is the same as =6-(5-1). Excel performs the left subtraction before the right subtraction so to the computer =6-5-1 is the same as =(6-5)-1, which evaluates to 0.

Here are the general rules that Excel follows when evaluating simple formulas:

1. Evaluate anything in parentheses first.

2. Evaluate the arithmetic operators in the following order:
    (a) negation (as in -7)
    (b) percent
    (c) exponentiation
    (d) multiplication or division
    (e) addition or subtraction

3. In case of tie, evaluate the operators from left to right.

YOU TRY EVALUATING A FORMULA

What would be the result of evaluating the formula

=23+((5+9)*3)/7-5

This problem uses each of the three general rules above. Try it before reading further. Write down your answer.

The computer first would add 5+9 to get 14. Then it would multiply the 14 times 3, which is 42. It would divide the 42 by 7 to get 6. Then it would add 23 and 6 to obtain 29. Finally it would take the 29 and subtract 5 to obtain the final answer of 24.

USING CELL ADDRESSES IN FORMULAS

Consider again the Price Quote worksheet in Figure 2-1. Suppose that in cell F6 instead of the formula =D6*E6 we put =100*1.19. (See Figure 2-7.) Would this formula work? It might first appear that this new formula works fine. After all, the result of evaluating this new formula would be the same as evaluating the original formula, namely 119. But, what would happen if we then changed the number in cell D6 from 100 to 300? The result of evaluating the original formula would change accordingly. But the result of evaluating the new formula =100*1.19 would not change at all, since the new formula does not refer to the numbers in the cells. It is very important that you use cell addresses in your formulas rather than the numbers that (now) are in the cells.

	A	B	C	D	E	F	G	H	I
1									
2		Price Quote							
3					Unit				
4		Product		Quantity	Price	Total			
5									
6		Widgets		100	$1.19	$119.00			
7		Grommits		50	$2.49	$124.50			
8		Connectors		200	$0.69	$138.00			
9									
10		Amount Before Tax				$381.50			
11									
12		Sales Tax				$22.89			
13									
14		Total Amount				$404.39			

Figure 2-7. A common mistake is to put the current values in formulas instead of the cell addresses. It looks as if this formula works, but if the value in D6 is changed, the value in F6 will not change accordingly.

SAVING THE WORKBOOK

When you enter information into a worksheet on the screen, the information is saved in the primary memory (also called RAM or Random Access Memory) of the computer. The primary memory is temporary, working memory. If you lose electric power or if Excel quits on you unexpectedly or if you turn off the computer then the information that is in primary memory will be erased. In order for the computer to remember a workbook from one session to the next, the workbook must be saved on disk. It is your responsibility to save the workbook on disk. It is advisable to save your work on the disk early and often.

The easiest way to instruct Excel to save your current workbook is to click on the **Save button**, usually the third button from the left of the standard toolbar, the button with a picture of a diskette. Alternatively, you can select *Save* in the *File* pull-down menu.

The first time you save a workbook you will be asked to fill in a file name and to select the disk and directory in which the workbook should be saved. File names are discussed in the next section.

The basic unit in Excel is the workbook. A workbook contains multiple worksheets. Thus far we have been working only with the first sheet, "Sheet1", of the workbook. When you click on the Save button or select *Save* in the *File* pull-down menu, Excel always saves the entire workbook on the disk, even though you may have used only a single sheet.

It is surprisingly easy and commonplace to lose files that are saved on disks. Removable diskettes can be misplaced or fall in a puddle. Hard disks can "crash". Files can be erased by mistake. I strongly advise you to buy an extra diskette or CD or two and routinely keep at least two disk copies of all of your work. Diskettes and blank CDs are very inexpensive. The $1 for an extra diskette or CD and the extra 20 seconds to save a second copy are an exceedingly good investment. Personally, I have been burned enough times that I will not leave the computer without having copies of my work on at least two disks. Forewarned is forearmed. To save the file a second time on a different disk or under a different file name, select *Save As...* in the *File* pull-down menu.

THE NAME OF THE WORKBOOK

In the process of saving a workbook for the first time you are asked to provide a name for the workbook. Excel provides an initial name like Book1, but it is better to change it to a name that will remind you of the contents of the workbook. If you are working on the first quarter sales report, a name like SalesQ1 is better than a name like Mary or John, even if you can't get Mary or John out of your mind.

File names can be up to 255 characters in length. You are not allowed to include various punctuation marks (/ ? : * " < > !) in the file names. Excel files have an extension, a last name, of .XLS, which indicates to the computer that it is an Excel workbook.

The name of the current workbook appears in the Title bar at the top of the window. (See Figure 2-5.)

The easiest way to change the name of the workbook is to select *Save As...* in the *File* pull-down menu, enter in the new name, and then save the workbook on the disk using that name. The new name will be retained for the current workbook.

PRINTING THE WORKSHEET

The simplest way to print the current worksheet is to click on the **Print button** in the Standard toolbar. The Print button has a picture of a printer.

Alternatively, you can select *Print...* in the *File* pull-down menu. On occasion computers have been known to hang up or freeze during printing, so always save your workbook on the disk before printing.

If you would like to see what will be printed before it actually is sent to the printer, click on the **Print Preview button**, which shows a picture of a magnifying glass over a sheet. The Print Preview button usually is just right of the Print button.

Alternatively, select *Print Preview* in the *File* pull-down menu.

Printing will be covered in greater detail in Chapter 7.

CLOSING THE WORKBOOK AND STARTING A NEW ONE

Suppose you just have completed one of the computer exercises that follow. You have constructed a worksheet, tested it, saved it, and printed it. Now you would like to start over on a new exercise. To do this you can select *Close* in the *File* pull-down menu. This closes the workbook you are working on. ("Close" means the workbook is erased from the primary memory of the computer and from the screen.) If you have not yet saved the workbook before closing it, the computer will ask you if you wish to save your work on the disk before it vanishes.

To start up a new workbook select *New...* from the *File* pull-down menu. Or, you can click on the **New Workbook button**. This button has a picture of a blank worksheet on it and usually is the leftmost button in the Standard toolbar.

If you would like, you can have two or more different workbooks open at once in different windows of your screen.

To resume work on a workbook previously saved on the disk, select *Open...* from the *File* pull-down menu. Alternatively, if you have worked on the document recently on this computer it might appear toward the bottom of the *File* pull-down menu, where you can select it directly.

EXITING FROM EXCEL

To exit from Excel, simply select *Exit* from the *File* pull-down menu. You will be asked if you would like to save any unsaved workbooks that you have been working on. Alternatively, you can click the **Close button** at the top right of the Excel window, in the rightmost part of the Title bar.

PAPER AND PENCIL EXERCISES

2-1. Consider the following worksheet:

	A	B	C	D	E	F	G	H
1								
2		Exercise 2-1						
3								
4	86	-4	-8	fun				
5	-47	5	26	37				
6	2.3	7	Excel	198				
7	computer	18	4.6	3				
8	56	102		-19				
9								

What would be the result of evaluating each of the following formulas? Write out your answers on paper. Do not use the computer.

(a) =B7+1

(b) =B6+2*D7

(c) =C4*(D7+B4)-6*C5+A8

(d) =C4*25%-3-B4

(e) =256/C4/2/B4

(f) =B5^2+B4^3

(g) =-B6-B4*-B3*2/C4+B5^D7-1

2-2.   Salespeople earn a base salary of $10,000 per year plus a commission of 4% of sales. The following worksheet has been created for our four salespeople. Columns E and G and row 11 contain formulas.

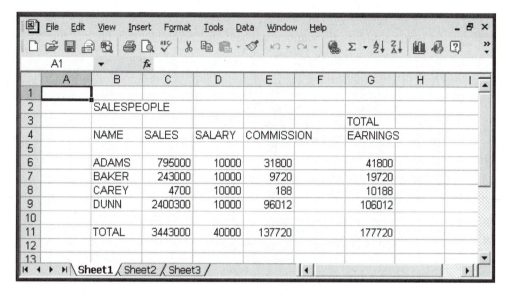

(a) Cell E6 gives Adams' Commission. What is the formula in E6?

(b) Cell E7 gives Baker's Commission. What is the formula in E7?

(c) Cell G7 gives Baker's Total Earnings. What is the formula in G7?

(d) Cell E11 gives the Total Commission. What is the formula in E11?

(e) Cell G11 gives the Grand Total of the Earnings. What is the formula in G11?

(f) Give an alternative formula for G11.

COMPUTER EXERCISES

2-3.   Start up Excel. You should see a blank Excel worksheet.

(a) Use the arrow keys to move the active cell right and left and down and up.
    Use the mouse to move the active cell.
    Move the active cell to F12.

Move the active cell to K23.

(b) Use the arrows, scroll bars, and mouse, or the Name bar to return to A1.

(c) Enter your name in cell D4.
Type Exercise 2-3 in cell D5.
(You should type your name and the exercise number at the top of each worksheet you do for homework.)

(d) Type the number 140 in cell B2.
Type the number 233 in cell B3.
Type the formula =B2+B3 in cell B5.
(The number 373 should appear now in B5.)

(e) Change the number in cell B2 to 56.
(The total in B5 should change automatically to 289.)

(f) Change the number in cell B3 to 375.6.
(The total in B5 should change again.)

(g) Save the workbook on your disk.

(h) Print the worksheet.

(i) Close the workbook.

2-4. Put your name in cell G2. Put Exercise 2-4 in cell G3.

(a) Enter the worksheet at the top of the next page exactly as shown. When you enter the formulas into cells D9, D13, and D17 the results of evaluating the formulas should show in the cells.

(b) Change the number in D6 to 31.
(The numbers in D19, D13, and D17 should change automatically.)

(c) Change the number in D11 to 43.
(The numbers in D13 and D17 should change.)

(d) Save, print, and close the workbook.

2-5. Enter the worksheet of Exercise 2-2 into the computer. Remember that columns E and G and row 11 contain formulas. Change Carey's Sales to 615,000. Do all the other numbers change appropriately?

2-6. Create a well-labeled worksheet that allows you to enter two numbers: the number of feet (for example, 6) and inches (for example, 2) in a person's height. The worksheet then should calculate the person's height in centimeters. Try your worksheet on the following heights: 5 feet 3 inches, 6 feet 2 inches, 7 feet 4.5 inches. One inch equals 2.54 centimeters.

2-7. Create a worksheet to convert a temperature from Fahrenheit to Celsius. The formula is $C = 5/9\ (F - 32)$. Try your worksheet on temperatures of 0 degrees Fahrenheit, 32 degrees, and 85 degrees.

2-8. Create a well-labeled worksheet that allows you to enter a person's weight in kilograms and height in centimeters and calculates the person's weight in pounds and height in inches.

2-9. The cash drawer at the local market has room for $20 bills, $10 bills, $5 bills, $1 bills, quarters, dimes, nickels, and pennies. Create a worksheet that allows a person to enter in how many of each type of bills and coins are in the cash drawer and calculates the total value of the money in the drawer. So for example if the drawer contains two $5 bills and three quarters, there would be $10.75 in the drawer.

2-10. At Louis' Discount Furniture Store, Louis, the owner, marks furniture at twice his wholesale cost plus $80. If you bargain with him, he'll drop the price as much as 15%. Create a worksheet that allows you to enter the wholesale cost and calculates the list price and the best discount price. Try your worksheet with a sofa that wholesales for $550 and then for a table that wholesales for $200.

2-11. When a star runs out of nuclear fuel, it may collapse into a black hole if its radius becomes small enough, below the event horizon so no light escapes. The event horizon depends on the mass of the star and is given by the formula

$$R = 2\, G\, M\, /\, c^2$$

where G is Newton's constant, M is the mass of the star, c is the speed of light, and R is the radius of the event horizon.

(a) Create a worksheet that allows you to enter the mass of a star in kilograms and determines the radius of its event horizon in kilometers. What would be the maximum radius of a black hole for a star with the same mass as our Sun?

(b) A black hole does emit some radiation. The "temperature" of a black hole depends only on its mass and is given by the formula

$$T = \hbar\, c^3\, /\, 8\, \pi\, k\, G\, M$$

where $\hbar$ is Planck's constant and k is Boltzmann's constant. Add to your worksheet a calculation of the apparent temperature of the black hole. What would be the apparent temperature of a black hole with the mass of the Sun?

2-12. Create a currency conversion worksheet. At the top of the worksheet put in the current conversions from dollars to euros and from dollars to yen in separate well-labeled cells. You should obtain these values off the web or from today's newspaper. Below that, your worksheet should have three parts. The first part should allow you to enter in a price in dollars and obtain the equivalent values in euros and yen. The second part should allow you to convert from euros to dollars and yen. The third part should allow you to convert from yen to dollars and euros. Try your worksheet on $29.98, €507, and ¥5,640,000.

2-13. People in cold climates often are concerned about the wind chill factor. People say, "Well it's 20 degrees out but because of the wind it feels like -5 degrees." The National Weather Service recently revised its formula for calculating the wind chill factor based on a year-long study involving volunteers with sensors on their faces doing 90-minute stints on a treadmill in a controlled climate chamber. The new official formula for calculating the wind chill factor from the National Weather Service is

$$W = 35.74 + 0.6215\,T - 35.75\,(V^{0.16}) + 0.4275\,T\,(V^{0.16})$$

where W is the wind chill adjusted temperature, T is the air temperature in Fahrenheit, and V is the wind velocity in miles per hour.

Create a worksheet for calculating the wind chill factor given a temperature and wind velocity. Try your worksheet for a 30 degree day with a 10 mile per hour wind and for a -5 degree day with a 40 mile per hour wind.

2-14. The atomic weight of carbon is 12.011. The atomic weight of hydrogen is 1.0079. The atomic weight of oxygen is 15.9994. Create a worksheet that allows you to enter the number of carbon atoms, hydrogen atoms, and oxygen atoms in a molecule and calculates (i) the total number of atoms in the molecule and (ii) the molecular weight of the molecule. Try your worksheet on ethane C_2H_6 and on sucrose $C_{12}H_{22}O_{11}$.

2-15. You recently were given a beautiful framed photograph of Tiger Woods signed by the man himself. You'd like to know what it will be worth in the future. The formula for calculating the future value of an investment that increases at a constant rate is $F = P\,(1 + R)^N$ where P is the present value, R is the annual rate of increase, and N is the number of years. Create a worksheet that has as input the present value of your Tiger Woods autographed photo, the annual rate of increase, and the number of years you will keep it and as output the future value.

(a) Try your worksheet with values of $500, 5%, and 10 years.

(b) Try your worksheet with values of $1,000, 7%, and 20 years.

(c) If the signed photograph is worth $1,000 today, at what annual rate must it increase to be worth $20,000 in 20 years? You should do this by trial and error to find the rate to the tenth of a percent that results in a value just over $20,000.

2-16. Create a worksheet for joggers that allows you to enter two numbers: a distance in miles and the number of minutes required to run the distance. The worksheet then should calculate two quantities: the average number of minutes per mile and the average miles per hour for the run. Try the worksheet on the following runs: 1 mile in 4 minutes, 3.5 miles in 42 minutes, and 26.21875 miles in 129.7 minutes.

2-17. The Widget Division factory purchases 25,000 couplers per year for use in its widget manufacturing process. The Director of Purchasing has determined that it costs $20.00 (in personnel and computer time) for the company to process an order to purchase couplers. It costs the company $4.00 per year to carry a coupler in inventory (including space allocation, breakage, theft, insurance). As the new Assistant to the Director of Purchasing, your job is to calculate how many couplers should be ordered at one time. If you order 100 couplers at a time, orders will be arriving almost daily so you will have low carrying costs but you will have to pay for 250 purchases per year. If you order 100,000 couplers at a time, you will have low purchase costs but very high inventory carrying costs.

The Economic Order Quantity (EOQ) is the amount that should be ordered at one time to minimize carrying and ordering costs. The EOQ is calculated by $\sqrt{2DO/C}$ where D is the annual demand, O is the cost for processing an order, and C is the annual carrying cost for a unit in inventory.

(a) Create a worksheet for determining the Economic Order Quantity. You should have an appropriate heading at the top. You should have separate well-labeled cells for the annual demand, order cost, and annual unit carrying cost. Your worksheet should work for any quantities entered. (Note that the square root of a quantity can be calculated by raising the quantity to the 0.5 power.) How many couplers should be purchased at a time? Try your worksheet on the numbers in the first paragraph.

(b) Suppose demand for widgets increases dramatically and now we need to purchase 100,000 couplers per year. How many should be purchased at a time? Change the value in the cell that contains the annual demand.

2-18. We would like to create a worksheet that will allow us to compare what we were supposed to sell in each region (our "goal") with what we actually sold.

(a) Enter the following worksheet with appropriate formulas in the blank cells in the bottom row and right column. Just as a check, the number calculated for Amount Over Goal for Africa should be 3.3.

Sales in $ Millions

Region	Goal	Actual	Amount Over Goal
Africa	24	27.3	
Antarctica	3	19.4	
Asia	20	33.5	
Europe	32	31.2	
Latin America	17	11.8	
North America	25	46.1	
Total			

(b) Change the Asia Actual sales to 56.7 and the Latin America Actual sales to 15.1. The numbers in the Total row and Amount Over Goal column should change automatically.

(c) Add formulas in a new column that calculate Percent Over Goal for each of the regions and for the Total. The Percent Over Goal calculated for Africa should be 13.75. For Europe it should be -2.5.

2-19. You are thinking of opening an ice cream stand and selling ice cream cones. You plan to sell single-scoop cones and double-scoop cones. You would like to know how much ice cream you would use for various size cones.

(a) Create a worksheet that allows you to enter three numbers: the height of the cone itself (without any ice cream), the diameter of the cone, and the diameter of the scoop. The output will be two numbers: the number of ounces of ice cream that would be used in a single-scoop cone and the number of ounces of ice cream that would be used in a double-scoop cone.

Assume that the cone is filled with ice cream so the top is level. Assume that each scoop is a perfect sphere. A pint of ice cream fits in a cylindrical container 4 inches high and 3 inches in diameter. The volume of a cone is $V = \pi r^2 h / 3$. The volume of a sphere is $V = 4 \pi r^3 / 3$. The volume of a cylinder is $V = \pi r^2 h$. To obtain the value of π you can use PI( ) in an Excel formula. There are 16 ounces in a pint. Try your worksheet on a cone that is 4 inches high and 2 inches wide with 2.5-inch scoops and on a cone that is 6 inches high and 3 inches wide with 4-inch scoops.

(b) You would like to know the projected cost for each of the ice cream cones. Assume that cones are bought by the gross (144 cones) and ice cream by the gallon (8 pints). Add separate cells for the price of cones per gross and price of ice cream per gallon. Try your worksheet on the above cones with costs of $15 per gross of cones and $4 per gallon of ice cream.

2-20. Create a worksheet to calculate the Break-Even Point for a product. Allow the user to enter three values: a unit Selling Price, the percentage of the selling price required for the Variable Cost of each unit, and the total Fixed Cost. The worksheet should be well-labeled and should contain formulas to calculate automatically two values: the Break-Even Point in units sold and the Break-Even Point in dollar volume sold. The worksheet also may calculate some intermediate values, if you wish. Print your worksheet with the following sets of input values: (a) Selling Price 200, Variable Cost Percent 60, Fixed Cost 40000, (b) Selling Price 250, Variable Cost Percent 50, Fixed Cost 50000. Write out by hand on your printout the formulas that appear in each cell.

2-21. The Body Mass Index (BMI) often is used by scientists and physicians to determine whether a person is underweight or overweight. The BMI is calculated as follows:

Step 1.   Multiply your body weight in pounds by 0.45.
Step 2.   Multiply your height in inches by 0.025.
Step 3.   Square the answer from Step 2.
Step 4.   Divide the answer from Step 1 by the answer from Step 3.

A healthy BMI is between 19 and 25. The BMI is said to work equally well for both men and women. Create a worksheet to calculate a person's BMI. There should be four values entered into the worksheet: the person's name, the person's weight in pounds, and the person's height in feet and inches. The worksheet should calculate the total height in inches, the values for each of the steps, and then show the resulting BMI.

(a) Try your worksheet for the following people: Jan, 115 pounds, 5 feet 8 inches; Fran, 325 pounds, 5 feet 1 inch; Dana, 240 pounds, 6 feet 4 inches; and Slim, 104 pounds, 5 feet 6 inches.

(b) A person is 5 feet 8 inches. Use the worksheet to determine the lowest healthy weight for this person and the highest healthy weight. Use trial and error. That is, try different weights until the BMI comes out to just above 19 and then to just below 25. Don't worry about fractions of a pound.

CHAPTER 3

CHANGING THE APPEARANCE OF THE WORKSHEET

OBJECTIVES

In this chapter you will learn how to:

- Change the width of columns
- Select ranges of cells
- Set the font, style, and size of text
- Change the alignment of text in cells
- Format numbers
- Place borders around cells
- Change the color of text and cells
- Give your worksheet a three-dimensional shading effect
- Display the formulas in your worksheet

Excel has many ways of changing the appearance of the information in the worksheet, both on the screen and as printed on the page. The general term for changing the appearance of information is **formatting**. Here we are not concerned with the contents of the information, but rather with how it appears. Proper formatting can make a worksheet easier to understand and more visually pleasing.

COLUMN WIDTH

Consider the Price Quote worksheet again. (See Figure 3-1.) Notice that cell B2 contains the text "Price Quote". But this text does not quite fit into the cell. When you start up Excel the columns are all set at the same width. Each cell holds about 9 or 10 characters, depending on the font that you use for the characters and the actual characters you are typing. If you type in text that is longer than what will fit in the cell, the computer will display the full text as long as the cell to the right is blank. If you look carefully you will notice that the line between cells B2 and C2 is missing, indicating that the extended B2 is being displayed on top of C2. If cell C2 contained some information, then all of B2 would not be displayed. Rather, only the information that fit within the cell boundaries would show. Similarly, you can see that the entries in B8, B10, and B14 are too long for the cells.

Figure 3-1. The Price Quote worksheet.

It is easy to change the width of the cells in column B so that all of the text fits. Simply move the mouse pointer up to the area right between column head B and C. The mouse pointer shape will change to a vertical line with arrows pointing left and right, as in Figure 3-2. Press the left mouse button, hold the button down, and drag the width of column B to the right to the size you would like.

Figure 3-2. When the mouse pointer assumes this shape you can change the width of the column to the left of the pointer by pressing the left mouse button and dragging.

Alternatively you can double click when the mouse pointer is in the position in Figure 3-2 and the width of column B will be adjusted automatically.

Now we can move the pointer up to the column head between the C and the D, and drag the pointer to the left to make column C narrower. (See Figure 3-3.)

We can make the rows different heights in the same way, but this technique usually is used only with columns. We can change the row heights automatically by changing the font size of the letters in the cells.

	A	B	C	D	E	F	G	H
1								
2		Price Quote						
3					Unit			
4		Product		Quantity	Price	Total		
5								
6		Widgets		100	$1.19	$119.00		
7		Grommits		50	$2.49	$124.50		
8		Connectors		200	$0.69	$138.00		
9								
10		Amount Before Tax				$381.50		
11								
12		Sales Tax				$22.89		
13								
14		Total Amount				$404.39		
15								
16								
17								
18								

File   Edit   View   Insert   Format   Tools   Data   Window   Help

G3

Sheet1 / Sheet2 / Sheet3 /

Figure 3-3. The Price Quote worksheet with the widths of columns B and C adjusted.

SELECTING CELLS

The characters (letters, digits, punctuation) are all of the same font, size, style, and color in the worksheet. To change the appearance of cells, we first need to select the cells to be changed. Cells can be selected by dragging across them with the mouse while the left mouse button is pressed. For example, to select the rectangular range of cells from B2 through F14, place the mouse pointer in B2, press down on the button, and drag the mouse to F14. Selected cells are darkened except for cell in the top left corner of the selection, which is white. In Figure 3-4, the range of cells in B2 through F14 has been selected.

Figure 3-4. The darkened area indicates that the range from B2 through F14 is selected.

It is possible to select a **noncontiguous range** of cells by holding your finger down on the **Ctrl key** ("Control" key) while you do the selection. For example, we could select B12 through B14 by dragging across the cells and then press down on the Ctrl key on the keyboard and with the Ctrl key pressed drag from D6 through F8. This selects two separate areas, as shown in Figure 3-5.

We can select all of the cells in the entire worksheet by clicking on the button above the 1 and to the left of the A, just to the top left of cell A1 in the worksheet.

	A	B	C	D	E	F	G	H	
1									
2		Price Quote							
3					Unit				
4		Product		Quantity	Price	Total			
5									
6		Widgets		100	$1.19	$119.00			
7		Grommits		50	$2.49	$124.50			
8		Connectors		200	$0.69	$138.00			
9									
10		Amount Before Tax				$381.50			
11									
12		Sales Tax				$22.89			
13									
14		Total Amount				$404.39			
15									

Figure 3-5. Use the Ctrl key ("Control" key) to select multiple areas.

FORMATTING CELLS

Once cells have been selected they can be formatted by selecting *Cells...* in the *Format* pull-down menu. For example, we would like to make cell B2, which contains "Price Quote", more prominent. So we click on B2 to select it. We select *Cells...* in the *Format* pull-down menu and then click on the tab for Font.

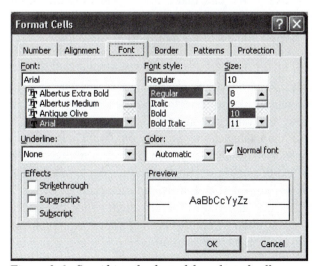

Figure 3-6. Specifying the font of the selected cells.

We see the Font selection sheet in Figure 3-6. Currently, cell B2 is in Arial Regular 10 point. We select Times New Roman in the Font: box and then Bold in the Font Style: box and 24 point in the Size: box. We click on OK. The text in cell B2 is changed accordingly to Times New Roman Bold 24. (See Figure 3-7.)

	A	B	C	D	E	F	G	H
1								
2		**Price Quote**						
3					Unit			
4		Product		Quantity	Price	Total		
5								
6		Widgets		100	$1.19	$119.00		
7		Grommits		50	$2.49	$124.50		
8		Connectors		200	$0.69	$138.00		
9								
10		Amount Before Tax				$381.50		
11								
12		Sales Tax				$22.89		
13								
14		Total Amount				$404.39		
15								

Figure 3-7. Changing the font, style, and size of cell B2.

Alternatively, we can make use of the **Formatting toolbar**. The Formatting toolbar contains buttons that provide shortcuts for formatting cells. The Formatting toolbar does not appear in the Excel window in Figure 3-7. To have the Formatting toolbar appear on the screen, select *Toolbars...* in the *View* pull-down menu. A sub-menu with all of the various toolbars available will appear. Click a check next to *Formatting*. The Formatting toolbar appears on the screen, as in Figure 3-8.

If you would like to have the tool buttons appear on two rows you can click on the **Toolbar Options** button to the left of the font box or on the far right of the toolbar and then select *Show Buttons on Two Rows*. (For more on Toolbars see the beginning section of Chapter 7.) Two rows of toolbars show in Figure 3-9.

With the Formatting toolbar visible, many formatting operations are available with a single mouse click. For example, to change the font of cells, select the desired cells by dragging the mouse across them (with the button depressed) so they are highlighted and then select the desired font from the **Font menu** on the left of the Formatting toolbar, as in Figure 3-9.

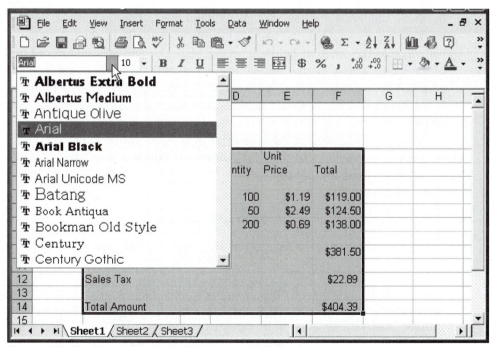

Figure 3-8. The Formatting toolbar contains many shortcuts for formatting cells.

Figure 3-9. The Font menu in the Formatting toolbar.

Figure 3-10. Font Size menu and style
buttons in the Formatting toolbar.

Similarly, we can change the size of the text by selecting the cells and then using the **Font Size menu** in the Formatting toolbar (see Figure 3-10). The Size menu is next to the font menu.

The button with a **B** is the **Bold** button. Pressing this button makes the selected cells appear bold. (Or it "unbolds" cells that already are bold.) The button with the *I* is the *Italics* button. The button with the U̲ is the U̲nderline button. Pressing this button causes the text in the selected cells to be underlined. (Or if the text already is underlined it removes the underline.)

ALIGNMENT

As you may have noticed, Excel automatically aligns text to the left of each cell and numbers to the right of each cell. This allows the user to see at a glance which cells contain text and which cells contain numbers. However, it also means that numbers usually do not line up under column titles. For example, in the Price Quote worksheet in Figure 3-8, the word "Quantity" in cell D4 is aligned on the left of the cell whereas the numbers below it, in cells D6, D7, and D8, are aligned on the right of the cells. Similarly, the titles "Unit Price" and "Totals" do not line up with the numbers below them. Here, we want to change the alignment of the titles in cells D4, E3, E4, and F4 so they are aligned to the right of the cells like the numbers below them.

If you wish to change the alignment of the text within cells, you can select the cells and then press one of the **Text Alignment buttons** to the right of the Underline button in the Formatting toolbar.

Figure 3-11. Text Alignment buttons.

The first Alignment button, the **Align Left button**, causes information in the selected cells to be aligned to the left of the cell. The second button, the **Center button**, causes information to be centered in the cell. The third of these buttons, the **Align Right button**, not surprisingly, causes information to be aligned to the right of the cell.

	File	Edit	View	Insert	Format	Tools	Data	Window	Help		

Arial ▾ 10 ▾ **B** *I* <u>U</u> ≡ ≡ ≡ 国 $ % , ⁺.⁰ .⁰⁰ ⊞ ▾ ◇ ▾ **A** ▾

D3 ▾ *fx*

Align Right

	A	B	C	D		F	G	H
1								
2		**Price Quote**						
3					Unit			
4		Product		Quantity	Price	Total		
5								
6		Widgets		100	$1.19	$119.00		
7		Grommits		50	$2.49	$124.50		
8		Connectors		200	$0.69	$138.00		
9								
10		Amount Before Tax				$381.50		
11								
12		Sales Tax				$22.89		
13								
14		Total Amount				$404.39		
15								

Sheet1 / Sheet2 / Sheet3 /

Figure 3-12. Aligning text to the right of the cells.

In the Price Quote worksheet, we can drag across D3 through F4 to select these cells. We then click on the Align Right button and the text is aligned on the right of the cells, as in Figure 3-12.

The rightmost of the Text Alignment buttons in the Formatting toolbar (see Figure 3-11) is the **Merge and Center button**. The Merge and Center button allows information to be centered across multiple cells. First, enter information into a cell. Then, select that cell and several blank cells to the right of the cell and click on the Merge and Center button. The selected cells will be merged. The text will appear centered across the selected cells, though it actually will remain located in the original cell. To "unmerge" the cells select the cell and click on the button again.

You also can change the alignment of cells by first selecting the cells and then using the Alignment tab in the window displayed by selecting *Cells...* in the *Format* pull-down menu. (See Figure 3-6.)

HELP!

Excel has a myriad of commands, menus, functions, and tools. No one could remember all of the features and details of operating Excel. Our brains can retain only so much.

Excel has a very extensive **Help system** to assist us. As usual with Excel, there are several ways to access the Help system. The easiest way is simply to click on the **Help button**, the rightmost button on the Standard toolbar. Clicking on the Help button usually brings up the dreaded **Clippit**, the animated paperclip character everybody loves to hate. (See Figure 3-13.) Just type your question in the place indicated and Clippit will try to answer it. Microsoft has been promising to eliminate Clippit, because so many people find it annoying, but "luckily" Clippit is still with us as of this writing. If you point to Clippit and right-click you can change to a different animated character, for example a robot or Merlin, or hide the animated characters completely.

Figure 3-13. Clippit, the Office Assistant, tries to be helpful.

Depending on the width of your Excel window, you may have a box to the right of your menus where you can type a question in directly to receive help.

You might have noticed that if you keep the mouse pointer over a button for a while without pressing the button, Excel will give you a little clue in yellow about what the button does, as with the Align Right button in Figure 3-12.

Also, notice that the rightmost menu is the Help menu. You can turn the Office Assistant on and off in the Help menu. If you turn off the Office Assistant (Clippit and his colleagues), then you get the more traditional interface to the Help system shown in Figure 3-14.

Figure 3-14. Searching for help on "Align" using the traditional Help interface.

FORMATTING NUMBERS

You may have noticed that some numbers in the Price Quote worksheet have dollar signs in front of them and some do not. These numbers have different formats. The cells with dollar signs are said to be in **Currency format**. The important point to be remembered here is that the format of a cell affects only how the cell is displayed. The format of a cell does not affect the actual contents of the cell. For example, a cell might contain the number 347.4725. If it is formatted as Currency to two decimal places, it will appear as $347.47. But the contents of the cell will remain unchanged. If the cell is used in calculations, the number used will be 347.4725 even though the number that appears in the cell is 347.47.

There are several ways to set the **Number format** of a cell. If the cell contains a number that you typed, the cell naturally will pick up any format you used in typing in the number. For example, if you enter $425.24 then the cell will be formatted automatically as currency. Five of the tool buttons on the Format toolbar affect the Number format of a cell (see Figure 3-15). To use the buttons to change the number format of cells, first select the cells and then click on the button.

Figure 3-15. Buttons on the Formatting toolbar for changing the format of numbers.

The **Currency Style button** changes the selected cells so that numbers in them are displayed with a dollar sign in front and with commas marking off every three places to the left of the decimal point. Two digits to the right of the decimal point are shown.

The **Percent Style button** changes the selected cells to Percent format. The contents of the cells will be displayed as multiplied by 100 and will be followed with a percent sign %. For example, if a cell contains 0.0789, it will be displayed as 7.89%.

The **Comma Style button** changes the selected cells to Comma format. Here, the numbers will be displayed with commas marking off every three places to the left of the decimal places. No dollar signs are displayed. Negative numbers are not displayed with parentheses around them, but rather with minus signs in front. This could be considered a "normal" format for numbers.

The **Increase Decimal button** increases the number of decimal places displayed in the selected cells by one for each time the button is pressed. For example, if a selected cell contains 304 and displays 304 and this button is pressed twice, the number will be displayed as 304.00.

The **Decrease Decimal button** decreases the number of decimal places displayed in the selected cells by one for each time the button is pressed. For example, if a selected cell displays 304.872 and this button is pressed twice, the number will be displayed as 304.9. The computer rounds off the number displayed but it leaves the actual number stored in the cell unchanged.

If a formatted number is too long to be displayed, then ######### will be displayed in the cell. This is a signal to you that you should widen the column of the cell or decrease the number of decimal places or change the format or the font size.

The five number format buttons displayed in the Format toolbar are only the tip of the iceberg of the number formats available. To reach the full range of choices for number formats, first select the cells in the worksheet to be formatted. Then select *Cells...* in the *Format* pull-down menu and click on the Number tab. (See Figure 3-16.)

Notice from Figure 3-16 that it is possible to change the way negative numbers are displayed in Currency format. (It might be difficult to see without color here, but some of the choices display negative numbers in red.) It also is possible using the Symbol drop-down list to change the currency symbol displayed from $ to £ or € or ¥ or any other symbol.

Figure 3-16. Many different formats for numbers are available.

There are many choices of formats for numbers. As you can see in Figure 3-16, there is an Accounting format for numbers as well as a Currency format. The differences are illustrated in the worksheet in Figure 3-17. Here negative numbers in Currency format are displayed with a minus sign.

If you are not satisfied with the choices, you can create your own **Custom format** by clicking on Custom at the bottom of the Category list in Figure 3-16.

Figure 3-17. Typical Currency vs. Accounting formats.

BORDERS

The **Borders button** in the Formatting toolbar allows you to put a border (lines) around selected cells. First select the cells in the worksheet around which you wish to place a border by dragging across them with the mouse. Click on the small downward-pointing triangle on the right of the Borders button in the Formatting toolbar. The **Borders palette** pops down. (See Figure 3-18.)

Figure 3-18. The Borders palette.

Each of these buttons causes a different type of border to be placed around the selected cells. The type is indicated in the picture on the button. For example, pressing the bottom right button in the Borders palette will put a thick box completely around the selected cells. If you don't like the selection provided, you can custom draw the borders by clicking on Draw Borders.

Note that borders are associated with cells. If the size of the cells changes, for example from changing the column width, the borders automatically are adjusted and redrawn.

To undo borders that were previously set, select the bordered cells and then press the top left button in the Border palette, the button with no borders around the cells.

COLORS

The rightmost two buttons on the Formatting toolbar let you change the colors of cells.

The **Fill Color button** has a paint can. This button allows you to change the color of the background of the selected cells. Clicking on the small downward-pointing triangle on the right of the button causes the **Color palette** to drop down (see Figure 3-19).

Figure 3-19. The Color palette
(printed in shades of gray, obviously).

To cause a group of cells in the worksheet to be displayed in yellow, select the cells by dragging across them, click on the right part of the Color button, and then click on the desired shade of yellow in the color palette. Note that the gridlines between the cells no longer show if any of the colors is selected, including white. To return to no fill with the gridlines showing between cells, highlight the cells and select No Fill.

As mentioned earlier, we can select all of the cells in the entire worksheet by clicking on the button above the 1 and to the left of the A just beyond the top left corner of the worksheet. Once all of the cells in the worksheet have been selected we can color all of them by selecting a color in the Color palette. Now the background of the entire worksheet will be a certain color. Coloring all the cells in white is one way of erasing the gridlines from the display.

The **Font Color button** allows you to change the color of the text that appears in the cell. With this tool you can cause the characters in a cell to be blue or yellow or whatever rather than the normal black. The button works essentially the same as the Fill Color button. Select the cells containing the text you wish to make a different color. Click on the triangle on the right part of the Font Color button. A color palette drops down. Select the desired color for the text from the palette.

Warning: If you make the font color the same as the background color, the text will seem to disappear.

EXAMPLE

We take the Price Quote worksheet. We make the background gray, change the font and size of cell B2, draw some borders, make some cells bold, make the font size of cells B14 and F14 larger. The result is shown in Figure 3-20.

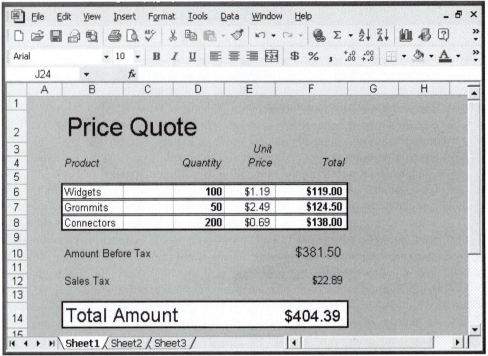

Figure 3-20. One approach to formatting the Price Quote worksheet.

3-D SHADING

It is possible to give your worksheets a three-dimensional effect by the judicious use of colors and borders. An example with the Price Quote worksheet is shown in Figure 3-21.

To begin, select the entire worksheet and color it with some neutral color, for example a medium shade of gray. To format a selection so it appears to be raised, to be above the worksheet, apply white borders on the left and top of the selection and black borders on the right and bottom of the selection. To format a selection so it appears to be sunken, to be below the worksheet, apply black borders to the left and top of the selection and white borders to the right and bottom of the selection. The Borders button in the Formatting toolbar does not provide enough options, enough power, to enable us to apply the borders we need. To apply a white border to the top of B2 and C2, we would first select B2 and C2 by dragging across them. Then we select *Cells...* in the *Format* pull-down menu and click on the Border tab. In the Border sheet we have many choices for the borders. (See Figure 3-22.)

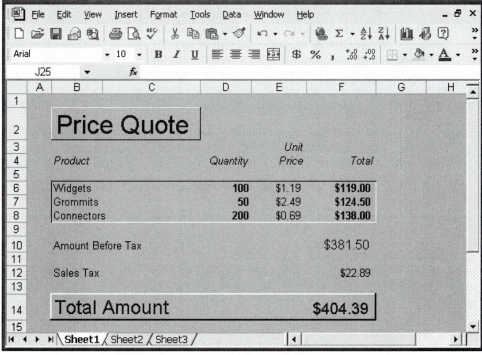

Figure 3-21. Three-dimensional shading of the Price Quote worksheet.

*Figure 3-22. The full range of Borders is available in the
Cells... selection in the Format pull-down menu.*

We first select the thickness of the line of the border in the Style: section of the Border sheet. The thicker the line, the more pronounced the three-dimensional effect will be. We next click on the white square in the Color: drop-down list. We click on the button with the border line on top of the cell and then click on OK. We will see a white border applied above B2 and C2. The order of selections here matters. In particular, it is important that we select the thickness and the color before selecting the location of the border.

We would use the same technique for each of the other borders. We select B2 and apply a white border to its left. We select B2 and C2 and apply a black border to the bottom of the cells. We select C2 and apply a black border to the right of the cell. This process is somewhat tedious, but the resulting worksheet in Figure 3-21 sure looks snazzy.

THE FORMAT PAINTER BUTTON

If you already have a cell that is formatted in a way that you like, you can capture that format and "paint" it on to other cells using the **Format Painter button**.

The Format Painter button is located on the Standard toolbar to the left of the Undo button. To use the Format Painter button: (1) select a cell or range of cells whose format you wish to duplicate, (2) click on the Format Painter button, and (3) click on the cell to which you wish to apply the format or drag across a range of cells to which you wish to apply the format. The format that is captured and then applied includes font, size, style (bold, italics), alignment, borders, and colors.

To apply a format to multiple ranges of cells: (1) select a cell or range of cells whose format you wish to duplicate, (2) double-click on the Format Painter button, (3) click on the cell to which you wish to apply the format or drag across a range of cells to which you wish to apply the format, (4) apply the format to other cells by clicking on them or dragging across them, (5) when you have finished applying the format, click once on the Format Painter button. The Format Painter button will stay depressed during this operation and the cell whose format you have captured will be identified with a dashed line moving around it.

DISPLAYING THE FORMULAS

We can instruct Excel to display the formulas in the cells by selecting *Options...* in the *Tools* pull-down menu and then clicking on the View tab. Clicking on Formulas in Window options, as in Figure 3-23, instructs Excel to display the formulas in the cells rather than the results of evaluating the formulas. The result of displaying the formulas is shown in Figure 3-24.

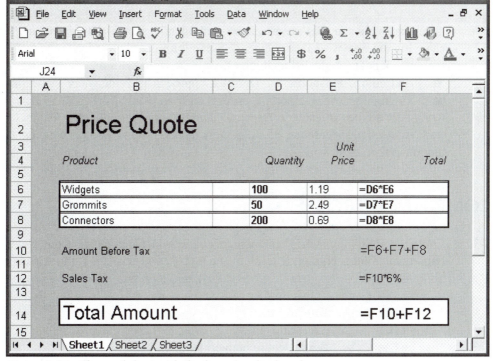

Figure 3-23. Specifying that formulas be displayed in the worksheet.

Figure 3-24. The worksheet with the formulas displayed.

This is a very useful way of seeing the formulas that underlie your worksheet. In the worksheet shown in Figure 3-24, we manually changed the column widths so all of the information fits on the screen. Instructing Excel to display the formulas causes the program to change the column widths and cell alignments, not always optimally.

If you print the worksheet in Figure 3-24, the formulas will be printed in the cells. If you hand in your homework on paper, your instructor might ask you to print out copies of the worksheet with both the values showing and the formulas showing.

If you are going to print the worksheet with the formulas displayed, you'll probably want to instruct Excel to print the Column Headings (A, B, C, ...) and Row Headings (1, 2, 3, ...) as well. You do this by selecting *Page Setup...* in the *File* pull-down menu and then selecting the Sheet tab and clicking on Row and Column headings. We will discuss the options in *Page Setup* in more detail in Chapter 7.

As you can see from Figure 3-23, there is a wealth of possibilities for changing the appearance of the worksheet in the *Options...* selection in the *Tools* pull-down menu. For example, you can instruct Excel not to display the gridlines in the worksheet by clicking on the box to the left of the word Gridlines so the check mark there vanishes.

FINDING A LOOK FOR YOUR WORKSHEETS

"Beauty lies in the eyes of the beholder." Excel provides many tools for changing the way worksheets appear. Sometimes people just leave the worksheets in the dry, standard style. Sometimes people go wild with an astonishing variety of fonts and colors and borders. The best approach is somewhere in between. You want to highlight the important information in your worksheet. You want the worksheet to be as easy to use and understand as possible. Some companies standardize the appearance of their worksheets. Some people develop their own unique look to their worksheets.

COMPUTER EXERCISES

3-1. Enter the following worksheet, which converts a temperature from Centigrade to Fahrenheit. Widen column B so all of the text shows. Make column A narrow.

CELL	CONTENTS
B1:	*Your Name*
B2:	Exercise 3-1.
B5:	Worksheet to convert temperatures

B7:	Hello
B8:	Please enter the temperature in Centigrade:
C8:	10
B10:	Equivalent temperature in Fahrenheit:
C10:	=(1.8*C8)+32

Cell C10 should show 50, the Fahrenheit equivalent of 10 degrees Centigrade.

(a) Change the format of cell C10 so it shows one decimal place to the right of the decimal point (for example, 50.0).

(b) Move to C8. Enter the number 20. The number in C10 should change to 68.

(c) Select cell B7. Press the Delete (or Del) key. The word Hello should be erased.

(d) Save the workbook on your disk. Give it a name you will remember, like Exer3_1.

(e) Print the worksheet.

(f) Display the formulas in the worksheet rather than the values. Print the worksheet again. Change the view back to the original, so the result of evaluating the formulas is displayed in the cells.

(g) Format the worksheet to make it as attractive as possible. Change the fonts and sizes. Draw borders. Color in the cells. Save the workbook as Exer3_1G. Print the worksheet again.

(h) Now take the original worksheet and format it with a completely different look. Perhaps you might use three-dimensional shading if you didn't in the previous part. Save the workbook as Exer3_1H. Print the worksheet again.

3-2.   Take a worksheet from the exercises at the end of Chapter 2.

(a) Format the worksheet to make it attractive and easy to understand.

(b) Format the worksheet in a second style.

(c) Which do you prefer? Why?

3-3.   Here is a strange one.

Cell D8 really does contain the formula =D5+D6.   Explain exactly how this is possible since 2 + 2 is not equal to 5.

CHAPTER 4

SIMPLE FUNCTIONS AND THE FILL OPERATION

OBJECTIVES

In this chapter you will learn how to:

- Use the SUM, AVERAGE, COUNT, MAX, and MIN functions
- Enter ranges for arguments of functions
- Point to cells in formulas
- Identify and avoid the error of circular reference
- Enter SUM functions automatically with the AutoSum tool
- Use the Function Wizard
- Fill formulas down columns or across rows
- Enter series of numbers using AutoFill

In the first three chapters we have seen how to create, use, and format simple worksheets. The basic idea is that each worksheet is organized as a two-dimensional grid made up of rows and columns. The intersection of each row and column is called a cell. Initially all the cells are blank. We can fill each of the cells with text, numbers, or formulas. The key to Excel is in the formulas. Whenever any cell is changed, all of the relevant formulas are recalculated.

In this chapter we begin to explore how to construct larger, more realistic worksheets. There are two important tools for doing this: built-in functions and the Fill operation. In many ways this is the key chapter of the book. Once you understand how to use built-in functions and the Fill operation you are well on your way to knowing Excel.

BUILT-IN FUNCTIONS SAVE YOU TYPING

Figure 4-1 is a worksheet that shows the monthly sales by region for the first half of the year. The total sales for Africa is in cell H6. What would be the formula in this cell? Clearly, it could be

$$=B6+C6+D6+E6+F6+G6$$

Suppose we would like to analyze sales for 60 months. Our formula would have 60 terms. Or, suppose we had 400 regions and would like to find the total sales for

	A	B	C	D	E	F	G	H	I
1									
2			SALES SUMMARY BY REGION						
3									
4		JAN	FEB	MAR	APR	MAY	JUN	TOTAL	
5									
6	AFRICA	4.6	3.4	4.2	5.4	3.9	4.9		
7	ANTARCTICA	1.1	0.8	0.7	1.3	0.9	1.3		
8	ASIA	43.2	46.4	45.4	47.6	47.1	46.3		
9	EUROPE	32.5	33.7	34.1	33.8	33.5	35.2		
10	LATIN AMERICA	14.7	13.6	13.4	17.5	15.2	18.9		
11	NORTH AMERICA	39.5	41.3	40.8	42.4	38.7	43.5		
12									
13	TOTAL								
14									

Figure 4-1. A worksheet showing the monthly sales by region.

January. The formula would have 400 cell addresses and 399 plus signs. We need an easier and shorter way of specifying formulas like this.

The best way to add up a list of numbers is to use **SUM**, which is a **built-in function**. The formula in H6 could be

$$=SUM(B6:G6)$$

This formula tells Excel that the number that should appear in H6 is the result of adding all the numbers from B6 through G6. Similarly, the formula in cell B13 could be

$$=SUM(B6:B11)$$

If we had 400 regions, we could add up all of the sales for January with the formula

$$=SUM(B6:B405)$$

Typing this formula clearly is easier than typing out 400 cell addresses and all the plus signs.

Built-in functions can save lots of typing. They help make large worksheets easy to construct.

THE VARIETY OF FUNCTIONS

There are hundreds of built-in functions in Excel. We will discuss five of the more common functions here. Other functions will be discussed in Chapters 11 through 15 and elsewhere in the book.

The most frequently used function by far is SUM. Other common functions include:

AVERAGE	Calculates the average or arithmetic mean of a list of values
COUNT	Counts how many numbers are in a list
MAX	Finds the largest value in a list
MIN	Finds the smallest value in a list

Thus, for the worksheet in Figure 4-1, =AVERAGE(B6:G6) would find the average monthly sales for Africa. The result of evaluating the formula would be 4.4. The formula =MAX(B6:G6) would find the highest monthly sales for Africa, namely 5.4. The formula =COUNT(B6:G6) would count the number of sales figures for Africa, namely 6.

The AVERAGE function is simply the SUM function divided by the COUNT function. The formula =AVERAGE(B6:G6) is exactly the same as the formula =SUM(B6:G6)/COUNT(B6:G6). This is important for understanding how missing values are treated in the AVERAGE function. If the number in F6, the May sales for Africa, was missing and the cell was blank, the average would be computed by adding the remaining numbers and dividing by 5, rather than 6. If one of the cells in the range of an AVERAGE function contains words or letters, it will be ignored (treated as if it is blank) because it does not contain a number. Similarly, any cells in the range of an argument of the SUM function (or MAX or MIN) that are blank or contain words or letters are ignored in the calculations.

Built-in functions not only save typing. They also provide a wide variety of calculations. Some of these calculations are impossible to specify using the normal arithmetic operators. For example, there is no formula using the normal arithmetic operators (+ - * / % ^) for calculating the largest number in a list. SUM saves typing. MAX provides a completely new capability.

ARGUMENTS AND RANGES

The inputs to a function are placed inside the parentheses and are called **arguments**. Multiple arguments in a function are separated by commas. For example, the formula =SUM(C6,3,4*B2) instructs Excel to add up the number in cell C6, the number 3, and the result of multiplying 4 times the number in B2. The SUM function here has three arguments: C6, 3, and 4*B2. The functions SUM, AVERAGE, COUNT, MAX, and MIN can have up to 30 arguments.

The most useful type of argument for these functions is a **range**. The argument in =SUM(B6:G6) is B6:G6, which is a range.

Ranges are very important in Excel. A range normally specifies a rectangular portion of a worksheet. The range B6:G6 consists of a cell address followed by a colon followed by another cell address. The first cell address gives one corner of the range. The second address indicates the diagonally opposite corner of the range. Usually, the first address is the top left corner of the range; the second address is the bottom right corner of the range.

The range B6:G6 is a one cell by six cell horizontal rectangle. The range B6:B11 is a six by one vertical rectangle. The range B6:G11 would contain 36 cells in a rectangle six cells across from column B through G and six cells down from row 6 through row 11.

What should be the formula in cell H13 in the worksheet in Figure 4-1? This is the grand total of the sales for the six months. There are three choices. The formula could be

=SUM(H6:H11)

This formula would calculate the grand total by adding up the product totals. The formula in H13 could be

$$=SUM(B13:G13)$$

This formula would calculate the grand total by adding up the monthly totals. The third possibility is for the formula in H13 to be

$$=SUM(B6:G11)$$

This formula would calculate the grand total by adding up the original 36 monthly sales numbers. All three formulas would give the same answer.

How many numbers would be added up in the formula

$$=SUM(23,C12,B4:B7,47,C2:E5)$$

There are five arguments:

1. the number 23   --   1 number
2. the cell C12   --   1 number
3. the range B4:B7   --   4 numbers
4. the number 47   --   1 number
5. the range C2:E5   --   12 numbers

Thus this formula instructs the computer to add 19 numbers.

Be careful with the commas and the colons. The formula =SUM(B6,G11) instructs the computer to add up 2 numbers, the values in B6 and G11. The formula =SUM(B6:G11) instructs the computer to add up 36 numbers, the values in the rectangular range of cells from B6 through G11.

In Chapter 8 we will see how to specify a three-dimensional range of cells through several worksheets.

POINTING

A convenient way to specify cell addresses in a range is to **point** to them instead of typing them. The idea of pointing is to use the mouse to point to the address that you would like to include in a formula. Pointing is especially useful when specifying a range, because when you point to a range Excel highlights the range on the screen.

To illustrate, consider the worksheet in Figure 4-2. We are in the process of entering the formula for cell H6.

Figure 4-2. Entering a range of addresses by dragging across the range with the mouse.

We have typed =SUM(and now are entering the range. Instead of typing the addresses of the range we simply drag across the desired range with the mouse (with the button pressed down). Excel automatically fills in the range pointed to in the formula, and, if you look carefully, you can see that as an added aid to the user Excel has placed dashed lines around the range selected. It also lists the arguments of the SUM function in a yellow box below the cell in which we are typing the formula. To complete the formula we type the closing) and press the Enter key or we can just type the Enter key and Excel will add the final parenthesis.

Pointing is not restricted to ranges. If you want to enter the formula =3*B2+C4, you can type =3*, then point and click on B2, type the +, point and click on C4, and then type the Enter key or click on the Enter button.

A COMMON ERROR: CIRCULAR REFERENCE

A common error made when entering a formula is to include the address of the cell in the formula itself. An example is shown in Figure 4-3. The formula in H6 should be =SUM(B6:G6). By mistake in H6 we have entered the formula =SUM(B6:H6). This typically occurs when we are pointing to the range and mistakenly extend the range over H6. The formula =SUM(B6:H6) instructs the computer that the value to be shown in H6 is the sum of the numbers from B6 through H6. That is, the computer needs to know the value in H6 in order to calculate the value in H6.

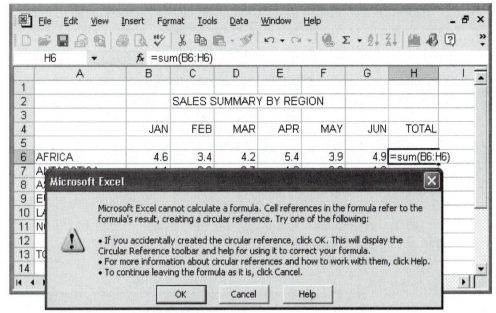

Figure 4-3. A mistake has been made. A circular reference occurs because the cell H6 contains a formula that refers to itself.

A formula that depends on its own value has a **circular reference**. As you can see, Excel warns you when it encounters a circular reference. There are a few cases where you want a circular reference, but normally it is a mistake that needs to be corrected.

OVERUSE OF THE SUM FUNCTION

Sometimes people become so enamored with the SUM function that they use it in every formula. If we want a formula that adds C4 and D6, we can simply use the formula =C4+D6. We could use =SUM(C4,D6) but it is a bit of overkill. Similarly, if we want to multiply the number in F5 by 3, we would write =F5*3. The formula =SUM(F5*3) would work, but the use of the SUM function here is wholly superfluous.

THE AUTOSUM TOOL

The SUM function legitimately is used so often that Excel provides a special tool button, the **AutoSum button**, for automatically entering the SUM function.

Simply select the cell in which you want a SUM function (as in Figure 4-1) and then click on the AutoSum button in the Standard toolbar. Excel will look at the worksheet and guess what row or column of numbers you want to add up. In this case if you select H6 and then click on the AutoSum button, Excel will guess that you want the formula =SUM(B6:G6) and this formula automatically will be entered in H6 for your approval. If you click on the downward-pointing triangle on the right of the button you will be able to select AVERAGE or COUNT or other functions as a shortcut.

THE INSERT FUNCTION TOOL

fx The **Insert Function** tool helps you enter functions into formulas and find out about their arguments. Selecting H6 and clicking on the Insert Function button, just to the left of the Formula bar, yields the dialog box shown in Figure 4-4.

Figure 4-4. Using the Insert Function tool.

The Insert Function tool works in two steps. In the first step we select the function we wish to use. Along the way it's easy to get information on a particular function by selecting the function and then by pressing the Help link at the bottom of the dialog box. After the proper function has been selected, press OK to proceed to the second step. In the second step we enter in the argument(s) of the function selected. This is particularly useful for functions with complicated arguments, as we will see in later chapters.

NESTED FUNCTIONS

The arguments of a function can include other functions. A function inside another function results in a **nested function**. An example of a nested function is

=MAX(SUM(C7:C10),SUM(D7:D10),SUM(E7:E10))

Here the MAX function has three arguments. Each of the arguments is a SUM function. The computer would add up C7 through C10. Then it would add up D7 through D10. Then it would add up E7 through E10. The value calculated by the whole formula would be the largest of these three totals. This is the number that would appear in the cell.

THE FILL OPERATION

Built-in functions with ranges provide an important tool for constructing large worksheets. They allow us to enter a formula that adds up 400 numbers by entering SUM and two addresses. The **Fill operation** allows us to make multiple copies of the formula so we do not have to type it over and over again into a column of cells or row of cells.

Return to our example of tabulating the monthly sales by region. In the worksheet in Figure 4-5 the final formula =SUM(B6:G6) in cell H6 is shown.

File Edit View Insert Format Tools Data Window Help									
H6		=SUM(B6:G6)							
	A	B	C	D	E	F	G	H	I
1									
2		SALES SUMMARY BY REGION							
3									
4		JAN	FEB	MAR	APR	MAY	JUN	TOTAL	
5									
6	AFRICA	4.6	3.4	4.2	5.4	3.9	4.9	26.4	
7	ANTARCTICA	1.1	0.8	0.7	1.3	0.9	1.3		
8	ASIA	43.2	46.4	45.4	47.6	47.1	46.3		
9	EUROPE	32.5	33.7	34.1	33.8	33.5	35.2		
10	LATIN AMERICA	14.7	13.6	13.4	17.5	15.2	18.9		
11	NORTH AMERICA	39.5	41.3	40.8	42.4	38.7	43.5		
12									
13	TOTAL								
14									

Figure 4-5. We are ready to fill the formula in H6 down the column.

We now would like to enter the formulas to total each of the other regions. The formulas for these cells would be as follows:

H7:	=SUM(B7:G7)
H8:	=SUM(B8:G8)
H9:	=SUM(B9:G9)
H10:	=SUM(B10:G10)
H11:	=SUM(B11:G11)

We could type each of these formulas, although it would be tedious. But suppose we had 400 regions? We would have to type the =SUM formula 400 times. A better solution than typing all of the formulas is to type the first formula and then use the Fill operation.

Once we have entered the formula in cell H6, we can use the Fill operation to tell Excel to fill the formula down the column into the other cells. But notice that we do not want Excel to fill an exact copy of the formula in cell H6 into the other cells. If it did fill an exact copy, then each of the cells from H7 through H11 would contain the formula =SUM(B6:G6) and the number that appeared in each of the cells would be the total for Africa. Rather, Excel has an "intelligent" Fill operation. As Excel fills the formula down the column it automatically adjusts the row numbers in the formula. So =SUM(B6:G6) in H6 becomes =SUM(B7:G7) in cell H7 and =SUM(B8:G8) in cell H8, and so on for each formula that is filled into the cells.

USING THE FILL HANDLE

The simplest way to fill a formula down a column or across a row is to use the **Fill Handle**. The Fill Handle is the small square at the bottom right of the active cell.

If we move the mouse pointer right on top of the Fill Handle, the mouse pointer becomes a thin cross.

JUN	TOTAL
4.9	26.4
1.3	
46.3	
35.2	
18.9	
43.5	

We press down on the left mouse button and drag down over the cells we would like to fill.

JUN	TOTAL
4.9	26.4
1.3	
46.3	
35.2	
18.9	
43.5	

We lift our finger off the mouse button and the formulas are filled down automatically.

JUN	TOTAL
4.9	26.4
1.3	6.1
46.3	276
35.2	202.8
18.9	93.3
43.5	246.2

We click somewhere else and we are finished. Sure enough, the formula =SUM(B6:G6) was changed as it was filled down the column. (See Figure 4-6.)

Now we would like to enter the row of monthly totals in row 13. First we click on cell B13. Click on the AutoSum button. The AutoSum button guesses that we want the formula =SUM(B6:B12) to appear in cell B14. We click on the Enter button to accept the formula and enter it into the cell. To fill the formula across the row, we move the mouse pointer on top of the Fill Handle in the bottom right corner of cell B13 until the mouse pointer becomes a thin cross. We press the mouse button and drag the Fill Handle to the right all the way over to H13. We lift our finger off the mouse button and click somewhere else. We are finished. Row 13 now contains appropriate formulas for calculating the column totals. (See Figure 4-7.)

Figure 4-6. When the formula in H6 is filled down, the addresses in the formula are adjusted automatically.

Figure 4-7. The worksheet with all formulas entered. The formula in B13 has been filled across the row.

FILLING BY DOUBLE-CLICKING

There is an even faster way to fill these formulas down or across. In Figure 4-8, simply point to the Fill Handle in H6 and double-click the mouse button. The formulas automatically are filled down. This trick works only if the cells to the immediate left or directly above are not empty.

	File	Edit	View	Insert	Format	Tools	Data	Window	Help		_ ⊡ ✕

H6 ▼ *fx* =SUM(B6:G6)

	A	B	C	D	E	F	G	H	I
1									
2			SALES SUMMARY BY REGION						
3									
4		JAN	FEB	MAR	APR	MAY	JUN	TOTAL	
5									
6	AFRICA	4.6	3.4	4.2	5.4	3.9	4.9	26.4	
7	ANTARCTICA	1.1	0.8	0.7	1.3	0.9	1.3		
8	ASIA	43.2	46.4	45.4	47.6	47.1	46.3		
9	EUROPE	32.5	33.7	34.1	33.8	33.5	35.2		
10	LATIN AMERICA	14.7	13.6	13.4	17.5	15.2	18.9		
11	NORTH AMERICA	39.5	41.3	40.8	42.4	38.7	43.5		
12									
13	TOTAL								
14									

Ⅰ◀ ▶ ▶Ⅰ \ Sheet1 / Sheet2 / Sheet3 /

Figure 4-8. A shortcut to filling down the formula is to double-click on the Fill Handle.

AUTO FILL

An interesting feature of Fill allows us to automatically create a series of values. For example, we might want to create a worksheet that has the weeks from 1 through 6 in a column. We could enter a 1 and 2 in successive cells. Then we select the cells by dragging down them.

We grab the Fill Handle in the bottom right corner of the selection and drag down four cells.

```
Week
   1
   2

        6
```

When we let up on the mouse button, Excel automatically fills in the values from 3 through 6.

```
Week
   1
   2
   3
   4
   5
   6
```

The annoying box at the bottom is the Auto Fill pop-up menu. If you click on it you will have various options. If you ignore it and click somewhere else, eventually the box goes away and the Auto Fill process is complete.

```
Week
   1
   2
   3
   4
   5
   6
```

The Auto Fill technique is remarkably flexible. If we had entered 2 and 5 instead of 1 and 2, Excel would have filled in the rest of the series as 8, 11, 14, 17. If we had entered Jan, Feb, Excel would have filled in the month names Mar, Apr, May, Jun. If we had entered in Q1, Q2, Excel would have filled in Q3, Q4, Q1, Q2, because it would interpret Q1 as Quarter 1. If we had entered A, B it would have filled in A, B, A, B. If you would like to enter your own custom series you can do so in the Custom Lists tab of *Options* in the *Tools* pull-down menu.

USING AUTO FILL TO FIT A STRAIGHT LINE

Remarkably, Auto Fill automatically will fit a straight line to a series of 3 or more values. For example, if we enter 3, 9, 6, 7 into successive cells, select those cells, and then drag the Fill Handle down four more cells, we will get the sequence 3, 9, 6, 7, 8.5, 9.4, 10.3, 11.2. Excel uses the values entered as the basis for its prediction of the new values.

SUMMARY

Two critical tools for creating larger worksheets are built-in functions and the Fill operation.

Excel provides built-in functions for many types of calculations. The inputs to a function are called arguments. The use of a range as the argument to a built-in function allows calculations to be performed on a large rectangular portion of the worksheet by specifying only the addresses of two of the diagonally opposite corners of the rectangle. For example, the formula =SUM(C101:AA1100) instructs the computer to add up the values of the 25,000 cells in a range 25 columns wide and 1,000 rows down. Ranges can be specified either by typing or by pointing.

The Fill operation allows a given formula to be filled down a column or across a row. For example, to find the sum of each of 1,000 rows of numbers we could enter the formula to sum the top row and then command the computer to fill the formula down through the remaining 999 rows. The Fill operation automatically adjusts the addresses in the new formulas created.

The Auto Fill feature allows us to easily create a series of values by entering just the first few values in the series, selecting those values, and then dragging the Fill Handle.

PAPER AND PENCIL EXERCISES

4-1. What is the value of each of the following formulas?

(a) =SUM(4,0,-2)

(b) =MAX(4,0,-2)

(c) =MIN(4,0,-2)

(d) =COUNT(4,0,-2)

(e) =AVERAGE(4,0,-2)

(f) =SUM(MAX(4,0,-2),5,MIN(4,0,-2),6)

(g) =COUNT(MAX(4,0,-2),5,MIN(4,0,-2),6)

(h) =AVERAGE(MAX(4,0,-2),5,MIN(4,0,-2),6)

(i) =AVERAGE(AVERAGE(1,2,3,4),AVERAGE(9,10))

4-2.   Consider the following worksheet.

	A	B	C	D	E	F	G	H	I
1									
2		Exercise 4-2							
3									
4	86	-4	-8	fun					
5	-47	5	26	37					
6	2.3	7	Excel	198					
7	computer	18	4.6	3					
8	56	102		-19					
9									
10									
11									

What would be the result of evaluating each of the following formulas? Write out your answer on paper. Please do not use the computer. The point of this exercise is to ensure that you understand what functions do.

(a) =SUM(A5:D5)

(b) =COUNT(A5:D5)

(c) =AVERAGE(A5:D5)

(d) =MAX(A5:D5)

(e) =MIN(A5:D5)

(f) =MIN(B7:C8)

(g) =AVERAGE(A3:A7)

(h) =COUNT(A3:A7)

(i) =SUM(AVERAGE(B4:B7),MAX(B4:B7),MIN(B4:B8))

(j) =SUM(3*B4,B4:C7,MAX(A5:C7),2*MIN(A4:B6))

(k) =AVERAGE(SUM(B4:B6),A8,MAX(B6:C8),MIN(B3:C5))

(l) =COUNT(SUM(B4:B6),A8,MAX(B6:C8),MIN(B3:C5))

COMPUTER EXERCISES

4-3.   Enter the following worksheet, adding the appropriate formulas. Use the built-in functions and the Fill operation. Test the worksheet by changing some of the numbers and checking the bottom two rows and the right two columns. Format the worksheet appropriately. Save and print the worksheet.

Sales Analysis
Product Line by Season
(All Sales in $ Millions)

Product	Winter	Spring	Summer	Fall	Total	Max
Golf	3.2	6.2	5.7	3.9		
Tennis	4.7	5.2	7.1	2.9		
Skiing	3.7	2.1	1.1	5.2		
Surfing	1.2	2.1	2.9	1.3		
Total						
Average						

4-4.   Set up a worksheet to help you track the amount of time you spend on computers this semester. Use the built-in functions and Fill. Enter appropriate values to test the worksheet. Save and print the worksheet.

Hours Spent on Computers

Week	Mon	Tue	Wed	Thu	Fri	Sat	Sun	Total
1								
2								
3								
...								
14								
15								

Total:
Average:
Max:

Maximum number of hours spent in any one day during the semester:

4-5. The following table shows the price of gasoline in several countries in 1990, 1995, and 2000. These are average prices, including taxes, of a U.S. gallon of unleaded regular gas in U.S. dollars.

Gasoline Retail Prices in Selected Countries
(Average price of unleaded regular gas: U.S. dollars per gallon, including taxes)

	1990	1995	2000
Australia	$ 1.91	1.95	1.94
Brazil	3.82	2.16	2.93
Canada	1.87	1.53	1.86
Germany	2.65	3.06	3.45
Japan	3.17	4.43	3.74
Taiwan	2.49	2.23	1.98
United States	1.16	1.15	1.51

(a) Add rows at the bottom for average price, maximum price, and minimum price. Use functions and the Fill operation.

(b) Use Auto Fill to show the predicted prices for 2005, 2010, 2015 for each country, assuming a linear trend. Fill the calculation rows out three columns to the right. Format all cells with two places to the right of the decimal point.

4-6. Create a worksheet to calculate the wages for hourly employees.

(a) Start off with a heading, the names of the employees, and the hours worked each day. Try using Auto Fill for the days of the weeks. Type in the numbers of hours worked each day. Use a variety of numbers.

Payroll

Week of

Name	Mon	Tue	Wed	Thu	Fri	Sat	Sun
Abel, Ann							
Jones, John							
Smith, Sam							
Wall, Joan							

(b) Add a column at the end to calculate total hours worked for each employee. Use the SUM function.

(c) Add a column with the hourly wage for each employee. Use a different wage for each employee. Be generous.

(d) Add a column to automatically calculate the gross wages earned for the week.

(e) Add a column for federal tax withholdings of 20%.

(f) Add a column for state tax withholdings of 5%.

(g) Add a column for medical deduction of $12 per week.

(h) Add a column for take-home pay (gross wages minus withholding and deductions).

(i) Add rows at the bottom for the total and the average of each of the columns. Use the SUM and AVERAGE functions and Fill.

(j) Format appropriate cells with $ signs and to two decimal places to the right of the decimal point.

(k) Format the worksheet so it is as attractive and readable as possible.

4-7.   Design and implement a worksheet to keep track of how much time you spend in each of your courses and favorite activities each day during a given week. You should have one row for each of your courses. You should have one column for each of the days of the week (Sun, Mon, Tue, ...). Add rows for sleeping and eating. Add rows for two other activities that you enjoy and participate in regularly. At the top of the worksheet should be your name and the dates of the week for the numbers in the worksheet.

Enter numbers into your worksheet (you can make them up). Include the time you spend in class for the hours for your courses.

Add a row at the bottom of your worksheet for Total. Use the Sum function and the Fill operation.

Add three columns on the right of your worksheet for Total, Average, and Maximum. Use the built-in functions and the Fill operation.

There are 168 hours in the week. Add a column that gives the percent of the week spent on each course or activity.

Now change some of the numbers in the worksheet. All of the formulas should automatically be recalculated.

CHAPTER 5

OPERATIONS ON CELLS

OBJECTIVES

In this chapter you will learn how to:

- Move cells in a worksheet
- Erase a range of cells
- Delete rows and columns
- Insert new rows and columns
- Attach a comment to a cell
- Use Copy and Paste to move information
- Link to files and web pages

In this chapter we will discuss some of the more commonly used operations on cells in Excel.

MOVING CELLS

Excel provides an easy way to move a group of cells to another location in the worksheet. First select the range of the worksheet you would like to move by dragging across it with the left mouse button down. Release the button and move the mouse so the mouse pointer is pointing to the very top of the selection. The pointer should change to a white arrow on top of a black figure with arrows pointing in four directions, as in Figure 5-1.

Now press the mouse button and drag the selected range to wherever you would like to place it. As you drag, you will see an outline of the range move along with the mouse pointer. Release the mouse button and the selected portion of the worksheet will move. This operation is a form of **drag and drop**. You can force scrolling by dragging the selected cells to the edge of the window.

After you move a range of cells within a complex worksheet, you should look to make sure that all the formulas still work correctly. Excel does its best to adjust all relevant formulas, both the formulas that are moved and the formulas in other cells that refer to the cells that are moved.

If you are unhappy with the results you can Undo the operation.

Figure 5-1. Getting ready to move a range of cells by dragging.

ERASING A RANGE OF CELLS

The easiest way to erase a range is to select the range by dragging across it and then with the button up move the mouse pointer down to the bottom right hand corner of the range. The pointer will change into a thin cross. Depress the mouse button and drag the mouse back through the range to the top left corner of the range. The range will turn gray as you drag. When you release the mouse button, the contents of the cells will be erased.

Alternatively, you can select the range of cells to be erased by dragging across them and then pressing the Delete key.

DELETING ROWS AND COLUMNS

To delete a row, first select the row by clicking on the row number to the left of the worksheet, as in Figure 5-2. Now select *Delete* in the *Edit* pull-down menu. The entire row will be deleted. All cells below the row will slide up one row.

Excel adjusts references in formulas as best it can. If you have referred to one of the deleted cells in a formula, the formula might evaluate to #REF!, meaning there is an unresolvable reference in the formula.

To delete multiple rows at once, drag across the row numbers to select the multiple rows and then select *Delete* in the *Edit* pull-down menu.

Columns are deleted in the same way.

	A	B	C	D	E	F	G	H	I
1									
2		SALES SUMMARY BY REGION							
3									
4		JAN	FEB	MAR	APR	MAY	JUN	TOTAL	
5									
6	AFRICA	4.6	3.4	4.2	5.4	3.9	4.9	26.4	
7	ANTARCTICA	1.1	0.8	0.7	1.3	0.9	1.3	6.1	
8	ASIA	43.2	46.4	45.4	47.6	47.1	46.3	276	
9	EUROPE	32.5	33.7	34.1	33.8	33.5	35.2	202.8	
10	LATIN AMERICA	14.7	13.6	13.4	17.5	15.2	18.9	93.3	
11	NORTH AMERICA	39.5	41.3	40.8	42.4	38.7	43.5	246.2	
12									
13	TOTAL	135.6	139.2	138.6	148	139.3	150.1	850.8	
14									

Figure 5-2. Click on the row number to select the entire row.

INSERTING ROWS AND COLUMNS

To insert a new row in a worksheet, select the row where you want a new row inserted. For example, if you would like a new row 6 inserted, select the current row 6 by clicking on the row number 6 on the left of the worksheet. Now select *Rows* in the *Insert* pull-down menu. A new blank row 6 will be inserted. Everything from row 6 down will be moved down one row. References in formulas will be adjusted.

If you would like to insert three rows beginning at row 6, simply drag across the row numbers 6, 7, and 8 so that these three rows are selected. Now select *Rows* in the *Insert* pull-down menu. Three new rows (6, 7, and 8) will be inserted. All information previously in row 6 and below will be moved down three rows. Formulas will be adjusted accordingly.

Alternatively, you simply can click on any cell in row 6 to make it the active cell and then select *Rows* in the *Insert* pull-down menu to insert a new row at the location of the active cell.

Ditto for columns.

ATTACHING A COMMENT TO A CELL

You can attach a **comment** to a cell. For example, if a formula in a cell is particularly complex, you can explain the formula in a comment. If you are making an important assumption about the inflation rate in a worksheet, you can add a comment to the cell with a statement about the assumption.

To attach a comment to a cell, click on the cell and then select *Comment* in the *Insert* pull-down menu. You will see a yellow box appear with the name of the user in bold. You can retype over the name and then add whatever comment you would like, as shown in Figure 5-3.

Cells that have comments attached are marked in the worksheet with a small red triangle in the top right corner of the cell. To see a comment just let the mouse pointer rest on the cell for a short period of time and the comment will appear.

Attaching comments is an excellent way to provide documentation for your workbook both for yourself and for other people who will be using it.

For people who work jointly on Excel workbooks comments provide an easy way to communicate with each other about the specific contents of various cells in the workbook. To change or add to an existing comment you can right click on the cell and select *Edit Comment* in the menu. Then you can add your name and your comment. To see all of the comments in the workbook at once select *Comments* in the *View* pull-down menu.

You can have comments printed with your worksheet by selecting Comments in the Sheet tab of *Page Setup* in the *File* pull-down menu.

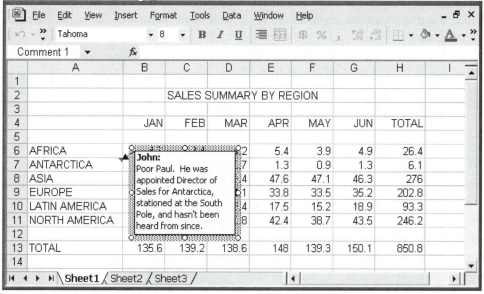

Figure 5-3. Attaching a comment to cell A7.

COPY AND PASTE

You may be familiar with the operations of Copy and Paste from other applications, for example word-processing. Copy and Paste is a common method for moving information from one place to another.

The basic idea is that there is a usually hidden part of the computer's memory called the **Clipboard**. The Clipboard holds recent information that was Copied (or Cut).

To Copy information into the Clipboard, first select the information by clicking on it or dragging across it and then click on the **Copy button** on the Standard toolbar or select *Copy* in the *Edit* pull-down menu.

The copied information is held temporarily in the Clipboard.

To Paste the information from the Clipboard into the worksheet, select the destination cell or range in the worksheet. Then click on the **Paste button** in the Standard toolbar or select *Paste* in the *Edit* pull-down menu.

Copy and Paste can be used to fill a formula down a column. In Figure 5-4, we click on cell H6 and then click on the Copy button to copy the contents of cell H6 into the Clipboard. We select cells H7:H11 by dragging down them and clicking on the Paste button. The result is shown in Figure 5-5. The formula from cell H6 has been copied and then pasted down column H. Note that this is an "intelligent" Copy and Paste, so the addresses in the formula have been adjusted. A moving dashed line appears around the most recent cell or range of cells copied into the clipboard.

Figure 5-4. Click on cell H6 to select it. Then click on the Copy button to copy the formula in H6 into the Clipboard.

Figure 5-5. Drag down across H7:H11 to select these cells. Click on the Paste button. The formula will be pasted from the Clipboard into the cells with the addresses adjusted.

In this instance we are using Copy and Paste as a substitute for dragging the Fill Handle, as a substitute for the Fill operation. Copy and Paste is more general than Fill because you can paste copied information anywhere in your workbook, or into any other workbook, or into any other program for that matter.

For example, we could copy the names of the regions in column A into the Clipboard by selecting A6:A11, dragging across those cells, and then clicking on the Copy button. Next we could scroll over to column T and click on cell T7. Now if we click on the Paste button, the names will be pasted from the Clipboard into cells T7:T12.

Similarly, we could copy a portion of a worksheet from Excel and then paste the values into a Word document.

PASTE OPTIONS

When we use the normal Paste operation, as in Figure 5-5, formulas are pasted into the cells. Clicking on the button on the right side of Paste button gives us a menu with various options. (See Figure 5-6.) For example, we could have Excel paste just the values into the selected area and not the formulas.

Selecting *Paste Special...* gives us even more options, as in Figure 5-7.

Figure 5-6. The Paste Options menu.

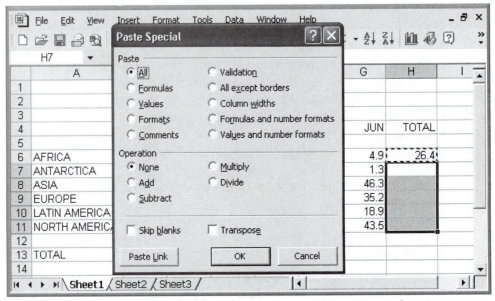

Figure 5-7. Paste Special. The trouble is, Microsoft never gives you enough options.

For example, in another situation we might want to paste the current values in the copied cells, rather than the formulas, but not the formats of the copied cells. And, we might want to add those values into the current values in the cells to which we are pasting. In this case, we would click on Values in the top left column and on Add in the middle left column, as in Figure 5-8.

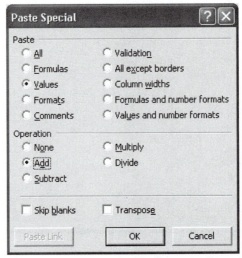

Figure 5-8. Changing options in the Paste Special menu.

COPYING AND PASTING FROM THE INTERNET

Sometimes we find data on the web that we would like to bring into Excel. The general technique is to Copy the data into the Clipboard by first dragging across it in the web browser and then selecting *Copy* in the *Edit* pull-down menu of the browser. Then paste it from the Clipboard into Excel by clicking on a cell in the Excel worksheet and clicking on Paste. The data should be pasted into the worksheet.

That's the theory. Sometimes it works in practice, but not always. There are many formats that the original data could be in on the web. If the original data is in Excel or is a table in Word, there should be no problem. On the other hand, if the original data is in a .pdf file and is being viewed in Adobe Acrobat then basically you are getting a picture of the data rather than the data values themselves so copying and pasting the values is hopeless. Alternatively, the data could be in a table in a webpage or it could be straight text. The best approach is trial and error. Try to Copy and Paste and see what happens. Since Internet Explorer is made by the same company as makes Excel (namely, Microsoft), I sometimes have better luck copying and pasting into Excel from Internet Explorer than I do from a Netscape browser.

As an example, suppose we want to analyze how much factory workers make in different countries. We find our way to www.bls.gov, the U.S. Bureau of Labor Statistics site. We find the basic data shown in Figure 5-9, which is just what we want. It shows hourly compensation for factory workers in various countries from 1992 through 2000 stated in U.S. dollars. We would like to bring the data into Excel to manipulate it. We drag across the data in the browser and copy it into the Clipboard. Then we open a workbook in Excel and paste the data into the worksheet. We obtain the worksheet shown in Figure 5-10. At first glance this worksheet looks OK, but there is a serious problem. All of the data really is text in column A. You can see in Figure 5-10 the active cell is in A1 and all of the data for that row is contained in the cell. With all of the data as text in column A, there is no way to refer to individual numbers in formulas. This is a common problem when the original data is simple text, as is the case here.

Excel provides a remedy in the form of a **Text to Columns Wizard**. A **Wizard** is a feature in Excel that takes a previously difficult operation and makes it easy by guiding you step by step. To access the Text to Columns Wizard, first select all of the cells with data in column A. Then select *Text to Columns...* in the *Data* pull-down menu, as in Figure 5-11. The Wizard shows you the text data, guesses where the column boundaries are, and asks you if it guessed correctly. It usually does. Simply clicking on Next or Finish in each of the three steps of the Wizard produces the worksheet in Figure 5-12.

The worksheet in Figure 5-12 has one number in each cell. The columns can be widened. The worksheet can be formatted. Most importantly, the cells with the numbers can be referred to in formulas so you can analyze the data.

Figure 5-9. Data as it appears in the browser.

Figure 5-10. After copying and pasting the data into Excel, there is a problem. All of the data is text in column A.

Figure 5-11. First select the data in column A and then invoke the Text to Columns Wizard in the Data pull-down menu.

Figure 5-12. The Text to Columns Wizard breaks the text up into separate cells. Now you can widen the columns and format the cells and enter formulas to analyze the data.

LINKING TO FILES AND WEB PAGES

Your worksheet can contain links to other files on your disk or local network or to pages at any site on the web.

Click on a cell. Now select *Hyperlink...* in the *Insert* pull-down menu or click on the **Insert Hyperlink tool**. You can either browse for the file you want or type it in directly. For example, I could type in C:\Music\BeethovensNinthFinale.mp3. This would appear in the cell as a link. Whenever I click on the cell the music would play using my default mp3 player software. You can link to any type of file, for example a movie or a Word document or another Excel workbook.

Alternatively I could type in http://www.cs.bc.edu/~gips. This is a link to my web page at Boston College. Whenever I click on the cell a browser window would open up with the web page in it.

Note that backslashes (\ ) are used for specifying file paths and slashes (/) are used for specifying URLs for web pages.

The **HYPERLINK** function is very useful here. The HYPERLINK function contains two arguments: the link location and a "friendly name". For example, if I put

=HYPERLINK("C:\Music\BeethovensNinthFinale.mp3","Play Ode to Joy")

in a cell, what will appear is <u>Play Ode to Joy</u>. Clicking on the cell will play the music in the file. Similarly, I could put

=HYPERLINK("http://www.cs.bc.edu/~gips","Click here for a good time")

into a cell, as in Figure 5-13.

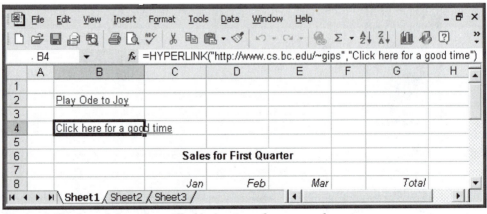

Figure 5-13. A worksheet that will play music and open a web page.

COMPUTER EXERCISE

5-1. We Love Plants, Inc. is a small company in the houseplant care business. People can arrange for the company to come into their apartment or house to care for their plants when they are away on business or on vacation or all-year around. The company has begun offering the same service to businesses and offices.

The most recent Income Statement for the company looks as follows.

WE LOVE PLANTS, INC.
Income Statement
For the Year Ended December 31

Revenues:		
Home plant care revenue	$197,329	
Office plant care revenue	65,545	
Total Revenues		$262,874
Expenses:		
Salaries expense	72,488	
Payroll tax expense	9,803	
Rent expense for office	7,800	
Utilities expense	1,377	
Advertising expense	23,103	
Automobile expense	35,292	
Supplies expense	24,550	
Misc. expense	8,500	
Total Expenses		$182,913
Pretax Income		$79,961
Income tax expense		15,992
Net income		$63,969
Earnings per share		$1.60

The company pays 20% in income taxes. There are 40,000 shares of stock.

(a) Create a "template" worksheet for the Income Statement where each of the numbers in the middle column is 0. All of the numbers in the right column should be the results of formulas and should appear as 0 also. The numbers should be formatted as they appear above. Save the worksheet on the disk.

(b) Now fill in the numbers in the middle column. The numbers in the right column should match. Save the worksheet. Print the worksheet.

(c) Select a rectangular range of cells that includes all of the non-blank cells by dragging across the cells. Move this entire range of cells two columns to the right and one row down.

(d) Erase the first four of the expenses categories and values by selecting the range containing the cells and dragging the Fill Handle back over the range.

(e) Undo the erase.

(f) Delete columns A and B. (They should be empty as the result of the move in part (c).)

(g) Insert a new row in the middle of the expenses. Enter in Insurance Expense 7,300.

(h) Attach the comment "We need to get better control of these." to the cell for Misc. Expense.

(i) Select the information in the two columns of numbers by dragging across it. Then click on the Copy button or select *Copy* in the *Edit* pull-down menu. Click on the cell two columns to the right of the top right cell of the copied range. Now click on the Paste button or select *Paste* in the *Edit* pull-down menu to paste a new copy of the information two columns over. This could be used as the basis for entering in next year's income statement to compare it with this year's.

(j) Erase the information just pasted either by selecting Undo or by erasing the range of cells.

(k) Save the worksheet on the disk.

(l) Format the worksheet so that it looks as attractive as possible. Save the worksheet again.

(m) Print the worksheet.

CHAPTER 6

RELATIVE VS. ABSOLUTE ADDRESSING

OBJECTIVES

In this chapter you will learn how to:

- Use absolute addressing in formulas
- Create worksheets for "What if" analysis
- Use the split bars to split the window
- Name cells and ranges of cells
- Use mixed addressing in formulas

What makes the Fill (or Copy and Paste) operation so powerful in making multiple copies of formulas is that Excel adjusts the addresses in the formulas as it makes the copies. For example, if the formula in H6 is =SUM(C6:G6) and we fill the formula down the column, then the formula in H7 will be =SUM(C7:G7), the formula in H8 will be =SUM(C8:G8), and so on. In Chapter 4, we referred to this as an "intelligent" Fill operation. The Fill operation as described usually works well. However, there are some cases where we do not want the address in the formula to be adjusted as the formula is filled, where changing the address causes an error in the formula. In this important chapter we will examine how to instruct Excel not to change an address in a formula when filling the formula down a column or across a row.

AN EXAMPLE WHERE THE FILL OPERATION SEEMS TO FAIL

We would like to know the proportion of the world's population in each continent. Some research yields the population for each continent shown in the worksheet in Figure 6-1.

Figure 6-1. *A worksheet for determining the proportion of the world population by continent.*

To find the total population on the planet we put the formula

$$=SUM(C7:C12)$$

into cell C14. There are approximately 6,157 million people on the planet, of whom 823 million live in Africa. To calculate the proportion of people in Africa, we divide the population of Africa by the total population for the planet. The formula in D7 can be

$$=C7/C14$$

as in Figure 6-2. Thus, 0.1336, or almost one-seventh, of the world's population lives in Africa.

Now we would like to Fill the formula down the column to calculate the proportion of the world's population living in the other continents. We click on D7 to select the cell. We move the mouse pointer over the Fill Handle in the bottom right of the cell and drag the Fill Handle down to D12. When we release the mouse button, the formula is filled down into D8:D12. Here is the key point. Filling the formula in D7 down the column yields the worksheet in Figure 6-3.

Figure 6-2. To find the proportion of the population in Africa, divide the Africa Population by the Total Population.

Figure 6-3. Filling down the formula just entered in D7 produces a very instructive error.

What has happened? The cells into which we filled the formula are full of #DIV/0! messages. These are error messages that indicate that we instructed Excel to divide a value by 0. Division by 0 is undefined and, so, produces an error message. What is the source of the problem? If we look at the formula in D8, we see that it is =C8/C15. The C8 is correct. But C15 is a blank cell. In evaluating the formula =C8/C15 the computer divides 3737, the number in C8, by 0, the "number" in C15. Dividing any number by 0 yields the error message.

What should the formula in D8 be? We would like it to be the population of Asia divided by the total population, =C8/C14, rather than =C8/C15. What happened in Figure 6-3? When the formula =C7/C14 in cell D7 was filled down the column, both of the addresses were adjusted by the Fill operation. So =C7/C14 in D7 became =C8/C15 in D8 became =C9/C16 in D9, and so on. We wanted =C7/C14 in D7 to become =C8/C14 in D8 to become =C9/C14 in D9, and so on. That is, we want the Fill operation to adjust the first address C7 in the formula in =C7/C14 but not the second address, C14. The cell address for the total population, C14, should remain unchanged. Excel has an "intelligent" Fill operation but not a brilliant Fill operation. Excel must be told which addresses to adjust and which to keep the same when a formula is filled.

ABSOLUTE ADDRESSING

An address written in the normal way (for example, C14) is adjusted automatically by Excel in a Fill operation and is called a **relative address** or **relative reference**. To instruct Excel that an address in a formula is not to be changed when filled, the address is written with dollar signs before the column name and row name, for example, as $C$14. An address that is not to be adjusted when copied is called an **absolute address** or **absolute reference**. The dollar signs have nothing to do with money or currency here. For reasons not apparent, the dollar signs were selected to denote an absolute address.

Returning to our example, now we see that the formula in cell D7 should be

$$=C7/\$C\$14$$

When filled down the column, this formula becomes =C8/$C$14 in D8, which becomes =C9/$C$14 in D9, and so on, as in Figure 6-4. The $C$14 is evaluated in the formula just the same as is C14, as the value in cell C14. The only difference in using an absolute address rather than a relative address occurs when the formula is filled or copied and pasted.

Figure 6-4. We do not want the reference to cell C14 to be adjusted when the formula in D7 is filled down, so we use absolute addressing.

Why are the terms "relative address" and "absolute address" used? Consider, again, the original formula in cell D7 in Figure 6-2. The formula =C7/C14 in D7 can be interpreted as "Take the number one column to the left and divide it by the number in the cell one column to the left and seven rows down" because the addresses are adjusted when the formula is filled or copied. Hence, the addresses C7 and C14 are "relative addresses". In contrast, the formula =C7/$C$14 in D7 can be interpreted as "Take the number one column to the left and divide it by the number in cell C14" because the address C7 is adjusted as the formula is copied but the address $C$14 remains the same. Hence, the address C7 is relative, but the address $C$14 is absolute.

To complete the example, we format the cells in column D as Percent with one decimal place and add up the percentages in D14 (see Figure 6-5). Note again that formatting a cell, for example as a percentage, only affects the way the cell appears in the worksheet, not the underlying value in the cell. While D10 appears as 7.9%, the value in D10 actually is 0.078934546, the result of dividing 486 by 6,157.

Figure 6-5. The completed worksheet for calculating the percentage of the population on each continent.

PETER MINUIT

Absolute addressing is especially important in worksheets where key numbers are put into separate cells. To illustrate this, let's do another example.

Peter Minuit was the director-general of the Dutch West Indies Company's settlements in North America. In 1626 he negotiated a deal with local tribal chiefs and purchased the island of Manhattan from them for pieces of bright cloth, beads, and other trinkets valued at 60 guilders, or about $24. Today the island of Manhattan forms the core of New York City and is worth a fortune. But did Peter make such a great deal? Suppose Peter had taken the money and put it into a Money Market Account at the Dutch National Bank. How much would it be worth today? What would be the value of the investment each year from 1626 to 2006?

We need one more piece of information. What interest rate would Peter have received on his money over 380 years? For now, let us assume a constant 3% per year. We will change this assumption later.

Figure 6-6 is a start toward a worksheet that calculates what Peter's investment would be worth. The years from 1626 through 2006 will be in column B. The corresponding value of the investment each year will be in column D.

Figure 6-6. Beginning the worksheet to calculate what the value of the $24 would be if Peter Minuit had deposited it in a bank instead of purchasing Manhattan.

How can we obtain the years in column B? We could type each one of them, but who wants to type 380 numbers? We could enter 1627 in cell B9 and then use AutoFill as discussed at the end of Chapter 4. Another solution is to put a formula into B9 and then fill the formula down the column. Each number in column B is to be one greater than the number in the cell above. So in cell B9 we put the formula

$$=B8+1$$

We then fill the formula down the column through B388. To do this, we click on B9, grab the Fill Handle in the bottom right of the cell by pressing down on the mouse button, and with the button held down we move the mouse pointer down column B below the bottom of the worksheet, forcing the worksheet to scroll down to B388. The further below the window we move the mouse pointer, the faster it scrolls. We then release the mouse button when we reach B388. Formulas will fill from B9 through B388. The formula in B10 will be =B9+1, the formula in B11 will be =B10+1, and so on. There will be a chain of formulas down the column, each adding one to the value of the cell above. The years from 1626 through 2006 will appear in column B.

How can we obtain the value of the investment each year in column D? We will follow the same technique of entering a formula for the cell in row 9 and then filling the formula down the column. How much money would Peter have in 1627? Peter would have the amount from the previous year plus the interest the money earned during the year. At 3% interest the formula for D9 would be

$$=D8+D8*3\%$$

We fill the formula from D9 down through D388. We format the values in column D as Currency with 0 decimal places, and widen the cells in column D. The resulting worksheet is shown in Figure 6-7.

Scrolling down to row 388, we can see the bottom of the worksheet in Figure 6-8. What would Peter's $24 investment in 1626 be worth today if he received 3% interest per year? Less than two million dollars. What does less than two million dollars buy in Manhattan today? A condo, an apartment in a nice building. It appears that Peter was wise in purchasing Manhattan. (Of course, the British fleet took over the city from the Dutch in 1664 and changed the name from Nieuw Amsterdam to New York. If the 60 guilders had been invested in the bank, at least the Dutch still would have had their money. And, in true New York fashion, it is said that the chiefs who "sold" Manhattan to Peter were from the Canarsie tribe in Brooklyn and had no claim to Manhattan.)

Figure 6-7. Calculating the value of the investment assuming a 3% interest rate.

Figure 6-8. Peter's investment would be worth less than $2,000,000 today at 3% interest.

But what if Peter had received 5% annual interest rate instead of 3%? What would Peter's account be worth now? To answer this question we need to change the worksheet. In particular, we need to change the formulas in column D. The formula in D9 could be changed to

$$=D8+D8*5\%$$

Then the formula would be filled down to D388. But suppose we then wanted to see what the value of the investment would be if the annual interest rate were 7% or 9% or 11%. In order to change the interest rate we would have to change the formula in D9 and then fill the new formula down the column each time.

A better approach is to put the interest rate in a separate cell and refer to that cell in the formulas in column D. Now if we want to see what would happen with a different interest rate, we would just need to change the number in the cell rather than changing all 375 formulas. This approach is shown in Figure 6-9.

This worksheet illustrates a good general rule: Any value that you might want to change should be placed in a separate cell, rather than being built explicitly into formulas.

Figure 6-9. A better approach is to place the annual interest rate in a separate cell and refer to the cell in the formulas using absolute addressing.

The Annual interest rate is in cell D5. The formula in D9 is

=D8+D8*$D$5

This formula has been filled from D9 down through D382. We refer to the interest rate as an absolute address ($D$5) so that the address is not adjusted as the formula is filled down the column. In Figure 6-9 the cursor is on D11 and indeed we can see that the formula in D11 is

=D10+D10*$D$5

SPLITTING THE WINDOW

Wouldn't it be nice to be able to change the interest rate and be able to see immediately the resulting value of the investment today? Excel has a **Horizontal Split Bar** and a **Vertical Split Bar** (see Figure 6-10). The Horizontal Split Bar is the small horizontal rectangle right above the up scroll arrow. The Vertical Split Bar is the small vertical rectangle to the right of the right scroll arrow.

Figure 6-10. The locations of the Horizontal and Vertical Split Bars.

Figure 6-11. The Horizontal Split Bar allows the display of two parts of the worksheet at once.

Dragging the Horizontal Split Bar down allows us to split the window in half. Each portion can be vertically scrolled independently. By scrolling the bottom portion down to row 389 we can see the two portions of the screen shown in Figure 6-11. At 5% interest Peter's $24 investment in 1626 would be worth over $2 billion today. With over $2 billion you could buy some major office buildings in Manhattan and a nice hotel or two.

In Chapter 1 we discussed how electronic spreadsheets were developed to facilitate "What if" analysis. Here is an example. We can easily determine "What if" Peter received some annual interest rate on his investment. To see "What if" we change the number in D5 to the annual interest rate we wish to try. As soon as we enter the new rate, the new values for the investment go rippling down the screen. With the worksheet designed so that the annual interest rate is in a separate cell and with the window divided into two portions, we can change the interest rate to 7% and see almost instantaneously that if Peter had invested $24 in 1626 at 7% annual interest, it would be worth some $3 trillion. (See Figure 6-12.) Now we're talking real money!

To remove the split in the window, we simply drag the Horizontal Split Bar back up to the top of the worksheet.

Figure 6-12. At 7% interest you might prefer the bank account over Manhattan. What would 9% produce? 11%?

NAMING CELLS

In larger worksheets it is easy to forget which cells contain which quantities. When reading the formulas in a larger worksheet it can be cumbersome to determine which quantities are referred to by cell addresses in the formulas. Excel provides the capability of giving names to cells and ranges of cells and using these names in formulas instead of the cell addresses. It is good practice to name key cells in larger worksheets.

For example, in this worksheet we could give cell D5 the name RATE. Then the formula in cell D9 would be

$$=D8+D8*RATE$$

rather than

$$=D8+D8*\$D\$5$$

Figure 6-13. To give a name to cell D5, select D5 and then click in the Name Box at the top left of the worksheet and type in the desired name, in this case RATE.

To give cell D5 a name, we first select D5 by clicking on it. Then we click in the **Name Box**. The Name Box is the box right above the A column heading. In the Name Box we type the new name of the cell, as in Figure 16-13.

The name can contain up to 255 characters. It should begin with a letter. The name can contain letters, digits, and underscores (_) but not spaces or arithmetic operators or most punctuation characters. Do be careful in naming ranges. Select a name that makes sense, that you will remember.

To use a name in a formula we can simply type the name instead of the cell address. Alternatively, we can select from the list of names by selecting *Name* in the *Insert* pull-down menu and then within *Name* selecting *Paste* and the name we would like.

Excel assumes that a name refers to an absolute address. In this case, Excel assumes that the name RATE refers to the absolute address $D$5. So if we use the name in a formula and then fill the formula, the name will continue to refer to the same cell in the filled copies of the formula. (See Figure 6-14.)

The Name Box contains a pull-down menu. (See Figure 6-15.) Just click on the downward-pointing triangle on the right of the Name Box to see the list of all the names that have been given to cells already. If you select a name in the menu the active cell will jump to the cell with that name so you can see which cells are referred to by the various names.

Figure 6-14. The name RATE is treated as an absolute reference to the cell D5. The reference is unchanged after the formula is filled down.

Figure 6-15. Use the Name Box pull-down menu to see the cell names that have been defined already and to find their locations.

Names also can be given to ranges of cells. For example, in the sales-by-region worksheet in the previous chapter we could have selected the range B6:G11 and given it the name SALES. Then instead of the formula =SUM(B6:G11) we could have written =SUM(SALES).

Incidentally, names in Excel are "case insensitive". This means that the name SALES is the same as Sales which is the same as sales.

MIXED ADDRESSING

On occasion we might want the column part of the address of a cell in a formula to remain absolute and the row part of the address to be relative. Or we might want the column part of the address of a cell in a formula to be relative and the row part to be absolute. An address in a formula that is to be absolute in one part and relative in the other dimension is called a **mixed address** or **mixed reference**.

The worksheet in Figure 6-16 illustrates a double use of mixed addressing. Each cell in the range B4:M15 is the product of the number in column A for the row and the number in row 3 for the column. Thus the formula in B4 is =$A4*B$3. The body of the table is produced by filling that formula across from B4 through M4 and then filling all of those formulas down from B4:M4 to B4:M15. As a check on your understanding, what would be the resulting formula in, say, cell H8? In the first address in the formula column A is absolute while the row is relative. In the second address in the formula the column is relative while row 3 is absolute. So the formula filled into cell H8 would be =$A8*H$3.

Figure 6-16. A simple worksheet that uses mixed addressing.

PENCIL AND PAPER EXERCISE

6-1.   The widget industry is dominated by two companies. United Widget (UW) has total sales of $87.2 million this year. However, their sales are decreasing by 0.8% per year. Widgets International (WI) has sales of $53.4 million this year. Their sales are increasing by 3.2% each year. We have developed a worksheet (using Fill) that shows their future performance if this trend continues. The growth rates are in separate cells. Changing one of the growth rates in C4 or D4 causes the predictions to change appropriately.

What is the formula in each of the following cells:

(a) B12
(b) C12
(c) D12
(d) E12
(e) C18
(f) E18

COMPUTER EXERCISES

6-2. There are eight students in your math class. They all took a quiz. Enter the eight names in one column and eight (different) scores in an adjoining column. At the bottom of the column calculate the class average. Now add a new column that calculates the points above or below the class average for each student. Use the Fill operation. Change one of the scores. Do the class average and all of the points above or below change accordingly?

6-3. The major regions of the earth and their areas in millions of square miles are shown below.

Pacific Ocean	64	Asia	17
Atlantic Ocean	33	Africa	12
Indian Ocean	28	North America	9
Arctic Ocean	5	South America	7
other oceans	9	Antarctica	5
		Europe	4
		Australia	3
		other land	1

(a) Enter this data into a worksheet. Add well-labeled cells for the total area covered by the oceans, the total area covered by land, and the total area of the earth. Name these cells.

(b) Add a column that shows the percentage of the earth covered by each of the 13 regions listed. Use the Fill operation.

(c) Add a column that shows the percentage of the total area covered by ocean that each of the ocean regions occupies. Use the Fill operation.

(d) Add a column that shows the percentage of the total area covered by land that each of the continents occupies. Use the Fill operation.

6-4. You are planning to deposit a fixed amount at the beginning of each year in a bank account for 20 years. Assume that you will earn a constant interest rate on your money. Design and implement a worksheet that will show you how much you will have accumulated at the end of each of the 20 years. You should have separate, well-labeled cells for the amount of your annual deposit and for the interest rate. If you change either of these cells, all the accumulations should change automatically.

Try your worksheet on

(a) a deposit of $5,000 per year and an interest rate of 5% per year,

(b) a deposit of $5,000 per year and an interest rate of 10% per year,

(c) a deposit of $10,000 per year and an interest rate of 5% per year, and

(d) a deposit of $10,000 per year and an interest rate of 10% per year.

(e) How much do you need to deposit each year to have exactly $1,000,000 in 20 years assuming that you earn 8% interest per year? Use trial and error.

(f) What annual interest rate would you need to obtain in order to accumulate $1,000,000 at the end of 20 years if you deposit $10,000 per year? Use trial and error.

6-5. The cost of a college education has been rising rapidly, as I am sure you are aware. You would like to estimate what it will cost you to put your children through college. First we will need to gather some data and make some assumptions. Find out the current cost of attending your favorite college or university in terms of (1) tuition and (2) all other expenses. If you do not have any children now, assume that your first child will be born five years from now and your second child will be born three years later. Assume that your children will enter college at age 18 and that they will attend for four years each and then graduate with high honors. (Of course they will be model students.) Further we will assume that there will be a single annual rate of increase over the years for tuition and other expenses.

Your worksheet will have a separate section at the top for parameters and data that might be changed. In particular, there should be well-labeled cells for current tuition, current other expenses, and rate of increase. The body of the worksheet should have four columns: year, tuition, other expenses, total expenses. The values that appear in these columns will depend in part on the values in the input section of the worksheet. At the bottom (or top) of the worksheet there should be a well-labeled output cell that gives the total projected cost of sending your two children to college.

Try your worksheet with an annual rate of increase of 6%. Now change the annual rate of increase to 9%. Do all of the appropriate numbers change? Don't worry. You will have a terrific job. The money you spend on college expenses for your children will be small change.

6-6. The country of Palladia has 3,750,000 people. The birth rate is 1.3%. That is, each year the number of babies born is equal to 1.3% of the people in the country at the beginning of the year. The death rate is 0.7%. Palladia is a wealthy paradise so lots of people are trying to enter from outside. The Minister of Immigration is proposing that 150,000 people be allowed to immigrate into the country each year.

(a) Create a worksheet for the Minister that predicts the population of Palladia for each of the next 10 years. There should be an input area at the top of your worksheet with cells for: starting population, annual birth rate, annual death rate, and annual immigration. Use the numbers above. There should be one row for each year. You can use as many columns as you would like. Print the worksheet.

(b) Suppose the birth rate is 1.1%, the death rate is 0.9%, and the annual immigration is 100,000. Print the worksheet.

(c) Suppose the birth rate is 1.0% and the death rate is 0.7%. The Prime Minister would like to see close to 5,000,000 people in the country at the end of 10 years. At what number should the annual immigration quota be set? Use trial and error to find a quota (in 1,000's) that results in a population that is as close as possible but just below 5,000,000. Print the worksheet.

6-7. Internet Shopping, Inc. has ambitious plans. This week they have 100,000 visitors to their website. Of their visitors, 2% place orders. These orders average $24.00 each. Thus they are taking orders for $48,000 this week (week 0).

For the next two years they plan to increase the visitors by 3% per week. They expect the percent who place orders to stay the same. They expect the average amount ordered to increase by $0.15 per week.

Create a worksheet to predict their growth over the next two years. You should have a separate input area with the two growth figures. You should have a row for each week. You should have columns for the week number (0 to 104), the number of visitors, number of shoppers, average amount ordered, and total ordered for each week. Changing either of the numbers in the input area should be reflected in changes in your worksheet.

6-8. Paul and Maria are married. Together they earn a salary of $85,000 per year. Their plan is to save enough money to retire to Bali for the rest of their lives. They believe that if they save $500,000 they should be set for life. Their expenses this year totaled $78,000, including taxes, living expenses, and everything else. They have decided to put the rest in a tax-free mutual fund to save up for their retirement.

Now Paul and Maria would like to do some projections to see when they can retire. They estimate that their salaries should go up by 8% per year. They hope to hold their expenses to an increase of 3% per year. Whatever is left at the end of each year, they will put into the account. They figure they should be able to earn interest of 4% per year on the money in the account, which will be accumulated in the mutual fund.

Your job is to set up a financial planning worksheet for Paul and Maria. You should have a separate input area with well-labeled cells for: current salary, current expenses, annual percentage increase for salary, annual percentage increase for expenses, and annual percentage interest rate earned in the mutual fund. Changing any of these numbers should result in changes throughout the worksheet.

The body of the worksheet should be the forecast for the next 25 years. Each row would represent a separate year. There should be separate columns for: Year, Salary, Expenses, Mutual Fund Interest Earned, Deposit in Mutual Fund, Mutual Fund End-of-Year Balance. All funds should accumulate in the mutual fund. You may assume that the deposit in the mutual fund from the difference between salary and expenses occurs at the end of the year.

Please try your worksheet three times: (1) assume the above numbers, (2) assume salary increases by 5% each year while expenses increase at 5% each year and they earn 5% in their mutual fund, and (3) one showing the percentage increase (or decrease) for expenses required if Paul and Maria wish to retire in only 8 years given that their salaries increase by 10% per year and they earn 6% per year in their mutual fund. This latter case can be solved by trial and error. For each of these last two cases you should need to change only cells in the input area.

6-9. Compsys is a start-up computer company. This quarter they expect Sales of $550,000. They expect their Sales to grow at a rate of 9% per quarter. Their Cost of Goods Sold is running at 34% of Sales and is expected to stay at that rate. Their Selling Costs are 12% of Sales and are expected to stay at that rate. Their General and Administrative Costs (including Research and Development) are $420,000 this quarter and are scheduled to rise at 2% per quarter.

(a) Design and implement a worksheet to make a 20 quarter income statement projection for Compsys. You should have a separate input area with well-labeled separate cells for each of the numbers above. You should have a separate row for each item in the income statement and a separate column for each quarter. The final row should be for Earnings Before Taxes. Use the Fill operation wherever possible.

In the initial quarters, Compsys should show operating losses (negative Earnings Before Taxes). Under the assumptions stated above, what is the first quarter in which Compsys shows an operating profit (positive Earnings Before Taxes)?

(b) Suppose Sales grow at 12% per quarter. Now in what quarter would Compsys first show an operating profit?

(c) Suppose Sales grow at 9% per quarter and General and Administrative Costs grow at 6% per quarter and Selling Costs are 15% of sales. Now in what quarter will Compsys first show an operating profit?

6-10. The Fibonacci series is named after Leonardo Fibonacci, an Italian mathematician of the thirteenth century. The Fibonacci series is an infinite series of numbers 0, 1, 1, 2, 3, 5, 8, 13, ... The first two numbers in the series are 0 and 1. Subsequent numbers are formed by adding the two previous numbers in the series. The Fibonacci series appears in many unexpected places. Indeed, there is a regularly published journal that is devoted to applications of the Fibonacci series.

What proportioned rectangle is the most aesthetically pleasing? What is the ratio of height to width that people most prefer in a rectangle? Since the Renaissance it has been claimed that The Golden Ratio is the most aesthetically pleasing ratio for a rectangle. The Golden Ratio has been shown to appear often in Western art. The Golden Ratio usually is defined as the proportion that results from dividing a line in two sections such that the ratio of the length of the smaller section to the larger section is the same as the ratio of the length of the larger section to the length of the line as a whole. Another way of computing the Golden Ratio is to take the ratio of successive terms of the Fibonacci series. Thus 0/1, 1/1, 1/2, 2/3, 3/5, 5/8, ... form closer and closer approximations of the Golden Ratio. (So, a 3 x 5 card or a 5 x 8 piece of paper should seem to be aesthetically pleasing rectangles.)

Create a worksheet with three well-labeled columns. In the first column should be the numbers 0, 1, 2, 3, 4, through 20. In the second column should be the successive terms of the Fibonacci series. In the third column should be the successive approximations to the Golden Ratio, printed as a decimal between 0 and 1. Use the Fill operation for all three columns.

6-11. Scientists at the Research Institute for Robotics have created a new type of robot that reproduces itself. The new robot takes two weeks to gather materials and then builds one new robot (exactly like itself) each week for three weeks. The first new robot is activated at the end of week 3, the second new robot is activated at the end of week 4, and the third new robot at the end of week 5. As soon as it is created, each new robot goes through the same cycle of gathering materials for two weeks and then creating three new robots, one per week. And so on for each of the new robots. At the end of the first five weeks of its existence each new robot ceases building new robots but retires and "lives" forever. The scientists plan to build only one robot with their own hands and then set it in motion. Create a worksheet that will tell you how many robots there will be in two years.

6-12. If you have been outside on a cold, windy day, you know that the wind makes it seem colder than it really is. After an extensive study (see Exercise 2-13) the National Weather Service has derived the following wind chill formula:

$$W = 35.74 + 0.6215\,T - 35.75\,(V^{0.16}) + 0.4275\,T\,(V^{0.16})$$

where W is the wind chill adjusted temperature, T is the air temperature in Fahrenheit, and V is the wind velocity in miles per hour.

Create a Wind Chill table that has columns for each temperature from 30 degrees down to -25 degrees in -5 degree increments and rows for wind velocity from 5 mph to 60 mph in 5 mph increments. These values should appear across the top (30, 25, 20, ... -25) and down the left column (5, 10, 15, ... 60) of your table. The body of the table should be the resulting wind chill adjusted temperatures according to the formula. The body of the table should use a single formula that is entered in the cell in the top left corner of the body of the table and then filled across and down.

6-13. To start her new business your aunt plans to take out a loan and pay it back in five annual installments of $50,000. These payments will be made at the end of each of the first five years of operation. She anticipates $180,000 in revenues for the first year and that revenues will grow at 12% per year. She estimates that her (non-loan) expenses for the first year will be $100,000 and will grow at 6% per year.

Design a worksheet that shows her revenues, expenses, loan payments, and pretax income during the first eight years of operation. There should be a separate input area for annual loan payment, initial revenues, initial expenses, annual growth rate for revenues, and annual growth rate for expenses. Changes in any of these values should result in appropriate changes in your worksheet.

(a) Try your worksheet with the above numbers.

(b) Try your worksheet with annual loan payment of $25,000, initial revenues of $100,000, initial expenses of $50,000, annual growth in revenues of 8%, annual growth in expenses of 5%.

6-14. Averosas are a new breed of small, furry animal that resemble guinea pigs. They are becoming all the rage as pets. You have decided to earn some extra money by raising averosas in your room. For Christmas you ask Santa Claus to help you out. You must have been good this year because sure enough on Christmas morning under the Christmas tree there is a one-month-old male averosa and a one-month-old female averosa in a cage.

Averosas are quite prolific, and predictably so. They have their first litter at six months of age. Every three months from then on, each female has a litter of on average four baby averosas (assume two males and two females). Of course, these babies will go through the same breeding cycle. At the end of each quarter (three months) you plan to sell all the averosas that have reached two years of age to the local pet stores. This is how you will make your fortune. You won't have any expenses because your roommate works in a restaurant and you figure your roommate can bring home the leftovers from the salad bar to feed the animals.

This sounds like a great scheme but your roommate would like to know (1) how many averosas will be born in your room each quarter and, more important, (2) how many averosas will be living in the room each quarter! You would like to know (3) how many averosas you'll be able to sell at the end of each quarter so you can plan what to do with all the money you'll earn. Incidentally, your roommate will be (somewhat) relieved to learn that averosas don't smell too bad if their cages are cleaned often.

Set up an Excel worksheet to answer these three questions. Assume you will have the averosa colony for the next five years. Of course you will use the Fill operation wherever possible. Use several columns. Label all columns clearly. Assume the quarter ends at January 1, April 1, July 1, and October 1.

Assuming everything goes as planned, what is the total number of averosas you will have owned during the five years? What is the maximum number of averosas that will be in your room at any one time? How long will it be before your roommate leaves?

CHAPTER 7

COMMON OPERATIONS

OBJECTIVES

In this chapter you will learn how to:

- Work with toolbars
- Add drawings to your worksheet
- Create textboxes on your worksheet
- Create WordArt
- Make your printouts more readable
- Protect cells in your worksheet from being changed

In this chapter we look at some common operations in Excel.

TOOLBARS

Toolbars provide buttons for performing different tasks. We can specify which toolbars we want displayed by selecting *Toolbars* in the *View* pull-down menu. The *Toolbars* sub-menu appears, as shown in Figure 7-1.

Figure 7-1. The Toolbars sub-menu.

Whichever toolbars we click a check next to will appear on the screen. Clicking on multiple toolbars can provide multiple buttons, but little space for your worksheet. (See Figure 7-2.) There obviously is a trade-off between the convenience of toolbars and the space they occupy in the window. Real estate on your computer display is a valuable and limited commodity.

Figure 7-2. Lots of toolbars. Not much worksheet space.

Toolbars can be dragged to wherever you like in the window. They can appear horizontal on the upper part of the window or they can be dragged into a rectangle that floats above a convenient location of your worksheet.

DRAWING

The Drawing toolbar (see Figure 7-3) provides a standard palette of drawing tools so you can add drawings to your worksheet (or chart). The drawings are not part of any cell, but rather float above the worksheet in a separate **drawing layer**. Drawings should not be confused with borders, which always are found around the outside of selected cells. Drawing is much more flexible.

To obtain the Drawing toolbar select *Toolbars* in the *View* pull-down menu and put a check by *Drawing*. The Drawing toolbar usually appears at the bottom of the window.

 Alternatively, you can click on the **Drawing button** on the Standard toolbar. Clicking on this button causes the Drawing toolbar to appear or disappear.

Figure 7-3. The Drawing toolbar.

The **Text Box button** allows you to add text boxes to your worksheet. Text boxes are boxes that contain text that float on top of your worksheet.

To create a text box, press the Text Box button. The mouse pointer becomes a down-pointing arrow and then when you press the button it becomes a crosshairs. The text box appears wherever you drag the pointer. You can type text into the text box. You can format the text the way you would like it to appear just as you can format any text that appears within a normal cell.

You can select a text box by clicking on the edge. The box should appear in outline with various handle points on it. Once the box is selected you can move it around or change its size by dragging on the handles.

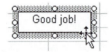

Figure 7-4. A text box.

 You can change the background color within the box by using the **Fill Color button** on the Formatting toolbar. If you want the text box to be transparent, select No Fill. You can select Fill Effects to create many different fill patterns.

 You can change the color of the text by selecting the text and using the **Font Color button**.

 You can change the thickness of the lines around the text box using the **Line Style button**.

 You can change the colors of the lines around the box using the **Line Color button.**

Thus you could have a textbox with red text on a yellow background with a thick blue box around it.

 This is only the beginning. The **Shadow Style button** allows you to put different shadows behind the text box (see Figure 7-5).

Figure 7-5. The Shadow Style pop-up menu.

The **3-D Style button** allows you to make the text box appear three-dimensional (see Figure 7-6).

Figure 7-6. The 3-D Style pop-up menu.

Selecting **3-D Settings ...** allows for even more controls of the rotations and lighting and variations on the three-dimensional style you selected (see Figure 7-7).

Figure 7-7. The 3-D Settings menu.

It is truly impressive how much work went into the Drawing feature. The Drawing toolbar is used not just in Excel but in Word and in other Office products.

 The **Arrow button** allows you to create different types of arrows to place on your worksheet or chart. First click on the Arrow button. Then drag the mouse where you would like the arrow to appear. It's best to drag in the direction of the arrow. (Start at the thin end and finish at the arrowhead.)

Double-clicking on the arrow gives you a box that allows you to change its thickness, color, the shape of the arrow point, and more other properties than you can imagine. Arrows can be dragged into the exact length, orientation, and location you like.

Arrows often are combined with text boxes, as in Figure 7-8.

The **Line button** on the Drawing toolbar allows you to draw lines of different sizes, widths, and colors.

Similarly for the **Rectangle button** and **Oval button**. These buttons work with the Shadow buttons and 3-D Style buttons described above. So you can first draw an oval and then make it into a cylinder using the 3-D Style button. Then you can use the Fill Color button and the Fill Effects tab to give it a colored texture.

	A	B	C	D	E	F	G	H	I
1									
2			SALES SUMMARY BY REGION						
3									
4		JAN	FEB	MAR	APR	MAY	JUN		
5								Good job!	
6	AFRICA	4.6	3.4	4.2	5.4	3.9	4.9		
7	ANTARCTICA	1.1	0.8	0.7	1.3	0.9	34.8		
8	ASIA	43.2	46.4	45.4	47.6	47.1	46.3		
9	EUROPE	32.5	33.7	34.1	33.8	33.5	35.2		
10	LATIN AMERICA	14.7	13.6	13.4	17.5	15.2	18.9		
11	NORTH AMERICA	39.5	41.3	40.8	42.4	38.7	43.5		
12									

Figure 7-8. Combining a text box with an arrow.

The text boxes, arrows, and other drawing elements float above the worksheet in the drawing layer. They can be dragged around and their sizes can be changed. At the same time their position is associated with the underlying worksheet, so that if, for example, a row or column width is changed or rows or columns are inserted or deleted, the positions of the drawings are adjusted accordingly.

The **AutoShapes button** in the Drawing toolbar allows you to add many different shapes to the drawing layer on top of the worksheet. For example, the Block Arrows are shown in Figure 7-9. First you select the basic shape that you want to draw. Then you click at the point on the worksheet where you would like it to appear and drag to indicate its size. The shape appears on the drawing layer with its various handles. You use the handles to size it and rotate it and move it. You can change the line width using the Line Style button and fill it with a color or texture using the Fill Color button or give it a 3-D shape or a shadow.

Another example of AutoShapes is shown in Figure 7-10. Here, a Ribbon is placed on top of a cell. The ribbon has No Fill selected in the Fill Color button so the underlying worksheet shows through.

The **Insert Clip Art button** allows you to place drawings that came with the software to be placed on top of the worksheet. When I searched for "book" in the Clip Art collection, the drawing at right was one of the selections found. This drawing seems typical of the Clip Art.

The **Insert Picture button** allows you to insert a photograph or other picture from your disk onto the drawing layer on top of your worksheet.

Figure 7-9. A Notched Right Arrow. The arrow was rotated and sized using the various handles and then the line width was made thicker using the Line Style button.

Figure 7-10. Placing a Curved Down Ribbon in the drawing layer over the cell. The line was made thicker using the Line Style button. No Fill was selected in the Fill Color button pop-up menu; otherwise you would not be able to see the underlying cells.

Alternatively, you can Copy and Paste a picture onto your worksheet, for example, off the web. All pictures can be selected, moved, and resized.

We have saved the best Drawing feature for last. The **WordArt button** allows us to make pictures out of words. Clicking on the WordArt button brings up the WordArt gallery.

Figure 7-11. The variety of WordArt templates.

Double clicking on one of the choices in the WordArt Gallery, for example the one in the fourth row where the arrow is in Figure 7-11, brings up a text entry box.

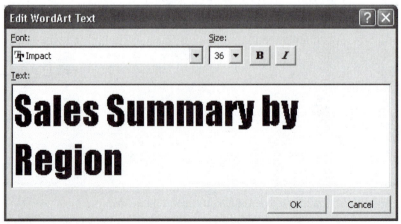

Figure 7-12. Enter the text for your WordArt here.

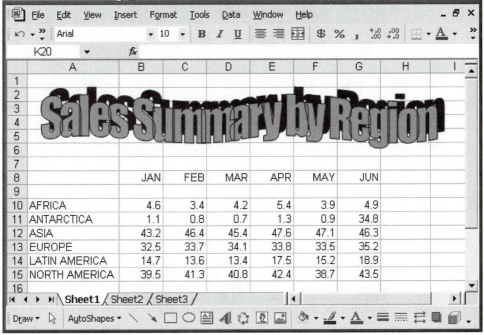

Figure 7-13. WordArt.

Click OK in the text entry box in Figure 7-12 and the WordArt in Figure 7-13 is created. To make room for the WordArt, the original title of the worksheet was deleted from C2 and four blank rows were inserted. The WordArt was selected and dragged into place.

The WordArt in Figure 7-13 contains light blue letters with a dark blue shadow. If you click on the WordArt picture itself a new **WordArt toolbar** will appear. The WordArt toolbar allows you to change the colors of the WordArt and to format it in other ways. You can explore the further wonders of WordArt on your own.

PRINTING: PAGE SETUP

Many options for printing the worksheet are found in the *Page Setup...* command in the *File* pull-down menu.

In the Page sheet of the Page Setup dialog box (see Figure 7-14) you can specify that the worksheet be printed in **Landscape** mode (sideways) rather than in the traditional **Portrait** mode. Since many worksheets are wider than they are long, this often makes sense. You also can inform Excel to shrink the printout by some fixed percentage or, more usefully, so it fits exactly on some number of pages. Usually it's a good idea to preview the printout first by clicking on the **Print Preview button** so you know that what will be printed is what you want.

Figure 7-14. Determining how your worksheet will be printed.

In the Margins sheet of the Page Setup dialog box (see Figure 7-15) you can specify the exact margins on the page and whether the worksheet should be centered on the page when printed.

Figure 7-15. Specifying margins and centering for your printout.

In the Header/Footer sheet of the Page Setup dialog box (Figure 7-16) you can select the **Header** and **Footer** for the printout. A Header is text that appears at the top of every page. A Footer is text that appears at the bottom of every page. By pressing Custom Header... or Custom Footer... you can specify the exact Header or Footer you would like on your printouts. The Header or Footer can contain information, such as the page number, the date, the time, the file name, your name, the exercise number, or any other text you would like to include with each page of the printout.

Figure 7-16. Specifying the header and footer for the printout.

In the Sheet sheet (sorry about that) of the Page Setup dialog box (see Figure 7-17), you can specify which area of the worksheet is to be printed. You can specify whether certain rows or columns are to be printed at the top or left of each page. (This is useful if the rows or columns contain titles for a very large range of numbers.) You can specify whether the gridlines (the lines between cells) are printed. You can specify whether the row numbers and column letters are printed. Printing the row numbers and column letters is especially useful if you are printing out a worksheet with the formulas displayed in the cells so you can easily determine which cells are referred to in the formulas. You can specify whether the Comments attached to cells are printed. You also can specify the order of printing for a large worksheet that requires multiple sheets of paper to print. Do you want Excel to print out the worksheet "Down, then over" or "Over, then down"? (See the illustration at the bottom of Figure 7-17.)

Figure 7-17. Even more choices for printing.

CELL PROTECTION

Cell protection is an important capability of Excel that should be used with almost all worksheets. Cell protection prevents the user from inadvertently changing or erasing cells in a worksheet. There are two steps to protecting cells in a worksheet. First we specify which cells should *not* be protected. Then we turn on the protection for the worksheet.

The first step is to inform Excel which cells we wish to be able to change, which cells should be **unlocked**. For example, in the Price Quote worksheet shown in Figure 2-1 or 3-19, only cells D6:D8 should be left unlocked because these are the only cells we wish the user to be able to change.

To cause the cells D6:D8 to be unlocked, we select D6:D8 by dragging across them and then select *Cells...* in the *Format* pull-down menu. We click on the Protection tab and then click to clear the Locked box in the dialog. Thus, cells D6:D8 will be the only cells in the worksheet that are *not* locked.

The second step in the process is to enable (turn on) the cell protection for the worksheet. This is accomplished in the *Protection* selection in the *Tools* pull-down menu. Once the protection is enabled then only the cells that are not locked can be changed by the user. If the user tries to change one of the locked cells Excel will display a warning box and not allow the user to make the change.

It is a good idea to change the color of cells that are unlocked, for example to a light green, so the user knows exactly which cells can be changed.

It even is possible to put **password** protection on the worksheet, so that the user must know the password in order to turn off protection of the worksheet. Password protection can be specified in the *Protection* selection in the *Tools* pull-down menu when the protection is turned on.

The method for cell protection can take time to get used to. Basically, you first unlock the cells you want to be able to change. Then you enable (turn on) the cell protection. You can think of the first step as building an electric fence around the cells that can be changed. The second step is turning on the electric power in the fence. If you simply enable protection without first unlocking specific cells, then all the cells will be locked and protected. In this case, nothing in the worksheet could be changed.

Cell protection is especially useful when a worksheet you create is going to be used by naive users. Only certain cells are meant to be input cells. These cells are unlocked. The other cells contain formulas that you have worked hard on, and you don't want the users mangling them with inputs. These cells are all locked and protected.

COMPUTER EXERCISE

7-1. Please enter the following worksheet.

(a) Align the column headings (Shares, Price, Total) on the right sides of the cells.

(b) Enter the formulas for column E for the Totals for E6, E7, E8, and E10.

(c) We just have purchased 1500 shares of Intel at $35.36 per share. Insert a new row between IBM and Microsoft. Fill in the new row 8 with appropriate entries, including a formula in cell E8. Inspect the formula in cell E11. Does the formula need to be adjusted? What happened to the formula when you inserted the row?

(d) Format the Price cells in column D and the Total cells in column E so they are displayed with dollar signs and two places to the right of the decimal point. Widen the columns if necessary to accommodate the formatted numbers.

(e) Save the worksheet on the disk.

(f) Print the worksheet.

(g) The stocks were purchased for the following amounts: Dell 22.30, IBM 81.50, Intel 35.36, Microsoft 9.65. Add a new column that lists the purchase price for each. Add a column that shows our total original investment in each stock and a column that indicates the amount of money we have gained (or lost) on each stock since we purchased it. Finally, add another column that indicates the percentage gain or loss from the purchase price. Your formulas should work whatever the values in the cells. Format the numbers in this column as percentages with two decimal places.

(h) Spend some time formatting the worksheet so it looks nice. Include different colors or shades for different cells. Include different fonts of different sizes and styles. Show the Drawing toolbar. Add a textbox and an arrow. Add at least two AutoShapes. Add some WordArt. Import an appropriate clip-art picture or photograph if you can find one. Add a header and footer.

(i) Save the worksheet on the disk. Print the worksheet.

(j) Protect the cells in the worksheet so that only the cells containing the current stock prices can be changed by the user. Try changing one of the other cells. Do you get the Warning box?

(k) Next day, the stock prices are as follows: Dell 29.26, IBM 124.58, Intel 35.61, Microsoft 68.75. Change the worksheet appropriately. Do the formulas calculate the appropriate numbers?

(l) Save your worksheet. Print your worksheet.

CHAPTER 8

WORKBOOKS WITH MULTIPLE WORKSHEETS

OBJECTIVES

In this chapter you will learn how to:

- Move between worksheets
- Insert new worksheets
- Make a duplicate copy of a worksheet
- Modify multiple worksheets at the same time
- Use cells from other worksheets in formulas
- View multiple worksheets and workbooks
- Link to data in other workbooks

So far, we have been doing all of our work on a single worksheet. An Excel workbook holds multiple worksheets, just as a printed book has multiple pages. Using multiple sheets can make many problems easier to solve in Excel.

MOVING BETWEEN WORKSHEETS

An Excel workbook starts out with three worksheets and can contain up to 255 sheets. Initially, the worksheets are named Sheet1, Sheet2, and Sheet3. To move to another worksheet simply click on the appropriate **worksheet tab** at the bottom of the window. In Figure 8-1, we have clicked on the tab for Sheet3. You can tell we are working in Sheet3 because its tab is white. Usually we can see at most six sheet tabs at a time. We can scroll so that other sheet tabs are visible using the four buttons to the left of the sheet tabs at the very bottom left of the window.

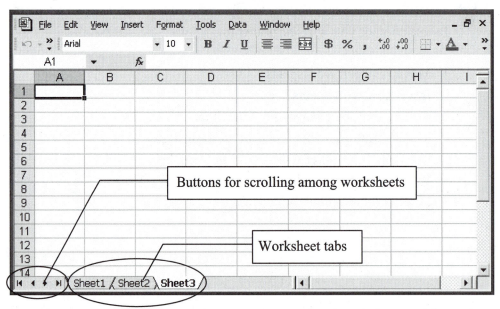

Figure 8-1. Select a different worksheet by clicking on the tab at the bottom of the window.

⏮   instructs Excel to scroll left all the way to the first worksheet tab.

◀   instructs Excel to scroll left one worksheet tab.

▶   instructs Excel to scroll right one worksheet tab.

⏭   instructs Excel to scroll right all the way to the last worksheet tab.

USING MULTIPLE WORKSHEETS

Audio International is a small but exclusive chain of stores that sells and installs top-of-the-line audio equipment. AI carries four types of products: home audio, automobile audio, personal audio, and commercial audio equipment. AI has stores in Beverly Hills, Dubai, Geneva, and Tokyo. Each quarter the stores send their sales data to world headquarters for compilation. For convenience, all stores report their sales in millions of U.S. dollars. We would like to create a workbook for keeping track of AI's sales for the year. A simple worksheet for keeping track of the sales in the quarter is shown in Figure 8-2.

		Home	Automotive	Personal	Commercial	Total
2			Audio International			
4	Q1		Sales in $ Millions			
6		Home	Automotive	Personal	Commercial	Total
7	Beverly Hills	2.3	4.2	0.6	1.5	8.6
8	Dubai	1.4	1.8	0.5	1.3	5.0
9	Geneva	3.7	5.1	0.2	1.7	10.7
10	Tokyo	3.0	3.8	0.6	3.8	11.2
11	Total	10.4	14.9	1.9	8.3	35.5

Figure 8-2. Audio International's sales for the first quarter.

Now the second quarter's sales are in and we would like to enter them. The best place to do this is on the next worksheet. First let's name the current worksheet. To change the name of the current worksheet, just double-click on the sheet tab, where it says Sheet1. The current name is selected. You can type in the new name.

We type in Q1 and the sheet is renamed Q1. The next step is to copy the information from the first sheet to the second sheet. One approach is to use Copy and Paste. We select the range A1:G11 by dragging across it. Now we select *Copy* from the *Edit* pull-down menu or simply click on the Copy button. This copies the range into the Clipboard. Now click on the tab for Sheet2 at the bottom of the window. Click on cell A1 of Sheet2 to select the cell. Now select *Paste* from the *Edit* pull-down menu or simply click on the Paste button. The range will be copied into Sheet2 beginning at A1, as in Figure 8-3.

	A	B	C	D	E	F	G	H	I
1									
2				Audio International					
3									
4		Q1		Sales in $ Millions					
5									
6			Home	Automotive	Personal	ommercial	Total		
7		Beverly Hil	2.3	4.2	0.6	1.5	8.6		
8		Dubai	1.4	1.8	0.5	1.3	5.0		
9		Geneva	3.7	5.1	0.2	1.7	10.7		
10		Tokyo	3.0	3.8	0.6	3.8	11.2		
11		Total	10.4	14.9	1.9	8.3	35.5		
12									

Figure 8-3. The result of copying and pasting from sheet Q1 to sheet Sheet2.

The Copy and Paste operation sort of worked, but notice that the column-width information was not transferred. Let's take another approach. We delete this entire worksheet by selecting *Delete Sheet* in the *Edit* pull-down menu. This command doesn't just erase the worksheet. It tears the entire worksheet out of the workbook.

A better approach to duplicating a worksheet is to use the *Move or Copy Sheet...* command in the *Edit* pull-down menu. This yields the dialog box in Figure 8-4. The name of the workbook we are working on is AISales.xls. We click on the *Create a copy* box at the bottom of the dialog box because we want to make a second copy of the worksheet rather than just moving it. We click on *Sheet3* because we want the new copy to appear just before Sheet3. (Notice that there is no Sheet2 because we just deleted it.)

Figure 8-4. Making a copy of a worksheet.

Click on OK and an exact duplicate of the worksheet Q1 appears with the name Q1(2), meaning the second copy of worksheet Q1. We double-click on the sheet tab and name the new worksheet Q2. Now we go in and change cell B4 to Q2 and enter in the sales figures for the second quarter. An even better approach might have been to create a copy of the sheet with no sales figures filled in and then used that to make the new quarterly sales worksheets.

As the third and fourth quarter sales figures come in, we copy the prior quarter's worksheets into new worksheets called Q3 and Q4 and fill in the appropriate sales figures. We now have a workbook with four worksheets.

We decide that we would like to insert a first sheet and make it a cover sheet for the workbook. We move to worksheet Q1 by clicking on the tab that says Q1 at the bottom of the window. To insert a new worksheet in front of Q1 we select *Worksheet* in the *Insert* pull-down menu. We name this worksheet Cover by double-clicking on the new tab. We enter information into the worksheet and format it.

WORKING WITH MULTIPLE SHEETS AT THE SAME TIME

We decide to jazz up the worksheets themselves. We'd like to place boxes, adjust the fonts, and so on. We would like the changes to take place on all four quarterly worksheets at once. We want to avoid formatting the worksheet for Q1 and then repeating the formatting for worksheet Q2 and so on. The secret is to select multiple sheets before doing the formatting.

There are two ways to select multiple sheets at once. If you hold your finger down on the Ctrl or Control key while you click on the sheet tabs, you can select Q1, and then Q2, and then Q3, and finally Q4. Using **Ctrl-clicking** you can select whichever sheets you would like one at a time. Alternatively, if you would like to select a sequence of sheets, you can click on the first sheet tab Q1 and then hold your finger down on the Shift key and click on sheet tab Q4. All of the sheets from Q1 through Q4 will be selected, as in Figure 8-5. This is **Shift-clicking**.

Figure 8-5. Changes are made simultaneously to all four selected worksheets.

Now whatever actions we perform on worksheet Q1 will be performed simultaneously on worksheets Q2, Q3, and Q4. After we are finished we click once on an unselected sheet tab (Sheet3) to undo the group selection and then click back on worksheet Q3 to see the result in Figure 8-6.

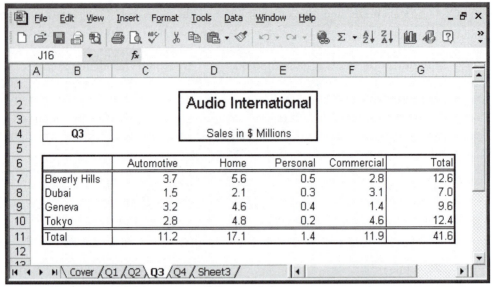

Figure 8-6. The result of formatting all four worksheets at once.

CALCULATIONS ACROSS WORKSHEETS

We would like a Totals worksheet that adds up the quarterly figures. We make a copy of worksheet Q4 and place it before the next sheet. We name the new sheet Totals. We enter Total for the Year in B4. We clear the data values in C7:F10 from the worksheet by selecting them and then dragging the Fill Handle back and up across them.

We are ready to enter the formulas into the body of the worksheet, into cells C7:F10. We want cell C7 in the Totals sheet to be the sum of C7 in the Q1, Q2, Q3, and Q4 worksheets. So we click on C7 in the Totals worksheet to activate it. We type in =SUM(and then we click on sheet tab Q1, hold our finger down on the Shift key, and click on sheet tab Q4. Thus far we have selected the four sheets Q1:Q4 in the formula. Now we click on cell C7 in sheet Q1 and then type the closing parenthesis and the Enter key. The formula in C7 in sheet Totals is

$$=SUM('Q1:Q4'!C7)$$

This formula instructs Excel to add four numbers together, the numbers in C7 in sheet Q1, C7 in sheet Q2, C7 in sheet Q3, and C7 in sheet Q4. The worksheet names usually are included within apostrophes (') in a formula. A range of worksheets is indicated by the colon (:). The names of the worksheets are separated from the addresses of the cells within the worksheets by the exclamation mark (!).

We now can fill this formula across row 7 in sheet Totals by dragging the Fill Handle at the bottom right of C7 across to F7. If we want to keep the existing formatting in place, including the existing borders, then we need to use the pop-up *Fill* menu that appears and select *Fill Without Formatting*, as in Figure 8-7.

Figure 8-7. Filling the formula in C7 across the row and then preserving the existing formatting, in this case the borders.

With C7:F7 still selected, we drag the resulting Fill Handle at the bottom right of F7 down to F10. Again we select *Fill Without Formatting* in the *Fill* pop-up menu. and click on D9 to unselect the range. The resulting worksheet is shown in Figure 8-8. You can see that the formula in cell D9 of the Totals worksheet adds up the four corresponding cells in worksheets Q1, Q2, Q3, and Q4.

There are several possible formulas for cell G11 in the Totals worksheet, for example =SUM(G7:G10) or =SUM(C11:F11) or =SUM('Q1:Q4'!G11). Another possible formula is

$$=SUM('Q1:Q4'!C7:F10)$$

This formula would instruct Excel to add up a 4 x 4 x 4 cube of cells, 64 cells, the cells in the range C7:F10 on sheets Q1, Q2, Q3, Q4. The four SUM formulas given should all result in the same values.

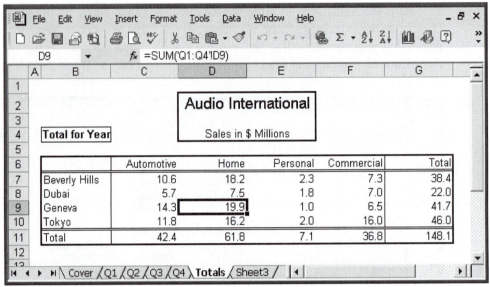

Figure 8-8. Calculating the sum of cells through four worksheets.

VIEWING MULTIPLE SHEETS AND WORKBOOKS

It is possible to view several worksheets at once. First select *New Window* in the *Window* pull-down menu. Each time you select *New Window* you will create a new window. The window will be named something like Sales:2, meaning it's the second view of the Sales workbook. If the second window is hidden you can click on the **Restore Windows button** at the top right of the worksheet and that will allow you manipulate the size of the worksheet window within the Excel window. Once multiple windows show, you can click on the worksheet tabs to see different worksheets at the same time. An example is shown in Figure 8-9.

You also can view multiple workbooks at once. Simply start a new workbook with an old one open or open a second workbook. Each workbook will appear in a different window within Excel.

You gain even more flexibility by starting up Excel multiple times. Now you have multiple Excel windows, each with different workbooks. This is convenient for copying information from one workbook into another or for linking multiple workbooks.

The exact behavior of multiple workbooks with multiple windows depends on the version of the operating system you are using and the version of Excel. You should be able to select among the different workbooks that are open by using the Excel task button(s) at the very bottom of your display window.

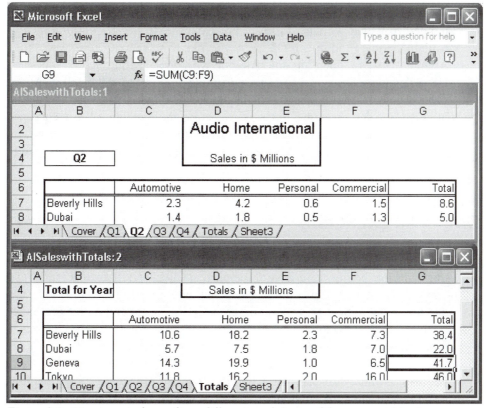

Figure 8-9. Viewing windows of two different worksheets of the same workbook.

LINKING WORKBOOKS

In addition to viewing multiple workbooks at the same time, it is possible to link workbooks. That is, it is possible to instruct Excel to obtain a value from a cell in some other workbook saved on the disk (or on the network). For example, in a cell we could enter the formula

='[Sales]Sheet1'!$H$7

This formula tells Excel that the value that is to appear in the cell is the value in H7 in the worksheet called Sheet1 of the Excel workbook called Sales. This link will be updated each time we open the workbook. Thus, to refer to a cell in another workbook, put the name of the workbook file in square brackets [ ].

In addition to typing in the link in the formula, it is possible simply to point to the cell to which we wish to link. For example, if we are working in a workbook called US_Sales and in cell D8 we would like to refer to a cell in a workbook called Atlanta, we can open up the Atlanta workbook within Excel, click on D8 in US_Sales, type the = sign to begin a formula, and click on the cell in Atlanta whose value we want to appear in D8 in US_Sales. The link will be entered in the formula in cell D8. We press the Enter key to enter the formula. We then can close the Atlanta workbook. The value that appears in D8 in US_Sales will be the current value in the linked cell in Atlanta. This link will be updated each time we open up US_Sales.

COMPUTER EXERCISES

8-1.   As a professional at a consulting firm, you would like to set up a workbook to keep track of your hours. You have three current clients (Acme, Beta, and Carlisle) that you bill by the hour. In addition you spend non-billable time cultivating new clients and non-billable time at work on other tasks, such as attending internal meetings and staring out the window (though you usually like to be thinking about a client's problem when you're staring out the window, so the time is billable).

Set up a workbook to help you keep track of your time and billing. Each worksheet should represent a different week. There should be five rows: one for each different client, one for time cultivating new clients, one for "nonproductive" time spent at work. You should have columns for each of the seven days of the week. Entries will be filled in for the number of hours spent each day in each of the categories. There should be row totals for the number of hours spent in each category and column totals for the number of billable hours, the number of non-billable hours, and the total number of hours you worked each day.

You bill your clients at $225 per hour. This value should be entered into a separate cell in the worksheet, because it is subject to change (upwards). You should have cells for the dollar amounts to be billed each client each day and for the week. The final cell should give the total amount to be billed for the week.

Your firm bills its clients every four weeks. You should have a worksheet in your workbook for each week in the cycle. Each of these worksheets should have the week number. After these weekly worksheets you should have a Totals worksheet that lists all useful totals, including the total accumulated hours for the cycle for each category, the total amount to be billed each client for the cycle, and the total amount billed for the cycle.

8-2. Design and create a workbook to keep track of the payroll for hourly employees. Each worksheet will correspond to a different week. You have six employees. List them in a column. Each employee makes a different amount per hour. List the hourly pay for each employee in a new column. Now add a column for each of the seven days of the week. In these columns enter the number of hours worked by each employee each day that week. To the right add columns that give the total number of hours worked by each employee and the gross pay for each employee. The federal government asks you to deduct 20% of gross pay for federal income taxes. Your state or province asks you to deduct 5% of gross pay for state income taxes. Add columns for these. Social Security deduction is 6.2% of gross pay. The deduction for medical insurance is $20 per week. Add columns for these. Each employee's take home pay is the gross pay minus the deductions. Add a column for take home pay. Add a row to total all of the columns. Add appropriate cells with headings for the worksheet.

Now use the worksheet for just created for one week's payroll to create a workbook for a month (four weeks). You should have an initial worksheet that gives a title and other information. There should be one worksheet for each week. Employees may work different hours from week to week. The final worksheet should be the totals for the four weeks. There should be six worksheets in all.

8-3. Design and create a workbook to keep track of how you spend your time. Each worksheet will correspond to a different day. There should be columns for each 6 hour period: night (midnight to 6 AM), morning (6 AM to noon), afternoon (noon to 6 PM), and evening (6 PM to midnight). The rows will correspond to your most common activities. For example, there might be rows for studying, going to class, sleeping (we'll assume no overlap in the activities), eating. You select at least six activities and a row for miscellaneous activities. The cells will contain the number of hours spent during each time period on each activity. Add cells with formulas for totals and averages for each row and for totals for each column. The columns should each add up to 6, the number of hours in each period.

Create a worksheet for one day. Then make copies for a full week. At the top of each worksheet give the date for the data in the worksheet and the day of the week. Fill in data for all of the worksheets. You can make up the data if you wish. Add a title worksheet at the front. Add a worksheet at the end for the weekly sums of the values and another worksheet for the weekly averages of the values and a third worksheet for the weekly maximums of the values. The final workbook should consist of eleven worksheets. Changing any of the data values should cause changes to ripple through the calculations in the worksheet that was changed and the three summary worksheets at the end of the workbook.

8-4.   Design and create a workbook to keep track of a stock portfolio. You own shares in five different companies:

Shares	Company	Purchase Price	Current Price
1000	Allied Networks	34.5	38.75
3500	Bionic Controls	8.25	56.50
9000	Cortical Connections	2.75	1.75
2000	United Housing	15.75	18.50
500	Energy Management	78.25	83.00

Create a workbook with multiple worksheets that allows you to keep track of your portfolio over the next 10 business days. During those 10 days the price of the shares will change, but you can assume that you will neither purchase nor sell any shares. Once the workbook is set up, you will enter in only 50 values, the closing price of each of the stocks on each of the days. All other cells should be protected and calculated automatically.

The workbook will tell you for each day the total value of each stock holding, the change from the previous day in both dollar amount and percent, and the change from original purchase price in both dollar amount and percent. There also will be cells that tell you the highest price of each stock over the 10 days and the highest value of your portfolio over the 10-day period.

There are several ways to organize the workbook in terms of what appears on each worksheet. The exact organization is up to you.

8-5.   Where does all the money go? Create a workbook to help keep track of weekly expenses. Each worksheet will correspond to one week's worth of expenses. In each worksheet you should have columns corresponding to the days of the week (Mon, Tue, ...). You should have rows for at least five different categories on which you spend money. Fill in values. (You can make up the numbers.) You should have sums and averages for the rows and columns. Now create a workbook for five weeks, with one sheet for each week. At the beginning add a colorful title worksheet. At the end you should have worksheets for overall totals and for overall averages. The workbook should consist of eight worksheets.

CHAPTER 9

THE PROBLEM-SOLVING PROCESS

OBJECTIVES

In this chapter you will learn:

- The process of developing workbooks
- Common forms of documentation for workbooks

In the first eight chapters we have looked at the basics of creating Excel workbooks. Now it is time to step back and look at the process of using Excel to help solve problems. This process usually involves five phases.

1. PROBLEM DEFINITION

What is the problem to be solved? What are we trying to accomplish? What information would we like to have? It is very important that you understand the problem before trying to solve it. You do not want to spend hours developing and perfecting a workbook that solves the wrong problem; that is of little use.

2. DESIGN

Is Excel the right tool to use to solve the problem? Sometimes people become so enamored with Excel that they try to use the program to solve problems that would be better solved by other means. There is an old saying "To a person with a hammer, everything looks like a nail." Excel is a powerful and useful tool, but it is not the solution to every problem. If a calculation is to be performed only once, sometimes it is easier just to do the calculation by hand, to use paper and pencil and a calculator. For problems that are better solved using the computer, several different types of computer software are available. Many problems are better solved using, say, a database program rather than Excel or by using some specialized software. For example, if you would like the computer to help you keep the books of a small business, you could create custom Excel workbooks, but you might save a lot of time and trouble by just buying a small business accounting program.

Once you decide that Excel is the right tool to use, it is best to design the workbook on paper first. What are the inputs? What information needs to be provided? What are the outputs? What are we trying to learn? What should be the format of the outputs? Are there any special printed reports that need to be produced? What should they look like? How do you get from the inputs to the outputs? Are there any key formulas to be developed? Could you perform the calculations by hand given enough time and a calculator? You want to be sure that there is nothing mystical in your workbook design, no key steps that need to be calculated but that you do not know how to specify.

As we saw in the Peter Minuit example in Chapter 6, an important principle for designing effective workbooks is that any number that might be changed should be placed into a separate cell. Do not put numbers that might be changed, like interest rates, directly into formulas. Rather put them into separate cells and always refer to these cells in the formulas. All of the numbers that might be varied should be placed together in a separate, well-labeled input area of the workbook.

In designing a workbook you might have four separate areas: introduction, input, calculations, and output. The introduction contains a description of the workbook, the name of the developer, the date, instructions to the user, and documentation. The introduction might encompass the entire first sheet of the workbook. The input area contains all of the cells that will be entered by the user. In a worksheet for "What if" analysis, the input area would contain all of the assumptions, all of the numbers that might be varied. The calculations area contains the formulas. The output area pulls the results of special interest out of the calculations area. The output area might be located next to the input area for easy viewing.

3. IMPLEMENTATION

Normally it is best to have the worksheets designed on paper before proceeding to the computer. Implementation should be straightforward. It is useful to name the important cells and ranges and to use these names in the formulas. Names should remind you of the contents of the cell or range. If a formula is going to be filled, be careful about using relative, mixed, or absolute addressing. Think about whether the address is relative, whether it is to be adjusted as it is replicated, or whether the address is absolute, always referring to the same cell or range of cells. Use the cell protection capability of Excel to protect all of the cells except the input cells from being changed by mistake.

It is customary to store a frequently used workbook as a template. A template is a workbook where all of the input values are set to zero. The user would retrieve the template workbook from the disk, enter in the input values, and save the filled-in workbook on the disk under a new name. The template would remain on the disk unchanged.

4. TESTING

Beginners often expect their Excel workbooks to work correctly the first time. Sometimes they do, but even the best planned and designed workbooks often contain errors. It is best to assume that a new workbook is full of errors and then test it extensively to make sure it is correct. Testing a workbook involves working out the numbers ahead of time with pencil, paper, and calculator before trying them on the computer. It is important that the workbooks be tested on a wide variety of inputs, on typical inputs and on extreme inputs.

There are several types of errors in Excel workbooks that can be uncovered. There can be errors in your understanding of the problem. Sometimes you create a workbook and then realize that you did not quite understand the problem. The workbook might "work" but it does not produce the answers you need. In this case, you would need to go back to step 1 to reanalyze the problem. There can be errors in your design of the workbook. You might have used an erroneous formula. You might have built a number that needs to be changed into a formula in a worksheet. You might not have foreseen some condition that might occur. In this case, you would need to go back to step 2 to modify your design for the workbook. There can be errors in your implementation of the workbook. You might have a number that is too large for the width of the column. You might forget to use absolute addressing where it is required. You might have made an error in typing a formula or pointing to an address. These errors in step 3 can be corrected right on the computer.

5. DOCUMENTATION

Documentation is the part of the problem-solving process that involves making the workbook understandable by people, rather than just by the computer. Documentation includes external paper documentation as well as instructions within the workbook itself. In a sense, documentation includes everything in a workbook except for the numbers and the formulas themselves. Documentation should not be an afterthought but rather an integral part of the entire development process.

The extent of the documentation required depends on the uses to which your workbook will be put.

If you are the only person who will ever use your work, then you should provide yourself with sufficient text, comments, and instructions so that the workbook will be understandable to you six months in the future.

If the workbook is being handed in as an assignment, your instructor will determine the level of documentation required. Certainly you should include your name, the date, and the assignment number. You should indicate any extra assumptions you have made and explain any tricky aspects of your work. Your instructor might ask you to hand in printed documentation, including printouts of the worksheets and their formulas, or you might submit disks, or you might submit the work over the network.

A workbook produced for class generally is seen by just two people—yourself and the person who grades the assignment. In industry there often are several people who use and modify the workbooks you will create.

In industry, workbooks often are used by people other than the creator of the workbooks. These people may have only a superficial understanding of Excel and its operation. Therefore it is important to include explicit instructions with your workbooks in these situations. The instructions should include where the data should be entered, how and where to save the work, and how to print out reports. Important instructions are best included as text in the worksheets themselves as well as on a separate piece of paper. Paper instructions can easily be separated from the workbooks or lost altogether. The cell protection capabilities should be used so that only input cells can be modified easily.

In industry, workbooks often are modified by people other than the person who creates them. You create an Excel workbook as part of your job and then you are rapidly promoted twice. Someone else is hired for your old position. This person inherits your work. Can this person make sense of your workbooks? Where did these data come from? What is this formula? What are the assumptions underlying this worksheet? What happens at the end of the year? Here you would like the work to be transparent, self-explanatory. List assumptions for the workbooks. List sources for data. Explain unusual formulas. Give explicit instructions. Put yourself in the place of the person who will succeed you. Could you understand this workbook the way it is written if you hadn't developed it yourself?

With important workbooks in industry it is customary to create a full documentation binder. The documentation binder could include:

- a description of the problem the workbook is designed to solve
- a general discussion of the workbook, its design and operation
- full, detailed instructions for a novice user
- full documentation for someone who will modify the workbook, including any assumptions, a discussion of formulas, any pitfalls or possible errors in the workbook, features that might be added
- a full printout of the worksheets with values displayed
- a full printout of the worksheets with formulas displayed
- two semi-sealed CDs or other removable storage media containing the workbook and documentation to be used for emergency backup.

Many people tend to provide too little documentation for their workbooks. The reason is simple. It takes a long time and a lot of effort to produce good documentation. It can take as long to document a workbook as it does to identify the problem, design the workbook, implement the workbook, and test the workbook all combined. A little extra effort with documentation can save users of your workbook many hours of work.

COMPUTER EXERCISES

9-1. Your courses each have different requirements—different types of assignments, quizzes, exams, etc. Create a workbook to keep track of all of the grades you receive. Every grade should appear in the workbook along with a description of what it is for, and the date received. You probably will want a different worksheet for each course. Your workbook should calculate your average in each class, if possible using the weighting system of the instructor. In the workbook all cells should be protected except for the input cells. Go through the process of problem definition, design, implementation, testing, and documentation.

9-2. Create a workbook to help keep track of a checking account. There should be separate entries for each check, deposit, ATM withdrawal, electronic transfer, debit card charge, and service charge. These entries should include the date, the amount, the check number (if any), the payee (if any), and the purpose. The workbook should keep track of the balance in your account and should help you check for errors in the statement you receive from the bank each month. Go through the process of problem definition, design, implementation, testing, and documentation.

9-3. Create a workbook that helps you budget income and expenses for each month. Include separate entries for income and expense items. Allow for both budgeted and actual. You may use fictional data if you wish. Go through the process of problem definition, design, implementation, testing, and documentation.

9-4. If you have a car, how much does it cost to operate? Create a workbook that will allow you to track operating expenses for your car for a year. Your workbook should allow you to record money spent for gas, oil, repairs, insurance, registration, and any other expenses. For each expense, you should record the date, the odometer mileage, the payee, a description of the expense, and an amount. The workbook should calculate subtotals for each type of expense, the total amount of money spent, and the cost per mile and the cost per day to drive your car. Go through the process of problem definition, design, implementation, testing, and documentation.

9-5. Perhaps you belong to a group, such as a campus organization or a church group, that is considering undertaking an activity, for example, a picnic or a dance or a raffle. Create a workbook that will allow you to model the financial aspects of the activity. You might have cells for the number of tickets sold and the price of the tickets and for any other revenue variables and for each of the different expense variables. The workbook should allow you to try out different scenarios. For example, what would happen if all of the tickets are sold? What would happen if only 20 tickets are sold? What would be the financial consequences if it rains on the day of the picnic? In the workbook all cells should be protected except for the input cells. Go through the process of problem definition, design, implementation, testing, and documentation.

CHAPTER 10

CHARTS

OBJECTIVES

In this chapter you will learn how to:

- Create charts using the Chart Wizard
- Modify charts
- Make and manipulate three-dimensional charts
- Chart data in noncontiguous areas of your worksheet
- Create separate chart sheets
- Use trendlines to forecast the future

Charts have visual impact. People often respond more favorably to charts than they do to tables of numbers. An important part of Excel is the ability to turn tables of numbers into bar charts and pie charts and other types of charts. Charting in Excel is easy, useful, and fun.

FUNDAMENTALS OF CHARTS

In Excel, charts are made from ranges of numbers in a workbook. Basically we need to specify (1) the cells that contain the values to be charted, (2) the type of chart we want drawn, and (3) the location where the chart is to be placed.

As an example, consider the Totals worksheet for Audio International, from Chapter 8, shown in Figure 10-1.

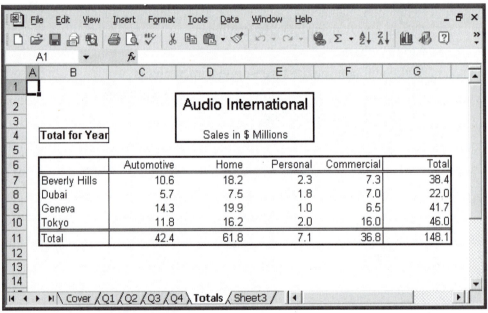

Figure 10-1. A worksheet to chart.

There are many different charts that could be drawn from this worksheet.

Let's start simple. Suppose we want to draw a vertical bar chart that has the locations along the horizontal axis and the annual sales of automotive audio equipment as the height of the bars, as in Figure 10-2. The data for this chart comes from B6:C10 of the Totals worksheet. Note that it is very important that you do not include any blank rows or columns in the data selected to be charted. If necessary, move the data around or delete the blank rows or columns.

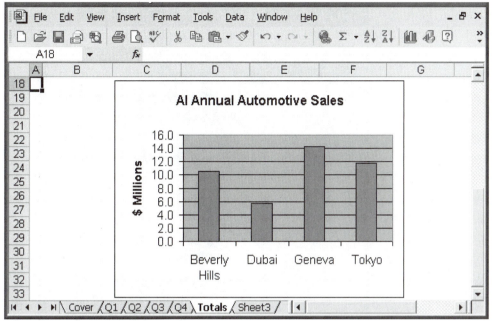

Figure 10-2. A simple chart.

Excel provides a **Chart Wizard** to guide us through the process of creating a chart. First, we specify the range of cells to be charted. We drag across B6:C10 to select the data to chart. Second, we select the Chart Wizard by clicking on the Chart Wizard button on the Standard toolbar. The Chart Wizard takes us through the rest of the process step by step. The Chart Wizard has four steps, four dialog boxes for us to respond to, before we are finished specifying our chart.

In Step 1 the Chart Wizard asks us to select a basic type of chart (see Figure 10-3). We select a Column Chart of the first type given in the Step 1 dialog box.

In Step 2 the Chart Wizard shows us a preliminary view of the chart and asks us to verify the source of the data to be charted. (See Figure 10-4.) The data comes from B6:C10 in the Totals worksheet and is to be organized by columns. Now we notice details of the chart we might want to change.

In Step 3 we first click on the Legend tab and inform the Wizard we do not want a legend. The legend is the box labeled "Automotiv" in the right of the chart shown in Figure 10-4. Legends are useful if we are charting multiple series of data but here we have only the Automotive sales. Next we go back to the Titles sheet and add a Chart title and a title for the Y axis, as shown in Figure 10-5.

The final step, in Figure 10-6, is to specify where we want the chart to appear. The chart can be displayed in its own new worksheet or as part of an existing worksheet. Displaying a chart in its own worksheet often is best if we wish to print the chart for inclusion in a report. Here we ask for the chart to be displayed in the Totals worksheet and end up with the chart in Figure 10-2.

Figure 10-3. Select the type of chart.

Figure 10-4. Verify the location for the data for the chart.

Figure 10-5. We eliminate the legend and then enter a Chart title and Value (Y) axis title for the chart.

Figure 10-6. We select where to place the chart and we are done.

MAKING CHANGES TO THE CHART

A chart in a worksheet is simply another graphical object that floats above the worksheet. To change the size, proportions, or location of the chart, first select the chart by clicking once on the chart. Handles appear around the edges of the chart. To change the size or proportions, point to one of the handles and drag with the mouse. To move the chart in the worksheet, simply point within the chart and drag the chart. The chart in Figure 10-2 was resized and dragged down to row 18.

To change some feature in the chart itself, first click on the chart to select it. A new **Chart toolbar** appears, as in Figure 10-7.

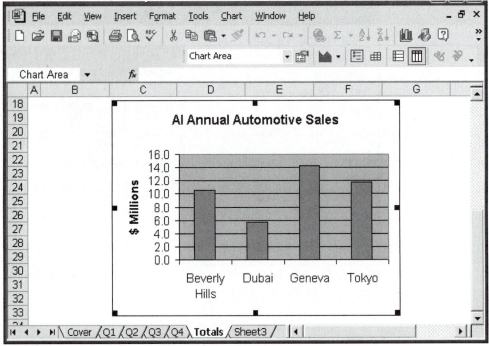

Figure 10-7. A Chart toolbar appears above the formula bar above the worksheet.

The **Chart Objects pull-down menu** (Figure 10-8) allows you to select the portion of the chart you wish to modify. Excel provides you with control over the minutest details in the chart.

Figure 10-8. The Chart Objects menu in the Chart toolbar.

Clicking on the **Format button** results in the dialog box in Figure 10-9. Here you can make dozens of alterations to the format of the chart area. For example, you can select a background color for the chart. If you click on Fill Effects… you can make the background of the chart appear to be marble or some other texture. This button allows you to format whichever part of the chart you select in the Chart Objects pull-down menu to its left.

Figure 10-9. Formatting the Chart Area. The colors don't show to their best here.

Clicking on the **Chart Type button** allows us to change the type of the chart being displayed, as in Figure 10-10.

Figure 10-10. Select a new chart type.

For example, selecting 3-D Cone Chart produces the chart displayed in Figure 10-11. This is the same data, but displayed as cones.

It is very important to note that charts are dynamic. This means that if the data that underlies a chart is changed, the chart automatically is redrawn. So, just as formulas are recalculated when the data in a cell changes, charts are redrawn.

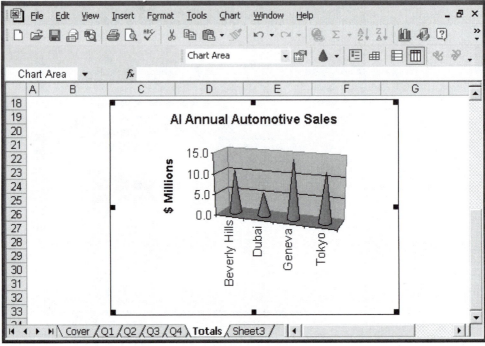

Figure 10-11. The chart redrawn as a 3-D Cone Chart.

    The **Legend button** allows you to put in or remove legends. Legends, again, are the data labels that often appear to the right side of the chart to identify which data are being drawn where.

    Clicking on the **Data Table button** will place a table with the data in your chart. An example is shown in Figure 10-12.

The remaining buttons in the Chart toolbar don't make any sense with the limited data we are displaying here. They will be discussed later in the chapter.

We really are only scratching the surface in the description of charting. Many kinds of changes in formatting can be made through the pull-down menu shown in Figure 10-8. For example, Excel has set the upper limit of the vertical axis automatically based on the data being charted. Note that in the Column chart in Figure 10-7 the upper value is 16.0 and the grids are drawn for values every 2.0 apart. In the Cone chart in Figure 10-11 the upper value is 15.0 and the grids are drawn every 5.0 apart. These were decisions made by Excel. If you would like to override these decisions–for example, you might want the vertical axis to go from 0 to 100 with grids 10 apart–you can select *Value Axis* in the pull-down menu of Figure 10-8 and then click on the Format button to its right and then go to town making changes in the vertical axis.

It should be noted that charting is one feature that Microsoft keeps changing so it's certainly possible that details are different in the version of Excel you are using.

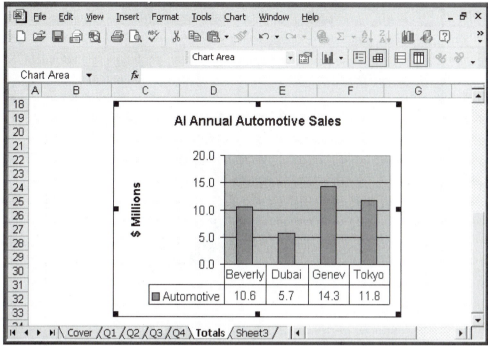

Figure 10-12. The chart with the Data Table showing.

MORE COMPLEX CHARTS

We charted only four values, Automotive sales, in the Totals worksheet. Suppose we would like to produce a chart that helps us visualize more of the data.

We begin by selecting B6:F10 in the original worksheet in Figure 10-1. We don't include the Total column and the Total row because if we include these values the computer would just consider "Total" to be the name of another city or product line, which would cause confusion in the charts. We go through the same process of clicking on the Chart Wizard and answering the questions in the four steps of dialog boxes. This time we select 3-D Column chart in Step 1 and request that the data be organized by rows in the worksheet. The Chart Wizard draws a 3-Dimensional Column chart. A little adjusting gives us the chart in Figure 10-13.

Note that the **By Row button** is selected in this chart as the result of a decision made in Step 2 (see Figure 10-4). This means that the data that was selected in B6:F10 is organized primarily by row, so that all of the sales figures for Beverly Hills are blue, all of the sales figures for Dubai are purple, and so on.

If we click on the **By Column button**, we get the chart in Figure 10-14. Here, the data has been reorganized by column, so that the sales figures for Automotive are in blue, for Home are in purple, and so on.

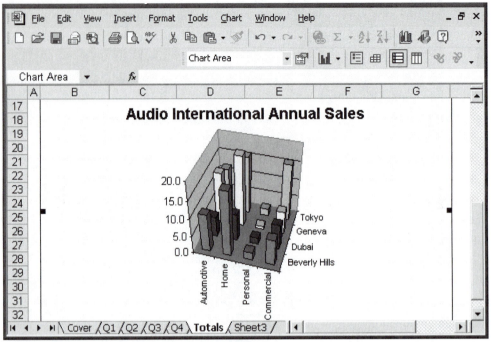

Figure 10-13. A 3-Dimensional Column chart.

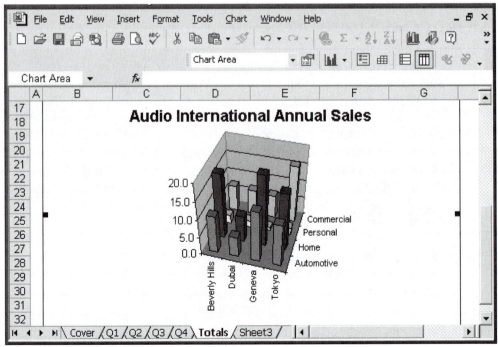

Figure 10-14. Clicking the By Columns button changes the organization of the chart.

We can change the three-dimensional orientation of the chart by clicking on the chart to select it and then by clicking on the bottom center corner (between "Tokyo" and "Automotive") and then dragging the corner. As shown in Figure 10-15, Excel displays a three-dimensional outline of the chart. The mouse pointer has become a + shape. Dragging the mouse changes the three-dimensional orientation. Holding down the Ctrl key while you drag lets you see the outlines of the bars. The new chart in Figure 10-16 seems easier to read than the original chart in Figure 10-14.

Figure 10-15. Changing the three-dimensional orientation of the chart.

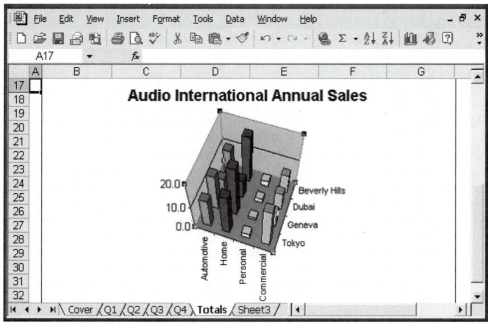

Figure 10-16. The same chart displayed with a different orientation.

CHARTING NONCONTIGUOUS RANGES

Often we want to chart noncontiguous areas of a worksheet, areas that are not next to each other. For example, we might want to chart only Dubai and Tokyo total annual sales in the worksheet in Figure 10-1. Dubai sales are in row 8. Tokyo sales are in row 10. The column headings are in row 6. To select noncontiguous portions of the worksheet use the Ctrl or Control key. That is, select the first portion of the worksheet by dragging across it and then hold your finger down on the Ctrl key while you drag across other portions. So with the Ctrl key pressed, we drag across B6:F6 and then B8:F8 and then B10:F10. The result will be that multiple rectangular ranges will be selected, as discussed in Chapter 3. Then we summon the Chart Wizard by clicking on the Chart Wizard button. The multiple ranges will appear in the Step 2 dialog box separated by a comma.

Another approach to charting different ranges of data from a workbook in a single chart is to set up a special area in a worksheet that contains just the data to be charted in just the order you want. The cells in this area can be copied and pasted from different sections of the workbook, or they can contain simple formulas that refer to the values to be charted. It is very important that no blank rows or columns be included in the data to be charted.

The result of charting Dubai and Tokyo sales as a **3-D Line chart** is shown in Figure 10-17.

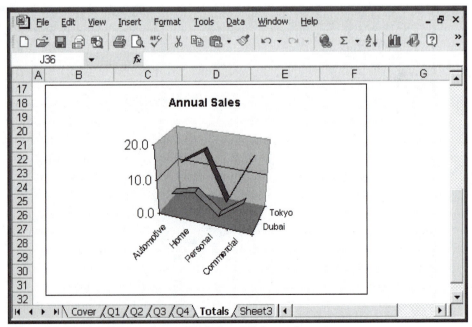

Figure 10-17. A 3-D Line chart of Dubai and Tokyo sales.

CHART SHEETS AND PRINTING

We have been placing the graphs on worksheets. It also is possible to have a separate sheet devoted just to a chart. A **chart sheet** does not contain rows or columns or cells. It just contains a single chart. You tell the Chart Wizard if you want a chart sheet in Step 4. (See Figure 10-6.)

Chart sheets are most useful if the end result is that the chart is going to be printed and included in a report. The text in chart sheets can be difficult to read on the screen unless you have a large monitor, but chart sheets generally print in the right size and proportions for a report.

If you want to use the chart in a presentation then it is better to have the chart placed on top of a worksheet. You can move a chart on a worksheet to another application, like PowerPoint or Word, by selecting just the chart and copying and pasting it. You can print just the chart on a worksheet by first clicking on the chart to select it before printing.

It is a good idea to select Print Preview before printing so you can ascertain that the printout will be what you want.

TRENDLINES

Audio International has gone public. We are considering purchasing some of its stock. We have obtained the closing price of the stock at the end of each of the 25 weeks since it was issued and entered the data into the worksheet in Figure 10-18.

Figure 10-18. Audio International goes public.

First, we would like to chart the stock so we can see what the change in price looks like. We select B4:C29 and click on the Chart Wizard button. We select an XY (Scatter) chart and go through the four screens in the Chart Wizard. The result is shown in Figure 10-19.

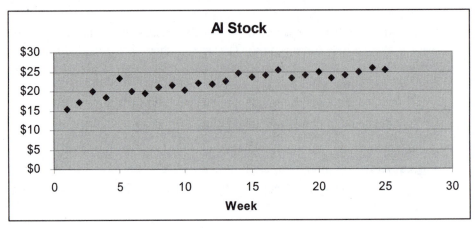

Figure 10-19. A chart of the stock prices.

That is the past. We are thinking of investing, so we are interested in forecasting the price of the stock for future weeks. One of the nicest features of Excel is that it will automatically compute and display **trendlines**. Trendlines are a way of using the past data to suggest what the future data will be.

To obtain a trendline, first we click on the chart to select the chart. Then we select *Series "Closing Price"* in the *Chart Objects* pull-down menu (see Figure 10-8). Now we select *Add Trendline...* in the *Chart* pull-down menu. The *Chart* pull-down menu appears whenever a chart is selected. Excel displays the Trendline dialog box shown in Figure 10-20.

In the Trendline dialog box we are being asked to select a type of trendline. The idea is that Excel will fit a trendline of the type we select to the existing data. There are half a dozen different types of trendlines based on common forms of equations. The nicest part is that Excel will do all of the math for us automatically. We select Linear, which means we want Excel to fit a straight line to the data. Now we click on the Options tab in Figure 10-20. Excel displays the dialog box shown in Figure 10-21.

We enter 20 in the Forecast Forward box. We want Excel to predict the prices for 20 weeks into the future. We also click on the Display equation on chart option and on the Display R-squared value on chart option. (There is no extra charge.) We click on OK and the result is shown in Figure 10-22.

Figure 10-20. Selecting the type of trendline.

Figure 10-21. We would like Excel to extend the trendline ahead for the next 20 weeks.

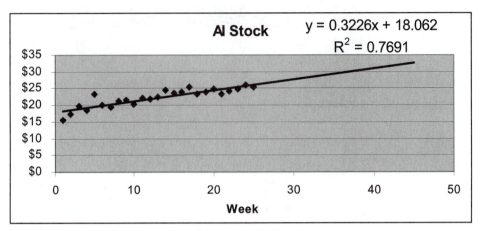

Figure 10-22. The linear trendline for the stock price data.

Excel has fitted a straight line to the data and has displayed the line for 20 weeks into the future. If the trend holds true, the price of the stock should be over $32 in 20 weeks. On the top right of the window is a text box that displays the equation and the R-squared value. The equation is

$$y = 0.3226x + 18.062$$

Here x is the week. The equation gives the formula that Excel found for predicting the price of the stock (y) given the week number (x). The R^2 value is 0.7691. R is the correlation between the values predicted by the equation and the actual values. The square of R is used as an indication of the goodness of fit of the line to the data. If all of the data points were right on the line and there was no deviance at all, the R^2 value would be 1. If the data values were randomly scattered and the line does not fit at all, the R^2 value would be 0.

If you are unhappy with the straight line trendline, you can select logarithmic, polynomial, power, exponential, or moving average. For example, fitting a polynomial of order 3 to the data gives us the trendline shown in Figure 10-23. (Order 3 means that 3 is the highest exponent of x in the polynomial equation.)

We have improved the R^2 value to 0.8247. The equation that Excel found is

$$y = 0.0009x^3 - 0.0482x^2 + 1.0206x + 15.732$$

The nicest aspect of this equation is that according to this trendline, in 20 weeks the stock price should be over $48 per share! And, it looks like the trend after 20 weeks is ever upwards!

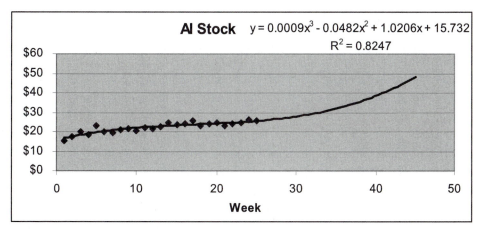

Figure 10-23. Fitting a polynomial equation of order 3 greatly improves the performance predicted for the stock price.

To determine what the trendline predicts for a longer period of time, we select *"Closing Price" Trendline* in the *Chart Objects* pull-down menu. Then we click on the Format button to the right. We click on the Option tab and change the number of Forward Units requested from 20 to 40. We click on *OK*. The resulting chart is shown in Figure 10-24. According to the trendline, the stock will rise to over $130 in just 40 more weeks!

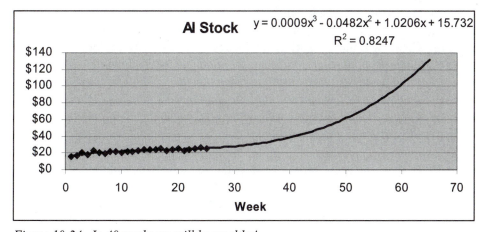

Figure 10-24. In 40 weeks we will be wealthy!

We'll make a fortune! *Caveat emptor.* Buyer beware. Trendlines based on past performance are not always good predictors of the future, as many people have discovered to their dismay.

COMPUTER EXERCISES

10-1. Enter the Audio International Totals worksheet in Figure 10-1. Duplicate the charts that appear in Figures 10-2, 10-11, 10-12, 10-13, 10-14, 10-16, and 10-17.

10-2. The following worksheet was used in Exercise 4-3. Either enter the worksheet with formulas or retrieve the worksheet from your disk.

Sales Analysis
Product Line by Season
(All Sales in $ Millions)

Product	Winter	Spring	Summer	Fall	Total	Max
Golf	3.2	6.2	5.7	3.9		
Tennis	4.7	5.2	7.1	2.9		
Skiing	3.7	2.1	1.1	5.2		
Surfing	1.2	2.1	2.9	1.3		

Total

Average

All of the following charts should be as understandable as possible and should be clearly identified with titles, legends, and so on. Be careful not to include blank rows or columns in the data to be charted. Delete them if necessary.

(a) Create a Column chart of total sales by season. Here, the total sales row would be plotted as columns (vertical bars) and the season names would be the X axis values. There should be four bars in the graph.

(b) Create a 3-D Column chart of sales for each of the different products by season. Do not include any totals. There should be 16 vertical bars in the chart.

(c) Display the chart in (b) as a Bar chart organized by columns.

(d) Display the chart as a Bar chart organized by rows.

(e) Display the chart in (b) as a Line chart.

(f) Which of the charts in (b), (c), (d), or (e) is most effective? Why?

(g) Display the Tennis sales as a 3-D Pie chart with one season for each slice.

10-3. (a) Enter the data in Exercise 6-3 on the major regions of the earth and their areas into a worksheet. Use the data to produce three charts of your own design that illustrate the data.

(b) Enter the continent population data in Figure 6-1 into the same worksheet. Use the population data to produce an additional chart.

(c) Now combine the data from (a) and (b) in the worksheet to obtain the population density of each continent. Assume that Oceania is the same as Australia combined with "other land". Produce a well-labeled chart on population density.

10-4. Produce a well-labeled chart that illustrates the difference in obtaining fixed annual compound interest rates of 5%, 10%, and 15% on an investment of $100,000 over the course of 10 years. Your chart should show three curves: the value of the investment growing at 5% per year, 10% per year, and 15% per year. You first should create a worksheet with all of the values to be charted.

10-5. Create a worksheet that keeps track of your major living expenses over the past five months. Include at least four different categories of expenses (for example, room and board, school, transportation, clothing, misc.). Fill in numbers. You may use fictional numbers if you wish. Calculate row and column totals. Print the worksheet. Create and print four well-labeled charts, as follows:

(a) A Pie chart of your expenses for the most recent month.

(b) A Line chart of your total expenses over the past five months.

(c) Some type of chart showing all the expenses over the past five months.

(d) A Bar chart of your choice.

10-6. The world population is estimated as follows:

Year	Population
1	200,000,000
1650	500,000,000
1850	1,000,000,000
1930	2,000,000,000
1975	4,000,000,000

2000	6,080,000,000

In the year A.D. 1, at the time of Jesus, there were fewer people in the entire world than there are in the United States today.

(a) Enter these values in a worksheet. (You may want to enter the populations in millions of people and leave off the six rightmost 0's.) Draw an X-Y (Scatter) chart of the population. The years should be the X axis values.

(b) Fit a trendline to the data. You choose the best type of trendline to use. Display the equation. Have Excel draw the trendline out past the year 2100. What will be the world population in the year 2100 according to the trendline? Does the trendline appear reasonable to you, to be a reasonable fit to the data? What do you think accounts for this?

(c) Create your own formula to fit the data. Your formula should be some function of the year and should yield the best possible approximation to the population in that year. Create a new column in your worksheet that shows the prediction made by your formula for each of the years in your worksheet. Now add the years 2010, 2020, through 2100 and your predictions for those years. Create an X-Y (Scatter) chart that has the year as the X axis values and both the actual population and your calculated population as data values. Does your formula appear to match the data? How does your trendline compare with the trendline calculated by Excel?

10-7. You have been asked to make a presentation to the United States Congress about the United States government finances and its trends. Enter the data and then fill in formulas for the Total Receipts, Total Outlays, and Deficit.

U.S. Government Receipts and Outlays in Billions of Dollars

	1980	1985	1990	1995	2000
Receipts					
Individual Income Taxes	244	335	467	588	1,004
Corporate Income Taxes	65	61	94	151	207
Social Insurance Taxes	158	265	380	484	620
Excise Taxes	24	36	35	58	69
Other	26	37	56	65	125
Total Receipts					

Outlays

National Defense	134	253	299	272	281
Social Security	119	189	249	336	442
Income Security	87	128	147	223	223
Medicare	32	66	98	157	190
All Other Government	166	181	275	317	290
Interest	53	129	184	234	362

Total Outlays

Surplus (Deficit)

(a) Use the worksheet to prepare four charts that best capture the most important historical points to be made about the U.S. budget. Your charts should be well thought out, well-labeled, and self-explanatory.

(b) Create a chart that shows the deficit or surplus over the past five time periods and then uses a trendline to forecast what the deficit or surplus would be up through 2020 if the trend continues.

(c) Prepare the text of your testimony. State in English the important points that your charts illustrate.

(d) Create a PowerPoint presentation to accompany your testimony. Include the charts in the presentation along with other appropriate screens.

10-8. The following are hourly compensation rates in U.S. dollars for production workers in selected countries. Hourly compensation includes wages, premiums, bonuses, vacation, holidays and other leave, insurance, and benefit plans.

Country	1975	1980	1985	1990	1995	2000
Canada	5.96	8.67	10.95	15.95	16.10	16.16
Hong Kong	0.76	1.51	1.73	3.20	4.82	5.53
Japan	3.00	5.52	6.34	12.80	23.82	22.00
Mexico	1.47	2.21	1.59	1.58	1.51	2.46
Switzerland	6.09	11.09	9.66	20.86	29.30	21.24
United States	6.36	9.87	13.01	14.91	17.19	19.86

Enter this information into a worksheet. Create a single well-labeled chart that best conveys all of this information as clearly as possible. This may take some experimentation on your part.

10-9. Obtain a recent financial statement or Annual Report for your college or university or for a company or organization with which you are familiar.

(a) Use the financial data to prepare four charts that best capture the most important points to be made about the financial situation of the organization. Your charts should be well thought out, well-labeled, and self-explanatory.

(b) Produce charts that use trendlines to show the future course of the organization if trends continue.

(c) Produce a written report on the financial health of the organization. Include your charts.

10-10. From the Internet, from a commercial on-line service, or from elsewhere obtain a series of prices for an individual stock or for the Dow Jones Industrial or some other standard average. Create a chart of the data. Fit an appropriate trendline to the data. What does the trendline predict for the future?

CHAPTER 11

LOGICAL FUNCTIONS

OBJECTIVES

In this chapter you will learn how to:

- Use IF functions to select between alternatives
- Create logical tests using comparison operators
- Use nested IF functions to select among multiple alternatives
- Implement complex conditions using the AND, OR, and NOT functions

Sometimes we would like a cell to display one of two or more alternative values. If you sell over $2 million you receive a bonus of $1,000, otherwise you receive no bonus. People caught driving at a speed over 80 miles per hour on the Interstate owe a fine of $200; people caught driving between 66 and 80 owe $90; otherwise, no fine. In this chapter we will look at functions that are designed to solve the problem of making decisions and selecting among alternatives.

THE IF FUNCTION

For orders under $100 there is a $5 Shipping and Handling charge. For orders of $100 or more there is no charge for Shipping and Handling. The total of the order is in cell D35 of a worksheet. What formula will calculate the amount of Shipping and Handling to charge?

The solution is to use an **IF** function, as follows:

$$=IF(D35<100, 5, 0)$$

The IF function always has three arguments:

$$=IF(logical\_test, value\_if\_true, value\_if\_false)$$

The first argument is a **logical test**. A logical test is an expression that evaluates to **TRUE** or **FALSE**. In this case the logical test is D35<100. If D35 is less than 100 then the logical test is TRUE, otherwise the logical test is FALSE.

Logical tests usually contain one or more of the following **comparison operators**:

operator	meaning
<	less than
<=	less than or equal to
=	equal to
>=	greater than or equal to
>	greater than
<>	not equal to

Note that the operators <= >= <> are formed by two consecutive keystrokes.

The second argument in an IF function is the value of the IF function if the logical test is TRUE. The third argument is the value of the IF function if the logical test is FALSE. That is, the result of evaluating an IF function is always either the second argument or the third argument. If the first argument is TRUE then the IF function evaluates to the second argument. If the first argument is FALSE then the

IF function evaluates to the third argument.

In the example, if the value in D35 is 34, then the condition (the logical test) in the IF function is TRUE and the value of the IF function is 5. If the value in cell D35 is changed to 200, then the condition becomes FALSE and the value of the IF function changes to 0.

The second and third arguments in the IF function can be any formula. For example, suppose orders under $100 are charged 5% for shipping. Then the formula would be

$$=IF(D35<100, 5\%*D35, 0)$$

A cell can contain just a logical test. That is, a cell could contain the formula =D23<>4 or a cell could contain =X17>(0.8*Q55). In this case, Excel would show either TRUE or FALSE in the cell. TRUE and FALSE are called **logical values**.

ANOTHER EXAMPLE

Suppose that salespeople who sell at least $2,000,000 are entitled to a free trip to Hawaii. The names of the salespeople and their sales figures are listed in the worksheet in Figure 11-1.

	A	B	C	D	E	F	G
	E15				=IF(C15>=$F$4,"Free trip to Hawaii","")		
1							
2		Salesperson Summary					
3							
4		Minimum sales required for free trip to Hawaii:				$2,000,000	
5							
6							
7			Annual				
8		Name	Sales		Result		
9		Aaron	$552,030				
10		Baker	$23,400				
11		Brown	$7,358,800		Free trip to Hawaii		
12		Carey	$1,488,900				
13		Chu	$3,500,400		Free trip to Hawaii		
14		Church	$995,000				
15		Dark	$7,560				
16		Davis	$1,557,100				
17		Delaney	$5,922,000		Free trip to Hawaii		

Figure 11-1. People with sales of at least $2,000,000 are entitled to a free trip to Hawaii.

What formula should be entered into cell E9 (and filled down) so that the cell contains "Free trip to Hawaii" if the person is eligible and appears blank otherwise? The answer is

=IF(C9>=$F$4, "Free trip to Hawaii", "")

The second and third arguments of the IF function are character strings that are enclosed in quotation marks. Thus if the logical test C9>=$F$4 is TRUE then the result of evaluating the function is the text "Free trip to Hawaii". If the condition C9>=$F$4 is FALSE the result of evaluating the function is the text that contains nothing, that is blank.

Text must be enclosed in quotation marks. The formula =IF(C9>=$F$4,Free trip to Hawaii,"") will not work. If the quotation marks were absent from the second argument then Excel would attempt to interpret Free trip to Hawaii as the name of a cell. Since no cell has that name (and indeed because the phrase contains a space it would be an illegal name anyway), if you try to leave the quotes off, the computer would display #NAME? in the cell, an error message meaning it does not recognize a name.

NESTED IF FUNCTIONS

Suppose that salespeople who sell under $100,000 are to be fired. Now there are three choices for the cells in column E. Cell E9 should contain "Free trip to Hawaii" if cell C9 contains a value of at least $2,000,000. Cell E9 should appear blank if cell C9 contains a value between $100,000 and $2,000,000. Cell E9 should contain "Fired" if cell C9 is under $100,000. This is illustrated in Figure 11-2. So far, IF functions have allowed us to create formulas that select between two possibilities depending on a logical test. In this example, we need a formula that allows us to select among three possibilities. The following formula in E9 will correctly select among these three possibilities:

=IF(C9>=$F$4, "Free trip to Hawaii", IF(C9<$F$5,"Fired",""))

This formula contains nested IF functions. This means that one IF function contains another IF function as an argument. The key to working with nested IF functions is to remember that IF functions always should have exactly three arguments.

The preceding formula can be read as follows: If C9 is greater than or equal to F4 then this cell should show "Free trip to Hawaii". Otherwise, if C9 is less than F5 then this cell should show "Fired", otherwise this cell should appear blank.

| | File | Edit | View | Insert | Format | Tools | Data | Window | Help | | _ 🗗 ✕ |

E14 ▼ fx =IF(C14>=$F$4,"Free trip to Hawaii",IF(C14<$F$5,"Fired",""))

	A	B	C	D	E	F	G
1							
2		**Salesperson Summary**					
3							
4		Minimum sales required for free trip to Hawaii:				$2,000,000	
5		People who sell under this amount are fired:				$100,000	
6							
7			Annual				
8		Name	Sales		Result		
9		Aaron	$552,030				
10		Baker	$23,400		Fired		
11		Brown	$7,358,800		Free trip to Hawaii		
12		Carey	$1,488,900				
13		Chu	$3,500,400		Free trip to Hawaii		
14		Church	$995,000				
15		Dark	$7,560		Fired		
16		Davis	$1,557,100				
17		Delaney	$5,922,000		Free trip to Hawaii		

| ◄ ◄ ► ►| \ **Sheet1** / Sheet2 / Sheet3 /

Figure 11-2. People with sales of under $100,000 are fired. Now there are three possibilities.

What are the arguments here? The outer IF function has three arguments:

1. The logical test: C9>$F$4
2. The value if the condition is TRUE: "Free trip to Hawaii"
3. The value if the condition is FALSE: IF(C9<$F$5,"Fired","")

The inner IF function is the third argument. It, too, clearly has three arguments:

1. The logical test: C9<$F$5
2. The value if the condition is TRUE :   "Fired"
3. The value if the condition is FALSE: ""

YOU TRY

A worksheet for tabulating the results of the Tiger football season is given in Figure 11-3. We would like the cells in column G to say "Win" if the Tigers won, "Tie" if the number of points each scored was equal, and "Lose" if the Tigers lost. What should be the formula in G7? Write out your answer before continuing.

Figure 11-3. What formula has been placed in G7 and filled down?

There are several possible correct answers. A good solution would be

=IF(D7>E7, "Win", IF(D7=E7,"Tie","Lose"))

Here the computer first checks to see if D7 is greater than E7. If that logical test is TRUE then the answer is "Win" and the evaluation is over. If D7 is not greater than E7 then the computer evaluates the third argument, the inner IF function. Now the computer checks the first argument of the inner IF function. The computer checks to see if D7 equals E7. If D7 does equal E7 then the answer is "Tie". If the first condition is FALSE and then the second condition is FALSE then the answer is "Lose". With nested IF functions the computer always makes its way from the outside in.

We could rearrange the order, for example, by checking for a tie first:

=IF(D7=E7, "Tie", IF(D7>E7,"Win","Lose"))

There are four other similar rearrangements that would work.

Suppose we want the cells in column G to contain the name of the team that won (or the word "Tie") as in the worksheet shown in Figure 11-4. What formula would you put in cell G7 and then fill down?

Here, what we would need to do is to change two of the arguments, as follows:

	A	B	C	D	E	F	G	H	I
1									
2		**Tiger Football Season**							
3									
4				*Tiger*	*Opponent*				
5	*Game*	*Date*	*Opponent*	*Score*	*Score*		*Result*		
6									
7	1	5-Sep	Eagles	27	31		Eagles		
8	2	12-Sep	Scorpions	17	17		Tie		
9	3	19-Sep	Wimps	10	35		Wimps		
10	4	26-Sep	Panthers	33	21		Tigers		
11	5	3-Oct	Hawks	14	7		Tigers		
12	6	10-Oct	Madmen	21	3		Tigers		
13	7	17-Oct	Bears	17	10		Tigers		
14	8	24-Oct	Gators	9	6		Tigers		
15	9	31-Oct	Warlocks	20	21		Warlocks		
16	10	6-Nov	Daisies	3	34		Daisies		
17	11	13-Nov	Braves	21	17		Tigers		

Figure 11-4. We would like the name of the winner to appear in column G or the word "Tie" if there is a tie. What is the formula in G7?

$$=IF(D7>E7, \text{"Tigers"}, IF(D7=E7,\text{"Tie"},C7))$$

The cell C7 contains the name of the opponent. Of course, when this formula is filled down, the row numbers of C7, D7, and E7 will be adjusted accordingly.

If we wanted to choose among four alternatives, we would need three nested IF functions. There can be up to seven nested IF functions in a formula. Again, each IF function should have three arguments. Any of these arguments can be other IF functions.

LOGICAL FUNCTIONS AND, OR, NOT

At the Tropical Resort there are 600 guest rooms. The guest rooms are classified as either suites, doubles, or singles. Some face the beach; some face the pool; some face inland (the parking lot). The resort manager has decided to charge $259 per night for suites that face the beach. All other rooms will be $179 per night. The worksheet in Figure 11-5 shows a list of the guest rooms. Each cell in column E should contain the price of the room. What formula should appear in cell E6 and then be filled down?

Figure 11-5. Suites that face the beach are $259 per night. All other rooms are $179 per night. What formula has been placed in E6 and filled down?

Clearly, we want to use an IF function here as there are two alternatives. The IF function would have the basic form

=IF(logical_test, 259, 179)

Now we need to fill in the logical test. There are two parts to the logical test, both of which must be TRUE for the logical test as a whole to be TRUE. That is, in order for the room to cost $259 the room both must be a suite and must face the beach.

First, we can check whether a cell contains a specific label with a logical test like C6="Suite". This logical test will be TRUE if C6 contains the word "Suite" and FALSE otherwise.

Excel provides the **AND** function for the purpose of testing whether two or more logical values all are TRUE. The completed formula would be

=IF(AND(C6="Suite",D6="Beach"), 259, 179)

The logical test is AND(C6="Suite",D6="Beach") This logical test will be TRUE only if both C6 contains the word "Suite" and D6 contains the word "Beach".

The AND function sometimes is called a **Boolean function**. (George Boole was an English mathematician who developed key ideas of symbolic logic. His best known book is *The Laws of Thought*, which was published in 1854.) Boolean functions work on arguments that are logical values, that are TRUE or FALSE, just the way that arithmetic functions like SUM and AVERAGE work on arguments that are numbers. The value produced by a Boolean function also is a logical value (just the way that the value produced by an arithmetic function is a number). An AND function always evaluates to TRUE or FALSE.

The AND function corresponds closely to the meaning of the word "and" in English. An AND function can have up to 30 arguments. Each of the arguments must evaluate to TRUE or FALSE. The value of the AND function is TRUE only if all of its operands are TRUE. The value of an AND function is FALSE if any of its arguments is FALSE. For example, for an AND function with two arguments:

Function	Value
AND(TRUE,TRUE)	TRUE
AND(TRUE,FALSE)	FALSE
AND(FALSE,TRUE)	FALSE
AND(FALSE,FALSE)	FALSE

So, for example, the value of

$$=AND(2+2=4,3+3=5)$$

would be FALSE.

There are two other Boolean functions: **OR** and **NOT**.

If we wrote the formula   =IF(OR(D6="Suite",E6="Beach"), 259, 179) then a room would cost $259 if it is a suite or if it faces the beach or both.

The OR function also corresponds closely to the meaning of the word "or" in English. An OR function can have up to 30 arguments. Each of the arguments must evaluate to TRUE or FALSE. The value of the OR function is TRUE only if any of its operands is TRUE. The value of an OR function is FALSE only if all of its arguments are FALSE. For example, for an OR function with two arguments:

Function	Value
OR(TRUE,TRUE)	TRUE
OR(TRUE,FALSE)	TRUE
OR(FALSE,TRUE)	TRUE
OR(FALSE,FALSE)	FALSE

So, for example, the value of

$$=OR(2+2=4,3+3=5)$$

would be TRUE.

The NOT function transforms TRUE into FALSE and FALSE into TRUE.

Function	Value
NOT(TRUE)	FALSE
NOT(FALSE)	TRUE

The NOT function can have only a single argument. The NOT function also follows normal English usage. I hold a black belt in the martial arts. Not!

ANOTHER EXAMPLE

Suppose the manager decides that suites that face the beach will be $259. All other suites will be $189. Doubles that do not face inland will be $189. All other rooms will be $149. (See Figure 11-6.)

Now we have three possibilities. The formula for cell E6 could have the form

$$=IF(logical\_test1, 259, IF(logical\_test2,189,149))$$

We need to fill in the logical tests. Logical_test1 is the same as before, namely

$$AND(C6="Suite",D6="Beach")$$

The tough one is logical_test2. Logical_test2 consists of an OR of two parts. The first part of logical_test2 is

$$D6="Suite"$$

The second part of logical_test2 is

$$AND(C6="Double",NOT(D6="Inland"))$$

So the entire formula would be

$$=IF(AND(C6="Suite",D6="Beach"), 259, IF(OR(C6="Suite",$$
$$AND(C6="Double",NOT(D6="Inland"))),189,149))$$

Alternatively, the formula could be written

	File	Edit	View	Insert	Format	Tools	Data	Window	Help		_	$\boxed{\exists}$	X

E6   ▼   *fx* =IF(AND(C6="Suite",D6="Beach"), 259, IF(OR(C6="Suite", AND(C6= "Double",NOT(D6="Inland"))),189,149))

	A	B			
1					
2		**Tropical Resort Room Charges**			
3					
4		*Room*	*Type*	*View*	*Rate*
5					
6		101	Double	Inland	149
7		102	Suite	Beach	259
8		103	Single	Inland	149
9		104	Single	Beach	149
10		105	Suite	Inland	189
11		106	Single	Beach	149
12		107	Suite	Pool	189
13		108	Double	Beach	189
14		109	Single	Pool	149
15		110	Suite	Beach	259
16		111	Double	Pool	189
17		112 Suite		Beach	259

|◄ ◄ ► ►|\ Sheet1 / Sheet2 / Sheet3 /

Figure 11-6. Suites that face the beach are $259 per night. All other suites are $189 per night as are doubles that do not face inland. All other rooms are $149.

=IF(AND(C6="Suite",D6="Beach"), 259, IF(C6="Suite",189,
IF(AND(C6="Double",NOT(D6="Inland")),189,149)))

Here we have treated the two parts of logical_test2 separately. Another nested IF has been added to accommodate this extra condition. This formula resembles the original statement of the problem on the previous page. Do you see how these two formulas are equivalent? If not, you might take a few minutes to work through the two formulas by writing out the arguments for each of the IF functions and applying the formulas to the examples in Figure 11-6.

TESTING IF FUNCTIONS

Testing worksheets that contain IF functions presents a challenge. Consider the worksheet for salespeople in Figure 11-2. The worksheet basically contains one nested IF function that has been filled down column E. To test this worksheet you should try Annual Sales values of (1) a number more than $2,000,000 (for example $5,000,000), (2) the number $2,000,000 exactly, (3) a number between $2,000,000 and $100,000 (for example $995,000), (4) the number $100,000 exactly, and (5) a number below \$100,000 (for example \$23,400). You also should try varying the value in C9 (the top cell in the column) and the value in C89 (the bottom cell in the column) and the value in a cell between just to be sure that the formula was filled down correctly. You also should try changing the threshold values in F4 and F5.

IF functions with complicated conditions require careful testing. Worksheets with many independent IF functions require very extensive testing to make sure that they are correct. It is quite possible and common for a worksheet with IF functions to work correctly most of the time but to fail when certain relatively unlikely conditions are true.

PENCIL AND PAPER EXERCISES

11-1. Consider the following worksheet:

	A	B	C	D	E	F	G	H	I
1									
2		Exercise 11-1							
3									
4	86	-4	-8	fun					
5	-47	5	26	37					
6	2.3	7	Excel	198					
7	computer	18	4.6	3					
8	56	102		-19					
9									

What would be the result of evaluating each of the following formulas? Assume that no errors will result from the formulas.

(a) =IF(B5>6,"Yes","No")

(b) =IF(B4<D6,C5,A6)

(c) =IF(SUM(B4:B7)>=D5,A4,"Nope")

(d) =B5<A5

(e) =(2*B6)>(C4+10)

(f) =IF(B7=12,47,IF(C4<D7,59,B7))

(g) =IF(C4=26,IF(B5=19,2,4),IF(A8=56,6,8))

(h) =AND(A8>B7,D6<B6)

(i) =IF(AND(K25<10,K25>20),A4,B7)

(j) =IF(OR(K25>10,K25<20),A4,B7)

(k) =IF(AND(OR(B6=7,C6="Excel"),NOT(B7>20)),44,33)

(l) =IF(OR(NOT(B5<6),D7>3),A7,IF(AND(C4=2*B4,D8>D7),C6,D4))

(m) =IF(D5="D5",D5,"D5")

11-2. What is the result of evaluating each of the following formulas?

(a) =IF(AND(6>3,8>2,2>7),"Mastering","Excel")

(b) =IF(OR(1>3,8>2),"yes",5)

(c) =IF(OR(AND(4>2,2>3),OR(4>7,4>5)),7,9)

(d) =IF(AND(6>3,4>7),IF(5>2,8,7),IF(5>3,3,9))

(e) =IF(SUM(3,5,7)=MAX(11,19,15),23,IF(NOT(OR(4=5,MIN(4,1,3)=1)),
     IF(4>2,6,7),9))

11-3. The ages of John, Juan, and Wan are in cells D4, D5, and D6. Give the Excel equivalents of the following conditions. I have answered (a) to give you the idea. Each of the parts is independent of the others.

(a) Juan is at least 18 years old. *Answer: (D5>=18)*

(b) Wan is not more than 55.

(c) John is at most 23.

(d) Juan is not 37.

(e) Both Wan and John are under 25.

(f) John is between 19 and 23, inclusive.

(g) At least one of the people is over 21.

(h) No one is over 65.

(i) Everyone is over 17.

(j) Juan and Wan are under 22 but John isn't.

(k) Exactly one of the people is 20.

(l) Wan is within three years of Juan.

(m) John is the oldest and Juan is the youngest.

(n) John and Wan are not over 21.

11-4. We are creating a worksheet to select stocks for our clients. We have gathered some of the relevant data in the following worksheet. The P/E Ratio is the closing price divided by this year's earnings.

	File Edit View Insert Format Tools Data Window Help _ ⎙ X

	A	B	C	D	E	F	G
F8			𝑓ₓ =E8/D8				
1							
2		**Our Stock Recommendations**					
3							
4	Stock	Earnings	Earnings	Earnings	Closing	P/E	We
5		2 yrs ago	Last yr.	This yr.	Price	ratio	Recommend
6							
7	AA Electronics	$3.47	$3.59	$3.83	$48.50	12.7	
8	Aardvark Intl	$0.69	$1.24	$0.53	$15.75	29.7	
9	Abaco	$4.23	$5.89	$5.92	$33.25	5.6	
10	Abandon Mines	$0.12	$0.15	$0.23	$2.25	9.8	
11	Abernathy	$1.27	$1.31	$0.98	$21.00	21.4	

Sheet1 / Sheet2 / Sheet3 /

What formula would go into cell G7 and be filled down for each of the following recommendations? Each of the cells in column G should contain "Buy", "Hold", "Sell", or appear blank. When no recommendation is made, the cell should appear blank. I have answered part (a) just to give you the basic idea. Each part is independent of the others.

(a) Buy if the P/E Ratio is below 10.   *Answer: =IF(F7<10,"Buy","")*

(b) Buy if the earnings have increased this year.
    Sell if the earnings have decreased this year.

(c) Buy if the earnings have increased for each of the two years and the P/E Ratio is
        below 10.
    Sell if the earnings have decreased for each of the two years.

(d) Buy if this year's earnings are up over 20% from last year and this year's
        earnings are up over 30% from 2 years ago or if the P/E ratio is below 8.
    Sell if this year's earnings are down over 20% from last year or if the P/E ratio is
        above 20.
    Hold otherwise.

11-5. In determining whether they are to receive a bonus, each of our 5,000 employees has
been rated between 1 and 100 on each of three factors.

	A	B	C	D	E	F
1						
2		*Employee Evaluations and Bonus Calculation*				
3						
4	*Employee*	*Effectiveness*	*Uniqueness*	*Value Added*	*Bonus*	
5	Aardvark, Aaron	95	58	91		
6	Able, Anna	86	67	42		
7	Acero, Avil	90	96	98		

Cell reference box shows: E5 with fx. Sheet tabs: Sheet1, Sheet2, Sheet3

Give the formula that can be entered in E5 and filled down to fulfill each of the following. Each employee's bonus depends on that employee's ratings. Each of the four parts below is independent of the other parts. You may use extra cells.

(a) If all the ratings are 90 or above then the person receives a bonus of $20,000.
    Otherwise if all the ratings are 80 or above the person receives $10,000.

Otherwise no bonus.

(b) If at least one of the ratings is above 90 and none of the factors are below 80 the person receives a bonus of $20,000.
Otherwise if at least one of the ratings is above 80 the person receives $10,000.
Otherwise no bonus.

(c) If at least two of the ratings are above 90 the person receives a $20,000 bonus.
Otherwise no bonus.

(d) If all three of the ratings are within 5 points of each other the employee receives a $20,000 bonus.
Otherwise no bonus.

COMPUTER EXERCISES

11-6. At Hill University students who register for at least 12 credits are considered Full-Time students and pay $4,320 tuition. Students who register for less than 12 credits are considered Part-Time students and pay $360 per credit. Create a worksheet that allows you to enter a student's name and the number of credits for which he or she is registering. The worksheet should then display (1) the status of the student (Full-Time or Part-Time) and (2) the amount of tuition owed. Try your worksheet on the following three students: Maria 15 credits, John 6 credits, Yu 12 credits.

11-7. At the Downtown Theater: Orchestra seats are $40, Mezzanine seats are $30, and Balcony seats are $20. Children (under 12) are half price. Seniors (65 or over) receive a $5 discount. Create a worksheet that allows you to enter the location of the ticket desired and the age of the person and gives you the price of the ticket. If the person types in an illegal seat location the worksheet should so inform the user. You can use as many cells as you would like. Try your worksheet for Orchestra for an 88-year-old, Mezzanine for a 7-year-old, Backstage for an 18-year-old, and Orchestra for a 21-year-old.

11-8. A company evaluates new graduates for positions according to three criteria. If the candidate has a Grade Point Average (GPA) of at least 3.3, the candidate receives point. On the interview, candidates who score 7 or 8 (out of 10) receive 1 point; candidates who score 9 or 10 receive 2 points. The company gives an aptitude test as well. A candidate who scores above 85 gets 1 point.

The company adds up the points to obtain a candidate's rating. A candidate who receives a rating of 0, 1, or 2 points is not given a job offer. A candidate who receives 3 points is given an offer as a Junior Salesperson. A candidate who receives 4 points is given an offer as a fast-track Manager in Training.

Create a worksheet that allows the Human Resources Department to enter in a candidate's name, GPA, interview score, and aptitude score and determines the employment decision.

11-9. Leary, Lebowsky, and Li are running for mayor.

(a) Create a worksheet that has the names of the candidates and next to the names the number of votes each receives. Now create another cell with a formula that gives the name of the winner, for example "Li wins!" You may assume there are no ties.

(b) Modify your worksheet so it allows for two-way ties ("Leary and Li tie!") or even for a three-way tie.

(c) Lopez has entered the race. Now there are four candidates. Create a worksheet that has the names of the candidates and next to the names the number of votes each receives. Now create another cell with a formula that gives the name of the winner, for example "Li wins!" You may assume there are no ties.

11-10. An employee is eligible for retirement if he or she satisfies at least one of the following three criteria:

     (i)   the employee has worked here for at least 40 years
     (ii) the employee is 65 or over
     (iii) the employee has worked here for at least 30 years and is 60 or over

(a) Create a worksheet that allows a person to enter in his or her age and the number of years worked here. A cell in the worksheet should respond either "Congratulations! You are eligible for retirement!" or "Back to work."

(b) Add a cell that will indicate how many years it will be until the employee is eligible for retirement if he or she is not now eligible. You may use extra cells in your worksheet.

11-11. At the county courthouse speeders pay a fine of $50 plus $5 for every mph above the speed limit. Anyone caught driving 90 mph or over pays an extra $200. Create a worksheet that will allow you to enter a driver's name, the speed limit on the road where the driver was caught, and the driver's speed. If the driver's speed did not exceed the speed limit, then the worksheet should display "Sorry! No fine." Otherwise the worksheet should display the fine owed.

Try your worksheet on the following five tickets: Alicia, Speed Limit 40, Driver's Speed 55; Bob, Speed Limit 55, Driver's Speed 97; Carlos, Speed Limit 65, Driver's Speed 65; Darlene, Speed Limit 25, Driver's Speed 28; Ernie, Speed Limit 45, Driver's Speed 17.

11-12. The Tigers and the Warriors are playing a three-game playoff for the league championship. Whoever wins the most games wins the championship. If any team wins the first two games, the third game is not played.

(a) The games cannot end in a tie. The scores are in a worksheet as below. Cell C8 must have a formula that determines the winner. You can use extra cells if you would like.

(b) The games can end in a tie and so can the championship. Modify your worksheet accordingly. Be sure to cover all possibilities, for example two ties and one win or one win by each team and a tie.

11-13. Just about all of us are fortunate to have lived in two years that are palindromes. Most people live in at most one. A year is a palindrome if it reads the same backwards as forwards. So 1991 and 2002 are palindromes but 2005 is not.

(a) Create a worksheet that gives in column B a list of all of the four-digit years that are palindromes, beginning with 1001 in B6 and extending on down in ascending order. You may use other columns as well, but the final answer for the row must be in column B. Furthermore, all rows below row 7 must be the result of filling the cells in row 7 down the worksheet. You may not use Auto Fill.

(b) Create a similar worksheet for all five-digit years that are palindromes, beginning with 10001 in B6.

11-14. Salespeople receive $10,000 base salary plus a commission of 2% of sales. Anyone who sells over $3 million receives a free vacation in Tahiti. Anyone who sells over $5 million receives an additional $5,000 bonus. At the end of the year salespeople are rated as follows: under $2 million "Dud", $2 million through $5 million "Star", over $5 million "Superstar". Create a worksheet that allows you to enter a salesperson's name and annual sales amount and then calculates the following:

Salesperson Summary

Name:	(input)
Annual sales:	(input)
Base salary:	$10,000
Commission:	(formula)
Bonus:	(formula)
Total pay:	(formula)
Free vacation?	(formula)
Status:	(formula)

11-15. The administration and faculty at New Ivy University have thought long and hard about their admission criteria. They have decided to forget about activities, athletics, parents who are alumni, interviews, recommendations, etc. in deciding which high school students should be admitted. NIU is going to decide admission strictly on academics. Only standardized test scores and grades will count.

Applicants will not have to write essays. All they will have to submit are five numbers: three test scores (Math SAT score, Verbal SAT score, and one SAT II subject test score), rank in graduating class, and number of students in graduating class. SAT test scores always range from 200 to 800.

The following criteria are used in deciding admissions:

1. If an impossible number is submitted, the applicant is refused admission.
2. If any test score is 800, the applicant is accepted.
3. If any of the test scores is below 300, the applicant is refused admission.
4. If the Math and Verbal SAT scores average above 600 and the applicant is in the top quarter of the graduating class, the applicant is accepted.
5. If any two of the test scores are below 400 or the applicant is in the bottom quarter of the graduating class, the applicant is refused admission.
6. Otherwise the applicant is put on the waiting list.

These criteria are applied in order. Thus, any impossible number disqualifies an applicant. If the five numbers are valid, then any test score of 800 means acceptance, regardless of the other numbers. If the first two criteria do not hold, then check the third criterion. And so on.

For this exercise you are to create a worksheet to decide whether an applicant is admitted. Your worksheet should be designed to accept the information for a single applicant. Thus a visiting high school senior could enter the information into your worksheet and find out the admission decision. In your worksheet you should have a different cell for each criterion. Then you should combine all six criteria into a final decision of either "Accepted", "Denied Admission", or "Waiting List".

Try your worksheet on each of the following 11 applicants:

Student	Math SAT	Verbal SAT	SAT II Subject	Rank	Class Size
A	520	480	450	103	298
B	640	120	800	3	137
C	250	300	800	492	506
D	590	600	720	352	440
E	590	800	740	193	160
F	650	680	240	53	800
G	590	700	550	120	410
H	310	520	390	42	77
I	430	290	450	10	240
J	470	510	420	−15	137
K	600	720	930	210	982

11-16. The number 371 is a "special" number because the sum of the cubes of the digits that compose it is equal to the number itself:

$$3^3 + 7^3 + 1^3 = 3*3*3 + 7*7*7 + 1*1*1 = 27 + 343 + 1 = 371$$

This is very unusual. Most numbers are not "special". For example, 502 is not "special" because $5^3 + 0^3 + 2^3 = 125 + 0 + 8 = 133$ rather than 502.

Create a worksheet that will find the highest three-digit "special" number. (Three-digit numbers are 100, 101, 102, ... 998, 999.) The answer should be calculated by the worksheet and appear automatically in an appropriately labeled cell at the top of the worksheet. This cell must have a formula in it, not just the answer typed in. All cells must have formulas in them and the same formulas must have been filled down for all 900 rows. Do not use Auto Fill. There are a couple of approaches to this problem. One uses the MOD function; others do not require learning new functions.

11-17. The Game of Life was invented by the Cambridge mathematician John Conway in the 1960s. The Game of Life takes place on an infinite two-dimensional grid. Each cell in the grid is either dead or alive. Each cell has eight neighbors, the cells that touch its sides or corners.

If a cell is alive it will survive into the next time period (next generation) if it has two or three neighbors that also are alive. If a cell is alive and has four or more neighbors that are alive, it will die of overcrowding. If a cell is alive and has zero or one neighbor that is alive, it will die of exposure.

If a cell is dead it will remain dead in the next generation unless exactly three of its neighbors are alive. In this case, the cell will be "born" in the next generation.

The rules are applied simultaneously to all cells from one generation to the next. We begin the game at Generation 1 with some configuration of living cells specified by the user. Each subsequent generation is determined by the rules established by Conway. The living cells can flourish and expand or stay the same or die off.

For example, suppose we start with the following configuration:

	A	B	C	D	E	F	G	H	I	J	K	L	M	N
1														
2			Generation					1						
3														
4														
5														
6														
7					1	1	1	1						
8														
9														
10														

Applying Conway's rules, cell E7 dies because it has only one living neighbor. Cell F7 survives because it has two living neighbors. Cell G7 survives. Cell H7 dies. New cells are born at F6, G6, F8, and G8 because all were dead but have three living neighbors. No other cells are born. The result is the following configuration:

	A	B	C	D	E	F	G	H	I	J	K	L	M	N
1														
2		Generation						2						
3														
4														
5														
6						1	1							
7						1	1							
8						1	1							
9														
10														

Applying the rules to these cells we get the following configuration:

	A	B	C	D	E	F	G	H	I	J	K	L	M	N
1														
2		Generation						3						
3														
4														
5														
6						1	1							
7					1			1						
8						1	1							
9														
10														

This configuration is stable. All of the living cells have two or three neighbors so all survive. No new cells are born. So the next generation looks the same as the previous generation.

	A	B	C	D	E	F	G	H	I	J	K	L	M	N
1														
2		Generation						4						
3														
4														
5														
6						1	1							
7					1			1						
8						1	1							
9														
10														

The colony is immortal. It stays the same forever.

Implement the Game of Life in Excel. Living cells should be represented by 1's. Dead cells should appear blank. (Hint: You might want to represent dead cells by 0's but not display the 0's by clicking off the Zero Values box in the View sheet in the *Options...* selection in the *Tools* pull-down menu.) You should use at least a 20 x 20 universe and draw a box around the universe. The universe should be surrounded by a blank row or column on all four sides so nothing leaks at the edges of the universe. At the top of each universe you should display the generation number.

The top left of the first sheet in the workbook should be a special universe for the user to enter in the initial configuration of 1's into Generation 1. The rest of the workbook should be protected from being changed. Any initial configuration of 1's should be acceptable. It is up to you how to design the rest of the workbook. You might want to use a separate worksheet for each generation. Or you might want to do all of the work in one worksheet. Or you might want to have one area of a worksheet where the universe changes over time. In this case you might want to turn off Automatic Recalculation in the Calculation sheet in the *Options...* selection in the *Tools* pull-down menu and have the formulas recalculate the next generation only when you press F9. The design of the workbook is up to you.

Be sure that the rules are applied only to cells in one generation to obtain the configuration of cells in the next generation. The workbook should be easy to use and should accurately portray the progress of life in the universe over at least a dozen generations, and preferably more, for any initial configuration.

(a) Try your workbook with the preceding initial configuration, with the three initial configurations that follow, and with three new initial configurations of your choice. For each of the initial configurations determine the ultimate fate of the inhabitants, for example whether the colony lives and expands forever, is stable, or dies off.

	A	B	C	D	E	F	G	H	I	J	K	L	M	N
1														
2			Generation					1						
3														
4														
5														
6														
7					E	1		G	1					
8					E	1	F	1	1					
9					E	1		G	1					
10														

	A	B	C	D	E	F	G	H	I	J	K	L	M	N
1														
2		Generation						1						
3														
4														
5														
6														
7					1	1	1							
8					1	1	1							
9					1	1	1							
10														

	A	B	C	D	E	F	G	H	I	J	K	L	M	N
1														
2		Generation						1						
3														
4														
5														
6				1										
7					1									
8		1	1	1										
9														
10														

(b) Determine the ultimate fate of the following initial configuration. You may need to modify your workbook. (Remember that the universe in the Game of Life is as large as necessary, as is the number of generations.)

(c) Find an original initial condition where the colony grows in number and expands forever.

CHAPTER 12

FUNCTIONS RELATED TO IF

OBJECTIVES

In this chapter you will learn how to:

- Use COUNTIF to count the cells that meet some criteria
- Use SUMIF to add cells meeting some criteria
- Create lookup tables
- Use VLOOKUP for inexact and exact matches
- Use the "IS" functions to check for error conditions

In this chapter we discuss the use of several functions that are related to the IF function in solving problems involving the selection of different values.

THE COUNTIF FUNCTION

The countries of the world are listed in order of Gross Domestic Product per Capita in the worksheet in Figure 12-1. That is, each country is listed, followed by the continent, the Gross Domestic Product for the country in $1,000,000,000, the population of the country, and the average Gross Domestic Product per person in the country.

We are interested in calculating various statistics about the countries of the world. For example, suppose we would like to have a cell that reports the total number of countries in Europe. There are several approaches to solving this problem, but an easy approach involves the use of the **COUNTIF** function. In a cell we could type the formula

=COUNTIF(C5:C232,"=Europe")

Figure 12-1. GDP and population of the countries of the world.

This formula instructs Excel to count up all of the cells in the range C5:C232 that contain the word "Europe". In fact, we could omit the = sign and enter the formula

=COUNTIF(C5:C232,"Europe")

The COUNTIF function has two arguments, a range and the criterion. The criterion is written in quotes. The value returned by the function is the number of nonblank cells in the range that meet the criterion.

As another example, suppose we want to have a cell that gives the number of countries that have a GDP above $100 billion. Since in the worksheet GDP's are given in billions of dollars, we could use the formula

=COUNTIF(D5:D232,">100")

This would return the number of values in D7:D189 that are greater than 100.

THE SUMIF FUNCTION

Now suppose we want to find the total GDP for Asia. To solve this problem we could use the formula

=SUMIF(C5:C232,"Asia",D5:D232)

The **SUMIF** function has three arguments: the range of the cells to be tested, the criterion to be used in the test, and the range that contains the cells to be summed. In this case, for each cell in the range C5:C232 that contains the word "Asia" the number in the corresponding cell in the range D5:D232 will be added into the total that is calculated by the function.

If we want a cell that calculates the total number of people who live in countries that have under $1,000 GNP per capita, we could enter the formula

=SUMIF(F5:F232,"<1000",E5:E232)

In fact, this worksheet is organized as an Excel list. There are many operations that can be performed with this data, as we will see in Chapter 16.

There is no AVERAGEIF function, but we could calculate the average per capita GDP for South America with the formula

= SUMIF(C5:C232,"South America",D5:D232)*1000000000 /
SUMIF(C5:C232,"South America",E5:E232)

USING IF FUNCTIONS IN EXTRA COLUMNS

Suppose we would like to have the largest GDP of any country in Africa appear in a cell at the bottom of the worksheet. Well, you might say, let's just use the MAXIF function. Unfortunately, there is no MAXIF function in Excel.

One approach is to use an extra column to pull out the GDP of the countries that are in Africa. (See Figure 12-2.) Here, cell G5 contains the formula

$$=IF(C5="Africa",D5,"")$$

which has been filled down column G. Thus the cells in column G contain the GDP for each country in Africa and are blank for each country not in Africa. In cell G234 we place the formula

$$=MAX(G5:G232)$$

	File	Edit	View	Insert	Format	Tools	Data	Window	Help					_ 𝔹 ×

| | Arial | | ▼ 10 ▼ | **B** *I* U | ≡ ≡ ⊞ | $ % , | +.0 .00 | ⊞ ▼ A ▼ | » |

| | G234 | ▼ | *fx* =MAX(G5:G232) |

	B	C	D	E	F	G	
1	**Countries of the World by Gross Domestic Product per Capita**						
2	(Source: The CIA Factbook)						
3			*GDP in*		*GDP per*	*Africa*	
4	*Country*	*Continent*	*$ billions*	*Population*	*Capita*	*GDP*	
5	Luxembourg	Europe	15.9	442,972	$ 35,894		▼
221	Mali:	Africa	9.1	11,008,518	$ 827	9.1	▲
222	Yemen	Asia	14.4	18,078,035	$ 797		
223	Afghanistan	Asia	21.0	26,813,057	$ 783		
224	Madagascar	Africa	12.3	15,982,963	$ 770	12.3	
225	Burundi	Africa	4.4	6,223,897	$ 707	4.4	
226	Comoros	Africa	0.42	596,202	$ 704	0.42	
227	Tanzania	Africa	25.1	36,232,074	$ 693	25.1	
228	Eritrea	Africa	2.9	4,298,269	$ 675	2.9	
229	Ethiopia	Africa	39.2	65,891,874	$ 595	39.2	
230	Congo	Africa	31.0	53,624,718	$ 578	31.0	
231	Somalia	Africa	4.3	7,488,773	$ 574	4.3	
232	Sierra Leone	Africa	2.7	5,426,618	$ 498	2.7	
233							
234			Maximum GDP of any country in Africa (in $ biilions):			369!	▼

| ◄ ◄ ► ►| \ **Sheet1** / Sheet2 / Sheet3 / | | ◄| | ►| |

Figure 12-2. Using IF in an extra column to select the GDP of African countries.

so that cell G232 contains the highest GDP of any country in Africa.

This technique of using an extra column containing IF functions is useful in solving many different problems.

THE VLOOKUP FUNCTION

It often is convenient to express a multi-way selection in a table. For example, we might have a tax rate table which indicates that if you earned so much money, then your tax rate is such and such. Or, we might give volume discounts, where the more you purchase, the lower the price. This could be expressed in a volume discount table that indicates how much you must purchase to qualify for the different discounts. Excel provides the special function **VLOOKUP** especially for making selections by looking up values in a table.

The VLOOKUP function has three arguments. The first argument is the number you want to look up. The second argument is the location of the **vertical lookup table**. The third argument indicates which column in the table contains the answer, the value to be returned by the function.

Suppose that the photocopy center charges are based on the number of photocopies ordered, as follows:

Photocopy Prices

Number Of Copies	Price Per Page
1 to 19	.06
20 to 99	.05
100 to 499	.04
500 to 999	.035
1000 or more	.03

In cell C15 we have the number of copies. We would like the price per page to appear in cell C17. What formula should go into cell C17?

We could solve this problem using a nested IF function. The cell would contain the formula

=IF(C15<20,.06,IF(C15<100,.05,IF(C15<500,.04,IF(C15<1000,.035,.03))))

This formula works, but it is cumbersome and does not indicate the price table explicitly in the worksheet. If the price changes we would need to find and change the formula. An alternative approach to solving this problem uses a vertical lookup table and VLOOKUP function, as in Figure 12-3. The formula in cell C17 is

Figure 12-3. Using the lookup table in E20:F24 to find the price per page for the number of copies in C15

=VLOOKUP(C15,E20:F24,2)

This formula instructs the computer to look up the number in cell C15 in the vertical lookup table located in cells E20 through F24. The value of the function will be the corresponding value in the second column of the vertical lookup table (column F).

A vertical lookup table has a definite organization. The values in the first column normally are in ascending order. The computer takes the number in C15 and compares it to the top left cell in the lookup table. If the number in the cell is less than C15, the computer proceeds to the next cell down. The computer keeps chugging down the left column until it finds a number that is greater than the value in C15. At that point it goes up one cell and over to the column in the vertical lookup table indicated by the third argument. The third argument is called the **column index**. This may sound confusing at first, but it works well.

In the example in Figure 12-3, the number to be looked up in the table is 325. The computer compares 1 with 325. 1 is less than 325 so the computer moves down a cell. 20 is less than 325 so the computer moves down another cell. 100 is less than 325 so the computer moves down a cell. At last, 500 is greater than 325. The computer moves up one cell. This is the row with the answer. Then it moves over to the second column in the vertical lookup table (because the third argument is 2). Finally the computer returns the number 0.04. The number 0.04 is the result of evaluating the VLOOKUP function in cell C17.

Suppose the number in cell C15 is 700. The result of evaluating the VLOOKUP function in C17 would be 0.035.

Suppose the number in cell C15 is 5000. The result of evaluating the VLOOKUP function in C17 would be 0.03. If the number to be looked up is larger than any number in the first column of the table, then the computer stops at the last row in the table.

Suppose the number in cell C15 is -25. The result of evaluating the VLOOKUP function in C17 would be the error message #N/A, which stands for "No value available." If the number to be looked up is less than the first value in the table, then the computer indicates an error.

Suppose the number in cell C15 is 100. The result of evaluating the VLOOKUP function in C17 would be 0.04. In this case the first number in the column that would be larger than the number we are looking up would be 500. The computer would then go up one cell and over to column F.

A major advantage of using a lookup table is that the numbers in the table are visible in the worksheet. The person using the worksheet can see the table rather than having the values hidden inside a nested IF formula. If the pricing policy changes, we can change the numbers in the table rather than trying to edit a complicated formula. For example, if the price per page for 100 to 499 copies is raised to $0.045, the number in cell F22 can be changed to 0.045. In the worksheet in Figure 12-3 the result of evaluating the formula in C17 would become 0.045.

What is the purpose of the third argument, the column index? Suppose we had two classes of customers, regular and preferred, and two sets of rates. The regular customers are "walk-ins", anyone who walks in the door. The preferred customers pay us an annual fee for special service and prices. We could assign regular customers a code of 2 and preferred customers a code of 3. Now we could determine the rate by making the code be the column index, as in the worksheet in Figure 12-4.

File Edit View Insert Format Tools Data Window Help							
Arial · 10 · B I U ≡ ≡ ≡ $ % ,							
C17 · fx =VLOOKUP(C15,E20:G24,C12)							
	A	B	C	D	E	F	G	H
12		Customer type	3				
13		(2=regular, 3=preferred)					
14							
15		Number of copies:	325				
16							
17		Price per page:	0.04				
18							
19					# Copies	$/page	
20					1	0.06	0.05
21					20	0.05	0.04
22					100	0.04	0.04
23					500	0.035	0.03
24					1000	0.03	0.025

Sheet1 / Sheet2 / Sheet3 /

Figure 12-4. The lookup table with two types of customers.

We entered the Customer Type in C12 and used that entry as the column index in the formula in C17

=VLOOKUP(C15,E20:G24,C12)

Note that we extended the lookup table over to column G in the formula. We could be fancier and have the person type in "regular" or "preferred" and then use an IF function to determine the column index.

This same technique would work for income tax tables where there are different rates for single taxpayers, married taxpayers filing jointly, and so on.

Warning! If a formula containing a VLOOKUP function is to be filled down a column, be sure that the table location is expressed as an absolute address. Otherwise, the address of the table will change as the formula is filled. This is a common but subtle error when using lookup functions.

It often is useful to name a lookup table as well as the other key cells. The formula in C17 could be

=VLOOKUP(COPIES,PRICE_TABLE,CLASS_CODE)

There is an **HLOOKUP** function that is similar to VLOOKUP. It works horizontally, scanning across the top row of a **horizontal lookup table**.

USING VLOOKUP FOR EXACT MATCHES

In the preceding example we wanted to look up a number in a range of values. Sometimes we want only an exact match. Suppose we have a list of the players on a team and their numbers. We would like to create a worksheet that an announcer can use to quickly find the name of a player given his number. We could create the worksheet shown in Figure 12-5.

Here we enter a number into the cell in C4. The computer automatically displays the name of the player in cell C6. The formula in C6 is

=VLOOKUP(C4,B10:C37,2,FALSE)

In this formula we are instructing Excel to look up the value in cell C4 in the first column of the vertical lookup table in B10:C37 and return the corresponding value in the second column, column C, of the table.

The VLOOKUP function call contains a fourth argument, namely FALSE. The VLOOKUP function has an optional fourth argument, which is either TRUE or FALSE.

Figure 12-5. When we look up the number of a player we want an exact match.

If the fourth argument is omitted, as in the photocopy example in the previous section, the fourth argument is assumed to be TRUE. If the fourth argument is omitted or TRUE, then we are instructing Excel that we want an approximate match and that Excel should find the correct range in the first column of the lookup table in which the value occurs. If the fourth argument is FALSE, as it is in this example, we are instructing Excel that we require an exact match.

For example, if we enter 7 for the player's number, and there is no number 7 in the first column of the lookup table because no player wears the number 7, we don't want the name of the player who wears number 6. We want an indication that we entered an erroneous number. In fact, if we were to enter the number 7 in cell C4 in the worksheet in Figure 12-5, we would get the error message #N/A (no value available) in cell C6.

Note that if we are requiring an exact match in a VLOOKUP function by including FALSE as the fourth argument, then the entries in the left column of the lookup table do not need to be in ascending order. If an exact match is required, as in the worksheet in Figure 12-5, the values in the left column of the lookup table can be entered in any order.

THE ISNA FUNCTION

We even could check for the potential error message in the worksheet in Figure 12-5 and insert our own error message by using the Excel function **ISNA**. The function ISNA has a single argument. The function ISNA returns TRUE if the argument evaluates out to #N/A and FALSE otherwise. We can embed the VLOOKUP function into the ISNA function and intercept the #N/A error message before it appears, as in Figure 12-6.

The formula in cell C6 now is

=IF(ISNA(VLOOKUP(C4,B10:C37,2,FALSE)), "No such player!",
VLOOKUP(C4,B10:C37,2,FALSE))

This formula instructs Excel that if the value of the VLOOKUP function is #N/A then Excel should display the message "No such player!" in the cell. Otherwise, Excel should display the result of the VLOOKUP function, the name of the player.

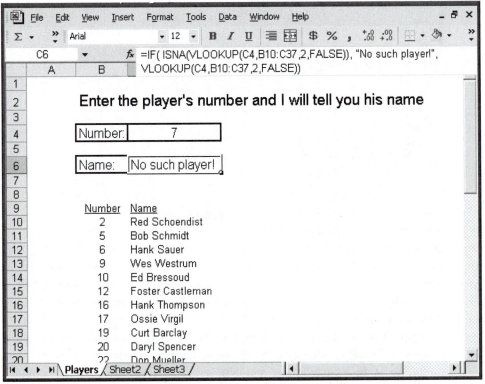

Figure 12-6. "No such player!" is more meaningful than "#N/A".

THE "IS" FUNCTIONS

There are several "IS" functions. Each of these functions has a single argument and returns TRUE or FALSE depending on the evaluation of the argument.

Function	Returns TRUE if
ISBLANK	The argument refers to an empty cell.
ISERR	The argument evaluates to any error value except #N/A.
ISERROR	The argument evaluates to any error value.
ISLOGICAL	The argument evaluates to TRUE or FALSE.
ISNA	The argument evaluates to #N/A.
ISNONTEXT	The argument refers to an item that is not text. (Note that this function returns TRUE if the argument refers to a blank cell.)
ISNUMBER	The argument evaluates to a number.
ISREF	The argument is a reference to a cell or range.
ISTEXT	The argument refers to an item that is text.

LOOKING UP TEXT

It is possible to search for text in a lookup table as well as numbers. An example is shown in the phone directory worksheet in Figure 12-7. Enter a name in C6. The computer then looks up the name in the table below and responds with the telephone number. The formula in C8 is

=VLOOKUP(C6,B11:C405,2,FALSE)

Excel looks up the value in C6 in the left column of the table in B11:C405. When it finds an exact match (because the fourth argument is FALSE) in B11:B405, Excel returns the corresponding value in column C, column 2 of the lookup table. If it does not find an exact match, Excel will return #N/A, as when looking up numbers.

Normally with text we want an exact match. If we do not want an exact match, we simply can make the fourth argument TRUE or leave it off altogether. If we are looking up the range within which a cell falls, in other words if the fourth argument is missing or TRUE, then the first column needs to be in ascending order. Ascending order for text is alphabetical order.

Excel is **case insensitive** in looking up text in a lookup table. That is, looking up "CAROL" is the same as looking up "Carol" or "carol".

Figure 12-7. Looking up text in a personal phone directory.

COMPUTER EXERCISES

12-1. The Weather Bureau would like a worksheet to help it keep track of some simple statistics. In column B from B8 through B38 enter the numbers 1 through 31. In column C from C8 through C38 enter the highest temperature recorded for your town for each day during the last month. (You can make up these temperatures.) In column D from D8 through D38 put Sunny, Cloudy, Rain, or Snow. In the top lines of the worksheet put appropriate titles and column headings. Beginning in cell B40 and continuing down put the following labels:

> Average Temperature for Month
> Highest Temperature
> Number of Sunny Days
> Number of Days above 50 Degrees
> Average Temperature of Rainy Days
> Highest Temperature of a Rainy Day
> Day of the Highest Temperature of the Month

Second Highest Temperature of Month

Widen column B appropriately. Your task is to enter formulas so that the appropriate statistics are calculated automatically in C40 through C47. The Day of the Highest Temperature of the Month would be 23 if the highest temperature of the entire month occurred on the twenty-third of the month. In case of a tie, select the latest day. Do not use the Sort command. You may use extra columns. Of course, your worksheet should work for any sequence of temperatures and weathers.

12-2. Contributors are classified as follows: under $100 Supporter, $100 to $399 Patron, $400 to $999 Fellow, $1,000 or more Blue Chip. Create a worksheet that allows you to enter a name and a contribution and then automatically displays the contributor's classification. Use a lookup table.

12-3. (a) Create a worksheet that gives a price quote. You will enter an item name and the quantity of that item purchased. Your worksheet should look up the item name in the Price Table to find the Unit Price. Then it should calculate the Total Before Discount. Look up this amount in the Discount Table to find the discount percent. Then your worksheet should calculate the Discount Amount, the Total After Discount, add in 6% sales tax, and give the final Total Due for the order.

Price Quote

Item: *(Input)*
Quantity: *(Input)*

Unit Price:
Total Before Discount:
Discount %:
Discount Amount:
Total After Discount:
Sales Tax:

Total Due:

Price Table

Item	Unit Price $
Connectors	3.98
Grommits	15.99
Hasps	0.35
Widgets	8.79

Discount Table

Amount $	Discount
0	0%
100	5%
500	10%
1000	15%

Try your worksheet three times, on the following orders: 100 Connectors, 2000 Widgets, 300 Faranges.

(b) Create a new workbook that allows the customer to order some quantity of each of the items at once. The discount should be applied to the total amount ordered. Try your workbook on one order of 30 Connectors, 0 Grommits, 50 Hasps, 5 Widgets.

12-4. Concert tickets are priced as follows:

	22 and under	over 22
Premier tickets	$65	$90
Floor tickets	$50	$70
Balcony tickets	$30	$30
Standing Room	$15	$20

(a) Create a worksheet that allows a person to enter in an age and a ticket location (Premier, Floor, Balcony, Standing Room) and automatically gives the price of the ticket. Use lookup.

(b) If the user enters an illegal ticket location the worksheet should put an appropriate error message in the cell.

12-5. On the Allied Student Cell Phone plan: if you use 60 minutes or less in a month you pay $17.99 in usage charge. If you use between 60 and 120 minutes you pay the $17.99 plus $0.25 per minute for each minute over 60 in usage charge. If you use more than 120 minutes you pay $29.99 plus $0.15 per minute for each minute over 120 in usage charge. In addition there is a $7 processing charge per month. Then there is an 8% sales tax on all charges. Create a worksheet that allows you to enter the minutes used and then shows you the usage charge, the processing charge, the tax, the total charge, and the average total cost per minute. Print out your results for 10 minutes, 100 minutes, 5000 minutes and also the formulas.

12-6. In the country of Freedonia, the national currency is the royal. Single people pay no taxes on the first 1,000 royals, 10% on any income between 1,000 and 3,000 royals, 20% on any income between 3,000 and 10,000, and 30% on any income over 10,000. Married people filing jointly pay no taxes on the first 1,000 royals, 8% on any income between 1,000 and 3,000, 15% on any income between 3,000 and 10,000 and 25% on any income in excess of 10,000 royals. So, for example, a single person with an income of 5,000 royals would pay 200 royals for the income between 1,000 and 3,000 and 400 for the income between 3,000 and 5,000 for a total tax bill of 600 royals. Create a worksheet to calculate the tax owed given the marriage status and income. The worksheet also should show the actual percentage of income owed in taxes. In the example given the 600 royals owed represent 12% of income.

12-7. At the Royal Pizza Parlor, pizzas are priced as follows:

	Small	Medium	Large
Triple Cheese	$7.95	8.95	10.95
Pepperoni	8.95	10.45	11.95
Goat Cheese and Fig	11.95	14.95	17.95
Sausage and Pepper	9.45	10.95	12.45
The Works	10.00	12.00	14.00
Cola	0.95	1.25	1.75

(a) Create a worksheet that allows a person to enter a type and a size and learn the price of the pizza. Use lookup.

(b) Give an appropriate error message if the person enters a type or size that the Parlor does not carry.

(c) Create a worksheet that allows a customer to enter up to six different pizzas (or drinks) with quantities and then calculates the total bill for the customer. For example the customer might order 2 Medium Sausage, 4 Large The Works, and 6 Large Cola.

12-8. The SoKo Cell Phone Company offers five anywhere/anytime plans. Plan A is $9.99 per month and each minute is $0.50. Plan B is $19.99 per month with the first 100 minutes free and each minute in excess of 100 costing $0.40. Plan C is $39.99 per month with the first 250 minutes free and each minute over 250 costing $0.30. Plan D is $79.99 per month with the first 1,000 minutes free and each minute in addition costing $0.20. Plan E is $159.99 per month with unlimited calls at no extra cost.

Create a worksheet that allows a person to enter in a name, the plan letter, and the number of minutes used in a month. The worksheet should calculate the total bill for the month. You may use as many cells as you would like in your design.

Try your worksheet on: John A 7 minutes, Luis B 80 minutes, Carla B 120 minutes, Shruti C 300 minutes, Omar D 1200 minutes, Suzanne E 2400 minutes, Kzyki E 12 minutes.

12-9. In your History course there are three hour exams, a paper, and a final exam. Each of these is graded between 0 and 100. In determining the final grade, the professor has decided to drop each student's lowest hour exam grade. The two highest hour exam grades will count 1/6 each, the paper will count 1/3, and the final exam will count 1/3 in determining the overall average for the course. The final letter grade for the course will be based on the overall average, as follows: below 60 is an F, 60 to 65 is a D, 65 to 75 is a C, 75 to 80 is a B-, 80 to 90 is a B, 90 to 95 is an A-, 95 and above is an A.

(a) There are 10 students in the course. Create a worksheet that automatically calculates and displays the overall average and final letter grade for each student. Enter 10 names and sets of grades that fully test the formulas in the worksheet. You should enter a name, three hour exam grades, a paper grade, and a final exam grade for each student. Everything else should be calculated automatically.

(b) In deciding the Grade Point Average, an A is worth 4 points, a B is worth 3 points, a C is worth 2 points, a D is worth 1 point, and an F is worth 0 points. An A- is worth 3.666 points and a B- is worth 2.666 points. Add formulas to your worksheet so that the course Grade Point Average is calculated and displayed. For example, the average grade for the 10 students in the course might be 2.8.

(c) To further encourage students to work hard on their papers, the professor has decided that whoever receives the highest grade on the paper will receive at least an A- in the course whatever the student's grades on the exams. Modify your worksheet so that the student who receives the highest grade on the paper automatically receives at least an A-.

CHAPTER **13**

DATES AND TIMES

OBJECTIVES

In this chapter you will learn how to:

- Use serial numbers to represent dates and times
- Enter dates and times into a worksheet
- Write formulas to perform calculations on dates and times
- Format cells as dates and times

The calendar we use was developed over 2,000 years ago by Julius Caesar and improved slightly by Pope Gregory XIII in 1582. We are so used to the system of 12 months per year and 28, 29, 30, or 31 days per month and leap days almost every fourth year that we don't think twice about it. Still, it is difficult to perform calculations in the calendar system. How many days is it until Christmas? A payment was due on November 27. When will the payment be 60 days overdue? How many days have you been alive? Not surprisingly, the calculations are difficult in the same way that doing arithmetic with Roman numerals is difficult.

Similarly, we are used to the division of the day into 24 hours (usually expressed as 12 hours AM and 12 hours PM), the hour into 60 minutes, and the minute into 60 seconds. But calculations using this time notation system are awkward too. How many minutes are there between 9:38 AM and 3:32 PM? A movie that is 2 hours and 27 minutes long begins at 8:46 PM. When will the movie end? How many seconds are there in a day?

The capabilities provided in Excel simplify date and time calculations. The secret lies in the use of serial numbers to represent dates and times.

SERIAL NUMBERS

In Excel, each day beginning at January 1, 1900 is assigned a sequential **serial number**. January 1, 1900 is serial number 1. January 2, 1900 is serial number 2. February 1, 1900 is serial number 32. January 1, 1901 is serial number 367. November 15, 2008 is serial number 39767. December 31, 2078 is serial number 65380.

Time of day is represented by a fraction of a serial number. The serial number 39767.5 is noon on November 15, 2008. The serial number 39767.75 is 6:00 PM on November 15, 2008. The serial number 39767.6650694444 is 3:57:42 PM on November 15, 2008. Strictly speaking, the serial number 39767 is actually 12:00 midnight at the beginning of November 15, 2008.

Can you see how serial numbers make date and time calculations easier? To determine the number of days between two dates just subtract one serial number from the other.

AN ERROR IN EXCEL

As you may have noticed, there is a minor error in assigning serial numbers. The serial number 60 is assigned to February 29, 1900. But that day never existed! There was no leap day in 1900, because 1900 was not a leap year. Years ending in 00 are not leap years unless they are divisible by 400. Thus, all dates after February 29,

1900 are assigned serial numbers one greater than they should be. If you think about it, this error is only rarely consequential. Calculations of the length of time between a date in January or February 1900 and a date in March 1900 or later are off by a day. All other calculations are unaffected. Still, in such a well-designed program any known error is worth noting, if only for some future trivia question. Actually, the developers of Excel are not responsible for the error. This dating system was used in Lotus 1-2-3 and adopted by Excel as is so that Excel would remain compatible with Lotus 1-2-3.

A SECOND DATE SYSTEM

To correct the error, but add to the confusion, there is an second date system that sometimes is used in Excel, especially on Macintoshes. This date system begins at January 1, 1904 rather than January 1, 1900. In this system, all of the serial numbers correspond to dates four years later. You can determine which date system you are using by selecting *Options...* in the *Tools* pull-down menu and then clicking on the Calculation tab. (See Figure 13-1.) If the 1904 Date System box is checked, you are using the **1904 Date System**. If the box is blank, you are using the **1900 Date System**. Just for consistency, if you are using dates in your workbook I suggest that at the beginning of your session on Excel you look to make sure that the box is not checked and that you are employing the standard 1900 Date System.

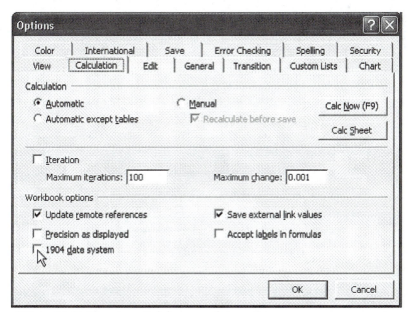

Figure 13-1. How to switch between date systems.

ENTERING DATES INTO THE WORKSHEET

How can we calculate how many days there are between September 23, 2004 and January 14, 2005? The short answer is to subtract the serial number for September 23, 2004 from the serial number for January 14, 2005. But how can we determine the serial numbers for those dates?

If we enter a date into a cell in the proper format, the computer recognizes the entry as a date and automatically converts the date into the corresponding serial number, as in Figure 13-2. Here we have typed 23-Sep-04 into cell D4 and 14-Jan-05 into cell D5. Excel recognizes these as dates and automatically converts them into serial numbers. Thus, the value of cell D4 actually is 38,253, the serial number for September 23, 2004, as is apparent if we format cell D4 in comma format, as in Figure 13-3.

Figure 13-2. To find the number of days between two dates, enter them and subtract.

Figure 13-3. A number can be formatted to appear as a number or as a date.

We have to be very careful here. The date has to be typed in just right. For example, if we type a space before the date, the computer will not recognize the entry as a date. Rather, the entry will be taken as text, as in Figure 13-4. Here, Excel is trying to subtract a label from a number, which yields the #VALUE! error message. You can tell that cell D4 now contains text because the entry is aligned to the left of the cell rather than to the right of the cell. Recall that Excel automatically aligns text on the left of the cell and numbers on the right of the cell, just so you can tell which cells contain text and which contain numbers.

What are the allowable formats for dates? It depends on the settings in Regional and Language Options in the computer's Control Panel. Different countries have different formats for dates. For a computer set to English (United States) Excel will recognize each of the following as a date:

September 23, 2004
23-Sep-04
9/23/04
Sept 23, 04
9-23-04

and automatically will convert the entry into the equivalent serial number. If you enter

9/23
9-23
September 23
23-Sep

or variants into a cell, the computer will interpret it as September 23 of this year.

Figure 13-4. If we type a space before the date then the entry is regarded as text.

USING DATES DIRECTLY IN FORMULAS

In the example in Figure 13-2, we entered the dates into cells and then used the cell addresses in the formula =D6-D4. Suppose we want to do the calculation in a single formula. If we type the formula

$$= 14\text{-Jan-05-23-Sep-04}$$

into a cell, we get a #NAME? error. Why? Excel interprets the dashes as minus signs. Excel tries to subtract the contents of the cell named Jan from the number 14, but there is no cell with the name of Jan so we get the #NAME? error. To do the date arithmetic directly in a formula, we need to place quotes around the dates:

$$= \text{"14-Jan-05"} - \text{"23-Sep-04"}$$

Now Excel will interpret the text in the quotes as dates, automatically convert these dates into their equivalent serial numbers, and perform the subtraction, yielding the value 113, the number of days between the two dates.

THE TODAY FUNCTION

The computer has a **system clock** which keeps track of the current date and time. This clock has its own battery so it stays current (excuse the mild pun) even when the computer is shut down. Excel can access the system clock using the **TODAY** function. If we enter the formula

$$=\text{TODAY( )}$$

into a cell, the cell will contain the serial number for today. The computer automatically will format this number as a date, so today's date will appear in the cell. The parentheses following TODAY are necessary to indicate this is a function and not the name of a cell. The function will be recalculated whenever all the other formulas are recalculated, so TODAY( ) will give you the current day rather than the day the worksheet was created.

THE DATE FUNCTION

The **DATE** function has three arguments: a year, a month number, and a day of the month. The result of evaluating the date function is the corresponding serial number. The formula =DATE(2005,1,14) calculates the serial number for January 14, 2005, which is 38366. Thus the following formula also calculates the number of days between September 23, 2004 and January 14, 2005:

$$=DATE(2005,1,14) - DATE(2004,9,23)$$

Entering this formula into a cell in Excel yields an answer of 113.

DATE FORMATS

Excel has several built-in formats for dates. If you specify a date format for a cell that contains a number, Excel takes the number as the serial number of a date, and displays the corresponding date. The formats are specified in the *Cells...* selection in the *Format* pull-down menu in the Number tab. In Figure 13-5 some of the formats available for English (United States) are shown.

Figure 13-5. Various date formats are available.

If you would like to use a different language or calendar system, Microsoft tries to accommodate you. Notice the Locale pull-down menu. This has over a hundred choices. If you are preparing a worksheet for clients in Bahrain and would like the date in Arabic, some of the date formats available are shown in Figure 13-6.

Figure 13-6. Alternative date formats for Arabic (Bahrain).

DATE FUNCTIONS FOR CONVERTING FROM SERIAL NUMBERS

There are three date functions that convert a serial number into the corresponding year, month, and day of the month.

The **YEAR** function converts a serial number into the corresponding year. For example, =YEAR(39014) is 2006 because the serial number falls in 2006.

The **MONTH** function converts a serial number into the corresponding month of the year. For example, =MONTH(39014) is 10 because the serial number falls in October.

The **DAY** function converts a serial number into the corresponding day of month. For example, =DAY(39014) is 24 because the serial number falls on October 24, 2006.

If the argument to any of these three functions is less than 0, then the function will evaluate to #NUM!.

For example, if we want to determine if the dates in C7 and C9 are in the same calendar year we could check with

=IF(YEAR(C7)=YEAR(C9), "Same year", "Different years")

EXAMPLE: HOW MANY DAYS UNTIL JULY 1?

Our organization uses a July 1 budget year. Budgets begin and end at midnight (at the beginning) of July 1. We would like to be able to calculate how many days are left before our current budget expires. If the current budget year ends on July 1, 2008, we could write the formula in one of two ways:

$$="1\text{-July-}2008" - TODAY(\ )$$

or

$$=DATE(2008,7,1) - TODAY(\ )$$

The only problem is that each year we would have to adjust the year in the quotes or in the first argument in the DATE function by hand. How could we write the formula so it always works automatically whatever the current year? As a first try we could substitute the current calendar year for the 2008 in the preceding formula, as follows:

$$=DATE(YEAR(TODAY(\ )),7,1) - TODAY(\ )$$

Here, YEAR(TODAY( )) evaluates to the current calendar year, to 2008 if this is 2008. This formula works if the current month is January through June, if we are in the same calendar year as the budget end. However, if this were October then the above formula would be incorrect. If the month were July through December, the formula would evaluate to a negative number because

$$=DATE(YEAR(TODAY(\ )),7,1)$$

would yield the serial number of the July 1 in the current calendar year, of the previous July 1 rather than the next July 1. To solve this problem we could use an IF function where the condition is TRUE if today's month is before July and FALSE if today's month is July or after.

$$=IF(MONTH(TODAY(\ ))<7,(DATE(YEAR(TODAY(\ )),7,1)-TODAY(\ )),$$
$$(DATE(YEAR(TODAY(\ ))+1,7,1)-TODAY(\ )))$$

If the month is before July, the computer calculates the serial number of July 1 of this year minus today's serial number. Otherwise, if the month is July or after, the computer calculates the serial number of July 1 of next year minus today's serial number.

HOURS, MINUTES, AND SECONDS

Serial numbers represent days. The fractions of a serial number represent fractions of a day. For example, 0.5 represents 12 hours. An hour is 0.0416666667, which is 1/24. A minute is 0.0006944444, which is 1/(24*60). A second is 0.0000115741, which is 1/(24*60*60) of a day.

Midnight is 0. 6:00 AM is 0.25. Noon is 0.5. 7:30 PM is 0.8125. 11:58:23 PM is 0.998877314814815.

The same types of built-in functions and display formats are provided for times as are provided for dates.

THE NOW FUNCTION

The **NOW** built-in function evaluates to the serial number for the date and time right now according to the system clock. The value of the formula

$$=NOW( )$$

changes each time the worksheet is evaluated. So, for example, if it is 8:00 AM on December 25, 2005, the value of NOW( ) is 38711.333333333.

To obtain just the current time we can use both the NOW( ) and TODAY( ) functions together. For example, if we wish the worksheet to greet the user we could enter the following formula into a cell:

=IF((NOW( ) – TODAY( )) < 0.5, "Good morning", IF ((NOW( ) – TODAY( )) < 17/24, "Good afternoon", "Good evening"))

Thus if it is before noon then Excel wishes the user "Good morning". Otherwise if it is before 5 PM (which is 17/24 through the day), Excel wishes the user "Good afternoon". Otherwise Excel wishes the user "Good evening". The greeting is updated each time the formulas in the worksheet are recalculated.

TIME FORMATS

There are several formats for displaying times in Excel. The time formats are reached through the *Cells...* selection in the *Format* pull-down menu in the Number tab. (See Figure 13-7.)

When a cell is displayed in a strictly time format, the digits to the left of the decimal point in the number in the cell are ignored. Only the fractional part of the

Figure 13-7. Time formats.

number is used to determine what is displayed. Thus a cell with the number 65.59 would appear the same as a cell with the number 42051.59 if the cells have the same time format. Both would be displayed as 2:09:36 PM, the time that is 0.59 through the day. There are some time formats that display both the date and the time represented by the serial number in the cell.

ENTERING A TIME INTO A CELL OR FORMULA

As with a date, a time can be entered directly into a cell. If you type 9:52 into a cell, Excel will interpret the entry as a time. The cell will contain the serial number for 9:52 AM, namely 0.4111111111. The cell will be formatted as a time, so 9:52 will appear in the cell, just as you typed it.

The **TIME** function has three arguments: the hour based on a 24-hour clock, the minute, and the second. The result of evaluating the TIME function is the equivalent serial number. For example, =TIME(19,12,0) evaluates to 0.8, as 7:12 PM is 80% through the day.

The movie began at 8:46 PM. The movie is 2 hours and 27 minutes long. When will the movie be over? A formula for determining the answer is

$$= \text{"8:46 PM"} + \text{"2:27"}$$

which yields the value 0.967361111111111 in the cell. Displaying this cell in a time format gives you the answer 11:13 PM. Another possible formula to use is

$$=TIME(20,46,0) + TIME(2,27,0)$$

which also yields 11:13 PM.

EXAMPLE: TESTING THE ENGINES

United Engines performs extensive tests on their products. They would like a worksheet to allow them to enter the starting date and time of a test and the number of hours for the test and then display the ending date and time for the test.

The worksheet is shown in Figure 13-8. The date at the start of the test is entered into cell C4. The time at the start of the test is entered into cell C5. The number of hours the test is to run is entered into cell C7. Cells F4 and F5 both have the same formula:

$$= C4 + C5 + C7/24$$

This formula adds the serial number for the date of the start plus the serial number of the time of the start plus the number of days that the test is to run. Cell F4 is given a date format. Cell F5 is given a time format. Both F4 and F5 contain the same formula and, hence, the same value, namely 37813.90625, which is the serial number for 9:45 PM on July 11, 2003.

Figure 13-8. Calculating the date and time of the end of the test.

TIME FUNCTIONS FOR CONVERTING FROM SERIAL NUMBERS

There are three time functions that convert a serial number into the corresponding hour, minutes, and seconds.

The **HOUR** function converts a serial number into the corresponding hour of the day. For example, =HOUR(39461.847) is 20 because the serial number falls between 8 PM and 9 PM.

The **MINUTE** function converts a serial number into the corresponding minute of the hour. For example, =MINUTE(39461.847) is 19 because the serial number falls between 8:19 PM and 8:20 PM.

The **SECOND** function converts a serial number into the corresponding second of the minute. For example, =SECOND(39461.847) is 41 because the serial number falls closest to 8:19:41 PM.

The serial number 39461.847 corresponds to 8:19:41 PM on January 14, 2008, to the nearest second.

PENCIL AND PAPER EXERCISE

13-1. Write down the formula that calculates each of the following quantities. Then identify the type of format in which the cell is to be displayed. You may use the computer to check the formulas. (You do not need to write down the result of evaluating each formula. You just need to write down the formula itself and the format in which the answer will be displayed.) I have answered part (a) just to give you the general idea.

(a) The date that is 90 days after December 23, 2006.
Answer: *The formula is* ="23-Dec-2006" + 90
Format the answer as a date.

(b) The number of days Franklin D. Roosevelt was President of the United States. FDR was inaugurated on March 4, 1933. He died in office on April 12, 1945.

(c) The date that is 1000 days from today.

(d) The date that was 1000 hours ago.

(e) The number of days until the year 2015.

(f) The date of serial number 10000.

(g) The serial number for April 3, 2046.

(h) The year for serial number 500000.

(i) The date of the 200th day of 2007.

(j) The number of days you have been alive.

(k) The number of hours between 11:52AM on 05-Nov-05 and 8:07AM on 25-Dec-05.

(l) The time 1000 hours from now.

(m) The hours:minutes:seconds between 6:46:32 AM and 10:23:15 PM.

(n) The number of minutes in the century beginning in 2000.

(o) The exact time 60% through the day.

(p) The time and date 100,000 minutes after 4:12 PM on November 12, 2004.

COMPUTER EXERCISES

13-2. Use the TODAY function to create the following worksheet. Your worksheet should work automatically whatever the day.

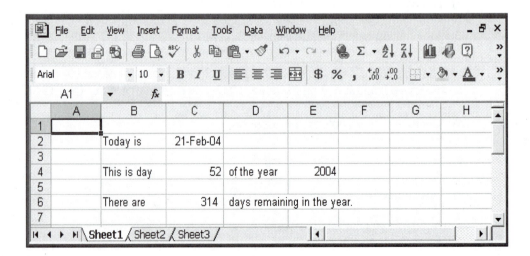

13-3. The local department store has hired you to create a well-labeled worksheet that displays in four cells the number of days, hours, minutes, and seconds from now until Christmas. The worksheet should be updated automatically each time it is opened. To update it once it is opened, press F9, the Recalculation key.

13-4. Create a worksheet that allows you to enter in any date into a cell and then in separate cells gives the date 30, 60, 90, and 120 days from the entered date.

13-5. NASA has commissioned you to create a worksheet for Mission Control. The design is given below. The time and date of launch will be entered as shown in C5 and D5. The worksheet should display the current time and date automatically. The elapsed length of the mission so far should be calculated and displayed in two ways: (1) in terms of days in C10 and then hours, minutes, and seconds in E10 and (2) in terms of hours and fractions of hours in C12. To update the display, you will need to press F9, the Recalculation key.

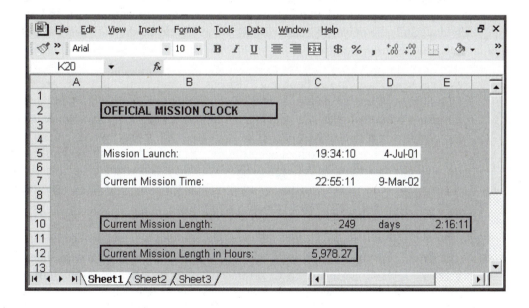

13-6. John loves riding on roller coasters. His lifetime dream is to set the world endurance record for riding a roller coaster and have his achievement be recorded in the *Book of World Records*. Now John has his chance. The local amusement park is excited about supporting John for the publicity his great accomplishment will bring. According to the book, the current record is 503 hours. The amusement park would like John to break the record at 8:00 PM on July 4. Create a worksheet to determine the date and time he should begin.

13-7. You have taken a part-time job as manager of the Happy Hamburger Stand. The Stand is open from 6 AM to 11 PM. Employees work all different odd schedules. Employees are paid at the rate of $8.00 per hour from the moment they check in to the moment they check out. So, for example, an employee who checked in at 6:00 PM and checked out at 9:15 PM would earn $26.00 for the day.

(a) Create a well-labeled worksheet that accepts two entries, the check-in time and the check-out time, as inputs. The worksheet should show the number of hours the employee worked and the amount of money the employee is to be paid for the day. No other inputs are allowed.

(b) The Stand is so popular under your management that you decide to stay open until 3 AM. Create a second worksheet that accepts check-in and check-out times between 6 AM and 3 AM. Again, the worksheet should show the total number of hours the employee worked and the amount of money the employee is to be paid for the day. Still, the only two cells used for input should be the entries for the check-in time and the check-out time.

(c) The Stand is doing a booming business at dinnertime, but you are having a difficult time hiring employees to work then. You decide to pay $10.00 per hour for any time worked between the hours of 5 PM and 8 PM. For example, an employee who checked in at 6:00 PM and checked out at 9:15 PM now would earn $30.00 for the day. Modify your worksheet accordingly. Your third worksheet should work for any check-in time and check-out time. You may use extra cells to hold partial results, but clearly label the final answer. Still, the only two inputs should be the entries for the check-in time and the check-out time.

13-8. You have been hired by Club 2010 to design and implement a worksheet for the "greeter" at the door to use to determine whether people are old enough to enter. Create a well-labeled worksheet that allows the greeter to enter into a cell the person's birth date as listed on the person's driver's license. In a separate cell should appear either "Welcome" if the person is at least 21 years old or "Sorry, you are underage" otherwise. Use TODAY and IF.

CHAPTER 14

FINANCIAL FUNCTIONS

OBJECTIVES

In this chapter you will learn how to:

- Create worksheets to solve problems involving the time value of money
- Use the PMT function to calculate loan payments
- Use the Function Wizard to assist you in entering functions
- Use the PV, RATE, NPER, and FV functions to analyze financial situations
- Make investment decisions using IRR and NPV

Excel often is used to help analyze financial problems.

A basic concept in finance is the **time value of money**. The value of money changes over time because of the potential of earning interest on the money. Which is more valuable, $1,000 today or $1,001 two years from now? The $1,000 today is more valuable because with almost no risk you could put the $1,000 in the bank, earn interest, and have over $1,050 two years from now.

Furthermore, if you leave the money in the bank, the interest compounds. During the second year you earn interest not just on the amount you deposited in the bank but also on the interest that you earned the first year. Suppose you decide to start saving for a down payment for a house. You open an account that pays 3% per year. Every year you put $2,500 into the account. How much money will you have in four years? How long will it be before you have $20,000?

Suppose you have $10,000 that you would like to invest for four years. The bank will guarantee you 6% interest per year. Your cousin has this great idea for starting a business. If you invest the $10,000 with her, she promises to pay you $2,000 after one year, $3,000 after two years, $4,000 after three years, and $5,000 at the end of four years. Which investment would pay the higher rate of interest? In making the decision of what to do with your money you may decide to invest in the bank because it is much less risky or you may decide to invest with your cousin because she is family, but at least you ought to be able to figure out how the options compare in terms of the rate of return on your money.

The calculations in financial analyses can be quite complex. A lot of money can be riding on making the correct calculations. To help in this important application area, several financial functions are provided in Excel. These functions facilitate many calculations involving the time value of money.

CALCULATING LOAN PAYMENTS WITH THE PMT FUNCTION

Wouldn't it be fun to drive around town in a bright red Ferrari 550 with a nice throaty V12 engine? Or maybe a yellow one? Red or yellow, I can't decide. Here is a new one advertised in the paper for only $227,500. Not bad. I can scrape up $3,000. My buddy just got an auto loan at 12% annual interest. Maybe I could take out a loan and then pay it back over four years. I wonder what the monthly payment would be on a $224,500 loan.

When borrowing money for an automobile loan or for the mortgage for a house or condo, the money usually is paid back in equal monthly payments. Part of these payments cover the interest that is owed. Part of the payments go to pay off the principal. The principal of a loan is the amount of money that was borrowed. After each payment, the amount owed on the principal is decreased. After the final payment the loan is paid off. The formula for calculating the fixed monthly payment is built into the **PMT** function.

The PMT function has five arguments (inputs): the periodic interest rate, the number of periodic payments, the present value, the future value, and the type:

PMT(rate, nper, pv, fv, type)

When using the PMT function, or any financial function, the first step is to decide on the period. All figures must be expressed in terms of a common period of time. If the payments are to be made each month, then the period would be a month. This means that the first argument to the PMT function, the interest rate to be paid, must be stated as the monthly interest rate. The second argument, nper, would be the number of monthly payments to be made, the number of periods of the loan.

How much would the monthly payment be for the Ferrari?

The interest rate is 12% per year. The monthly interest rate would be 12%/12 or 1%. This could be written in the formula either as 1% or as .01.

We would make monthly payments for four years, for a total of 48 monthly payments.

The present value of the loan would be the principal, the amount borrowed, which would be 224500. Here, we need to be careful not to include a dollar sign or any commas. If we put in a dollar sign, Excel will think it's the beginning of an absolute address and give us an error message. If we include a comma to mark off the thousands, Excel will think the comma is separating two different arguments.

The future value is the amount of money that will be exchanged at the end of the loan. Here, the future value would be 0 as the loan will be all paid off after 48 months. In some cases there is a "balloon payment", an amount to be paid off at the end of the loan period. This would be included as the future value.

Finally, the type of the loan is either 0 or 1. The type is 0 if the payment is due at the end of each month. The type is 1 if the payment is due at the beginning of each month. Normally the bank would require you to make your first payment at the end of the first month and subsequent payments would be due at the end of each succeeding month, so the type would be 0.

The formula for calculating the monthly payment for the Ferrari would be

=PMT(1%, 48, 224500, 0, 0)

Entering this formula into a cell yields the answer ($5,911.95). The parentheses mean this is a negative number. That is, each month we would need to pay the finance company $5,911.95. Taxes and insurance and gas and tune-ups are extra. You know, I've always wanted an eight-year-old Chevy.

One of the tricky parts of using financial functions in Excel is the sign of the number. A positive number represents money you are receiving, cash coming into your wallet. A negative number represents money you are paying, cash going out of your wallet. In this example we are receiving $224,500 from the bank at the beginning of the transaction of the loan so the present value would be +224500. Each month we are paying money to the bank out of our wallet so the monthly payment is represented in Excel as a negative number.

The last two arguments in the PMT function are optional, in the sense that if they are 0, you can leave them off. Thus, we could write the formula

$$=PMT(1\%, 48, 224500)$$

Rather than entering the numbers for the loan directly into the formula, we could put them into separate cells and refer to the cells in the formula, as in the worksheet in Figure 14-1. The advantage of this approach, of course, is that to change the specifics for the loan, we would just need to change the numbers in the cells rather than going in and editing the formula. Also, these numbers show on the worksheet and in a printout of the worksheet. Most lending institutions state the interest rate and the length of the loan in years so the worksheet in Figure 14-1 is designed accordingly. The interest rate and length of the loan are converted to monthly figures in the formula. The actual data in the worksheet in Figure 14-1 show the figures for a $200,000 mortgage at 8% per year over 30 years.

Note that a balloon payment would be entered as a positive number in C7. It would be money out of our pocket at the end of the loan period, negative cash flow for us. The balloon payment is converted to a negative number in the formula in C10 by placing a minus sign before the entry for C7 in the fourth argument in the formula.

Figure 14-1. A worksheet for calculating the monthly payment for a loan. In this case, the loan is for $200,000 for 30 years.

USING THE INSERT FUNCTION TOOL

 The Insert Function tool was introduced in Chapter 4. It is especially useful with financial functions in specifying the arguments. The Insert Function button is just to the left of the Formula bar.

The first step is to select the function you wish to use. You either type the name of the function in the top box or you can select the category of the function in the pull-down menu and then find the function in the list below, as in Figure 14-2. The list of arguments and a brief description of the function is shown at the bottom of the dialog box. You can ask for Help to find out all about the function if you wish. Click on OK once you have identified the correct function.

Figure 14-2. Find and select the function.

The second step of the Insert Function tool is the Function Argument dialog box, shown in Figure 14-3. The dialog box gives you the arguments and their order. It is critical that the arguments be in the correct order in the formula. To enter cell addresses in the arguments, either you can type the addresses or you can click on the cells themselves. If the cells you need to refer to are hidden by the dialog box window, you can drag the window to one side and scroll the worksheet. Or, if you click on the button to the right of the argument box, the Function Arguments window temporarily will roll up out of your way. The result of evaluating the function is shown at the bottom of the dialog box. The optional Help facility really is helpful here and explains the functions and their arguments. Click on OK in the dialog box of Figure 14-3 and you have the formula in Figure 14-1.

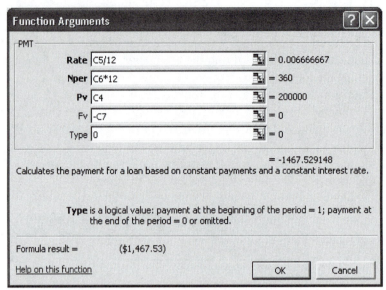

Figure 14-3. The Insert Function tool shows and explains the list of arguments and lets you fill them in by typing or pointing.

CALCULATING FUTURE VALUES USING THE FV FUNCTION

I have $40,000 to invest right now. Each year I plan to invest $5,000 more. I figure I can earn 8% per year on my investment. How much will I have accumulated in 10 years?

To solve this problem we would use the **FV** function. The FV function calculates the future value of an investment assuming constant periodic payments and a constant interest rate throughout the life of the investment. The FV function has five arguments:

FV(rate, nper, pmt, pv, type)

Again, the first step is to determine the time period involved in the investment. Since all of the information is stated in years, we will use a time period of a year. So, the rate and number of periods will be stated in terms of years. The annual rate is 8%. The number of years of the investment is 10. The annual payment is $5,000 out of our wallet, so we'll enter -5000 into the formula for pmt. The present value is -40000, our initial investment. We plan to make our annual investment at the end of each year. That is, the first payment of $5,000 will be made one year from now rather than right now. So the type of the investment is 0 rather than 1.

Using the FV function to solve the problem of the future value of our investment, we get the formula

$$=FV(8\%, 10, -5000, -40000, 0)$$

Entering this formula into Excel tells us we will have accumulated $158,789.81 after 10 years. We have deposited a total of $90,000 (that is, $40,000 initially and $50,000 over 10 years) so the remaining $68,789.81 is the amount we have earned in interest.

Suppose we are uncertain about being able to make the $5,000 deposit each year. We just want to see what an initial deposit of $40,000 would earn in 10 years at 8% if we left it alone. Now the formula would be

$$=FV(8\%, 10, 0, -40000, 0)$$

Here there is no periodic payment, so the third argument, pmt, is 0. Excel tells us that at 8% interest in 10 years the $40,000 investment would turn into $86,357.

If we change the periodic payment to +5000, as in the formula

$$=FV(8\%, 10, 5000, -40000, 0)$$

it would mean that we want to deposit $40,000 in an account earning 8% per year and withdraw $5,000 at the end of each year. Here we would have $13,924.19 at the end of 10 years.

THE BASIC IDEA OF THESE FINANCIAL FUNCTIONS

These investments (or loans) have five basic parameters:

pv   the value or cash flow at the beginning of the investment
rate   the interest rate per time period
nper   the total number of time periods
pmt   the payment that is made each time period
fv   the value or cash flow at the end of the investment

Given any four of these parameters, there is a financial function to calculate the fifth. For the PMT function we know the present value, the interest rate, the number of periods, and the future value. PMT tells us the amount of the periodic payment. For the FV function we know the present value, the interest rate, the number of periods, and the periodic payment. FV tells us the future value of the investment.

THE NPER FUNCTION

My goal is to become a millionaire, to accumulate 1,000,000 dollars. I have $100,000 saved up in an investment earning 10% per year. If I deposit $25,000 additional each year, how many years until I have the $1,000,000?

The **NPER** function has five arguments:

$$NPER(rate, pmt, pv, fv, type)$$

Filling in the arguments

$$=NPER(10\%, -25000, -100000, 1000000, 0)$$

we find it will take 13.4 years until I am a millionaire!

Suppose by some good fortune I find myself with a million dollars. I decide to put it in a safe investment at 5% per year and retire to a tropical island. I figure I will need $80,000 per year to live the tropical lifestyle to which I would like to become accustomed. How many years will it be until I run out of money?

This is still a problem for NPER. Entering the formula

$$=NPER(5\%, 80000, -1000000, 0, 1)$$

yields an answer of 18.5 years before I run out of money. The fifth argument, the type, is 1 because I want that first withdrawal right away and each subsequent withdrawal at the beginning of the year.

Suppose I could earn 10% per year on my money. The formula

$$=NPER(10\%, 80000, -1000000, 0, 1)$$

yields an answer of #NUM!. This is an error message. In this case it means that there is no such number. If you think about it, at 10% interest per year I will be earning more than I am spending so I can withdraw $80,000 per year forever and my investment will continue to increase in value! NPER has no value; the number of periods the investment will last is infinite.

THE RATE FUNCTION

Suppose we have $20,000 to invest and we would like to grow it into $50,000 in five years. What interest rate would we need to receive?

The **RATE** function has six arguments:

RATE(nper, pmt, pv, fv, type, guess)

The final argument, the guess, is optional. The guess is the user's guess about what is the correct answer. There is no algebraic formula for calculating the rate, so the computer does it iteratively, by trial and error. The guess is the starting point for the computer's attempts to find the correct answer. If the user leaves off the guess, the computer automatically will begin with a guess of 10%.

To solve this problem we enter

=RATE(5, 0, -20000, 50000, 0)

and the computer informs us we will require an annual interest rate of 20.11%.

If we had wanted to grow the $20,000 into $5,000,000 in five years, then we would enter

=RATE(5, 0, -20000, 5000000, 0)

Now the computer evaluates the formula to #NUM!, meaning it couldn't come up with an answer. The problem is that the computer started with a guess of 10% but the required rate is much higher. If we instruct the computer to begin with a guess of 100% per year

=RATE(5, 0, -20000, 5000000, 0, 100%)

then the formula evaluates to 202%, meaning we need to receive more than 200% interest each year. We must triple our money each year to achieve this rather ambitious objective.

We need to enter a number for the guess in the RATE function if the final answer is not close to 10%.

THE PV FUNCTION

Mike is hoping to spend 18 months on a Greek island programming the great new computer game (and tasting a little ouzo). Mike figures he will need $3,000 per month to live and $800 at the end of the period for transportation home. How much money would Mike need to deposit initially in an account paying 6% interest per year to be able to withdraw $3,000 per month for 18 months and have $800 left at the end?

The **PV** function has five arguments:

$$PV(\text{rate, nper, pmt, fv, type})$$

The formula would be

$$=PV(6\%/12, 18, 3000, 800, 1)$$

Here the time period is the month so we divide the annual interest rate by 12. The formula evaluates to ($52,507.20), meaning Mike must now deposit $52,507.20 in the account to be able to make the desired withdrawals.

MAKING INVESTMENT DECISIONS USING IRR

Let's return to the investment decision we posed in the beginning of the chapter. You have $10,000. The bank will pay you 6% interest per year if you deposit your $10,000 there for four years. Your cousin says that if you invest the $10,000 in her new business she promises to pay you $2,000 after one year, $3,000 after two years, $4,000 after three years, and $5,000 at the end of four years. Which investment would pay the higher rate of interest? Here we have periodic (annual) payments being made, but the payments are not equal. This frequently is the case in proposed investments in business. Thus the set of five functions just discussed (PMT, FV, NPER, RATE, PV) would not pertain here, because they require all of the periodic payments to be the same.

A different set of functions in Excel is designed to help analyze situations where there is an arbitrary stream of cash flows.

The **IRR** function is used to calculate the interest rate returned on an investment involving various positive and negative payments that are made on a regular basis. The IRR function calculates "internal rate of return". The use of the IRR function to calculate the internal rate of return for the investment in your cousin's business is shown in the worksheet in Figure 14-4.

The cash flows are listed explicitly in column D. As usual in Excel, any investments you make, money you pay out, are entered as negative numbers. Any returns on your investment, money you receive, are entered as positive numbers. Using the IRR function in the worksheet we can see that investing in your cousin's business under the terms proposed would result in a rate of return of 12.83%. The bank is paying only 6% so you would receive a higher rate of return from your cousin.

The IRR function has two arguments:

$$IRR(\text{cash flows, guess})$$

Figure 14-4. Using the IRR function to calculate the rate of return on an investment in your cousin's business, assuming she pays you back as promised.

The first argument to the IRR function is the range of addresses where the series of cash flows is located on the worksheet. The cash flows should be in sequential cells, either down a column or across a row. The period of time from one cash flow to the next must be the same. The resulting rate of return is for that period. That is, if the time between each payment in the cash flows is one year, then the result of evaluating IRR will be an annual rate of return. If the time between each payment in the cash flows is one month, then the result of evaluating IRR will be a monthly rate of return. Note that in the worksheet in Figure 14-4, the year numbers in column B are there just to help make the worksheet understandable by people. The numbers in column B are not used by the computer in the IRR calculations.

The IRR function assumes that the initial cash flow in the range occurs right now and not at the end of the first period. The initial cash flow usually is negative and represents an initial investment.

There must be at least one negative number (representing an amount invested) and one positive number (representing an amount received) within the cash flows. Otherwise you'll get the dreaded #NUM! error message, because there would be no rate of return.

It is possible to list the cash flows explicitly within the function argument by putting them within curly brackets { }. Thus, we could do the entire calculation using the formula

=IRR({-10000,2000,3000,4000,5000})

Figure 14-5. Your cousin is so successful and grateful to you for the loan that she pays you back $10,000 in year 4.

Of course, the advantage to using the worksheet in Figure 14-4 is that it is easy to play "What if" by changing one of the values in the cells. Suppose your cousin is so successful in her business and so grateful for your investment that she decides to give you $10,000 at the end of year 4 instead of the $5,000. Now, what would be the annual rate of return on your investment? To find out we can just change the number in D9 to 10,000, as in Figure 14-5. The internal rate of return of the series of cash flows -10,000, 2,000, 3,000, 4,000, 10,000 is 23.54%.

If at the end of the second year you would need to invest another $2,000 rather than receiving $3,000, you would change the number in D7 to -2,000.

The second argument is the guess. IRR is basically an extended version of the RATE function that works when the payments throughout the investment are of different amounts. Just as with the RATE function, there is no closed algebraic formula for calculating the IRR. The computer uses trial and error and begins with the guess. Entering a guess is optional. If none is included by the user, the computer assumes a guess of 10%.

NET PRESENT VALUE

An alternative approach to analyzing an investment in terms of its internal rate of return is to calculate its **net present value**. In a present value calculation you state future cash flows in terms of their value in today's dollar. If money earns 10% per year, then $500 today would be worth the same as $550 a year from now. So the present value of $550 a year from now using a **discount rate** of 10% would be $500. Similarly, the present value of $605 two years from now using a discount rate of 10% would be $500. (1.10 * 500 is 550. 1.10 * 550 is 605.) The net present value of an investment is the total value of each of the cash flows for the investment stated in terms of today's dollars.

When making a present value calculation, you must use a discount rate. The discount rate is the rate at which money changes in value each year. Roughly speaking, the discount rate is the interest rate the bank will pay or it is the inflation rate in the economy.

If the net present value of an investment is greater than zero, then it is a good investment relative to the discount rate. If the net present value is less than zero, then it is a poor investment relative to the discount rate. Or, alternatively, if you are comparing the merits of two potential investments, you would select the investment with the higher net present value.

A net present value analysis of the investment in your cousin's business is shown in the worksheet in Figure 14-6. The net present value of the investment is calculated by finding the present value of the future cash flows and subtracting the $10,000 initial investment.

Figure 14-6. Analysis shows a positive net present value of $1,876 using a 6% discount rate. The investment would make you $1,876 in today's dollars.

The **NPV** function is used to calculate the present value of a stream of possibly varying future cash flows.

NPV(discount rate, cash flows)

The first argument is the discount rate, the rate at which money changes value each period. After the discount rate comes the future cash flows. These arguments can be the addresses of the values in the worksheet, as in the function used in cell E13 of the worksheet in Figure 14-6.

=NPV(E4,E8:E11)

Or, unlike in the IRR function, the cash flows can be listed explicitly as a sequence of arguments in the NPV function (without the curly brackets). So, we also could perform the calculation in one formula

=NPV(6%,2000,3000,4000,5000) - 10000

The NPV function is similar to the PV function discussed earlier. However, where the PV function assumes that the cash flow each period is a constant, the NPV function allows for different amounts each period. If in each year you would receive $4,000, then you could use the PV function. If, as is the case in the current example, the cash flows are not the same from year to year, you would use NPV to calculate the present value.

In the worksheet in Figure 14-6 we use a discount rate of 6% because that is the rate the bank would pay. The net present value for the investment is calculated by taking the present value of the future cash flows and subtracting the initial investment required. In cell E17 we see that the net present value of the investment is $1,876. Investing in your cousin's business would be worth $1,876 more in today's money than investing the money in the bank at 6% interest.

Unlike the IRR function, the NPV function assumes that the first of the cash flows occurs at the end of the first period rather than right away. Note that the NPV function is somewhat misnamed. The NPV function does not calculate the net present value of an investment. Rather, the NPV function calculates the present value of a series of possibly different future cash flows that occur at fixed intervals. The net present value is then calculated by subtracting any initial investment that might be made right now.

The IRR function and the NPV function are closely related. The NPV function is used in the series of calculations made for the IRR function. Indeed, if we use the internal rate of return of the investment as the discount rate, then the net present value of the investment will be 0.

WINNING THE LOTTERY

We now have covered seven of the financial functions available in Excel. All of the functions are designed to facilitate analyses involving the time value of money. These calculations take practice so let's do one more example.

Many states have lotteries. Typically you pay $1 to select the numbers that you think will be drawn. If you select all the numbers correctly you win a fortune! But do you? Suppose you have selected your numbers and the day after the drawing you learn that they have drawn your numbers and you have won $1,000,000! You are a winner! You head down to the state lottery office to collect your million dollars. But at the office you learn that the lottery commission does not give you the million dollars all at once. Rather they pay the money to you in 20 equal annual payments. You receive $50,000 now and $50,000 per year at the end of each of the next 19 years.

How much have you really won? Clearly that last $50,000 payment 19 years from now is not going to be worth very much if inflation picks up. It is legal to sell your winning ticket. There are companies that will pay you cash now for a winning ticket. Suppose someone offered you $100,000 right now for your ticket (and all the winnings). Would you take it? No, your winnings are worth more than $100,000 even though they are spread out over 20 years. Suppose the person offered you $900,000 right now for your ticket. Yes, $900,000 today is worth more than $1,000,000 paid out in 20 equal annual payments.

How can we figure out how much your lottery winnings would be worth in terms of today's money? What we are asking for is the present value of the winnings. There are two functions that calculate present value, NPV and PV. The NPV function calculates the present value of a series of possibly unequal future cash flows. The PV function calculates the present value of a series of equal cash flows. The lottery winnings are paid in equal amounts so PV is the function to use. A worksheet to calculate the present value of winning the lottery is shown in Figure 14-7.

The formula in C12 calculates the present value using the PV function. The final argument of the PV function is the type. In this case the type is 1 because the first payment is made right now, at the beginning of the first period.

Assuming a discount rate (inflation rate) of 5%, the present value of 20 annual payments of $50,000 each is $654,266.04. Another way of looking at the problem is that you would have to deposit $654,266.04 in an account earning 5% per year to be able to withdraw $50,000 today and $50,000 at the end of each of the next 19 years. So if you believe the discount rate to be 5% for the next 20 years, you might want to accept an offer of $700,000 for your winnings and decline an offer of $600,000. Of course, our analysis has not taken into account the income taxes you would have to pay on your winnings.

Figure 14-7. The present value of winning $1,000,000 in the lottery paid out in 20 annual payments. This is the amount it would be fair to pay for 20 equal annual payments of $50,000 assuming a discount rate of 5%.

Look at the situation from the state's point of view. The state can take a million dollars and put it in the bank. If they earn 5% per year, they would make $50,000 per year in interest, which they pay you. At the end of the 20 years the state would still have its $1,000,000 intact.

OTHER FINANCIAL FUNCTIONS

Understanding the time value of money is critical to being able to analyze many financial situations. The financial functions of Excel provide important tools. We have looked at just the basic financial functions. There are dozens of additional financial functions built into Excel and included in the Analysis ToolPak add-in.

PENCIL AND PAPER EXERCISES

14-1. Write down the formula that calculates each of the following quantities. You may use the computer to try your answers. You need only write down the formula. You do not need to calculate the result of evaluating the formula.

(a) The monthly payment on a 30 year mortgage for $4,500,000 at 8% per year.

(b) The value of your Michael Jordan basketball card in 30 years if it is worth $20.00 today and appreciates at 9% per year.

(c) The annual rate of increase in the value of a house that was purchased for $59,000 in 1983 and sells for $232,000 today.

(d) The value of your retirement account in 50 years if you deposit $2,400 each year and receive 6% annual interest on your money.

(e) The value of your retirement account in 50 years if you deposit $200 per month for 50 years and receive 6% annual interest on your money.

(f) The annual interest rate you must receive to triple your money in 10 years.

(g) The monthly interest rate you are paying to Joe the Shark if you borrow $10,000 today and pay back $1,000 each month for 11 months and then pay back $10,000 a year from now.

(h) The amount of money you would need to accumulate to be able to retire for the rest of your life on $100,000 per year if your money earns 10% per year.

(i) The number of months a new company could last if it raised $2,000,000 and had a burn rate (spending rate) of $60,000 per month, assuming it kept its cash in an account earning 5% per year.

(j) There are two major companies in the widget market. United Widgets had sales of $20 million last year and is expected to grow at the rate of 4% per year. Widgets International had sales of $14 million last year. Give a formula that will indicate the annual rate at which Widgets International must grow to catch up to United Widgets in seven years.

(k) The year in which the country of Corinth will reach 8,000,000 people given that it has 3,488,710 people today and its population is increasing by 2.4% per year. For example, your formula might tell us that Corinth will reach 8,000,000 people in the year 2025.

(l) The rate of increase required for Corinth to reach a population of 8,000,000 in the year 2025 given that it has a population of 3,488,710 today.

14-2. Evaluate each of the following by hand. The idea here is for you to learn how these functions really are calculated. If you get stuck you can check your answer out on the computer, but eventually you should be able to do these problems and other problems like them without a computer or calculator.

(a) =FV(10%,1,0,-2000)

(b) =FV(10%,2,0,-2000)

(c) =FV(10%,1,-500,-2000)

(d) =FV(10%,1,-500,-2000,1)

(e) =FV(10%,2,-500,-2000)

(f) =FV(10%,2,500,-2000)

(g) =PMT(0%,5,-2000,7000)

(h) =NPER(5%,0,-1000,1102.50)

(i) =NPER(5%,-1050,1000,0)

(j) =PV(10%,2,0,4840)

(k) =RATE(5,100,-2000,1500)

(l) =RATE(2,0,8000,-8160.80)

14-3. Write down the formula that calculates each of the following quantities. You do not need to calculate the result of evaluating the formula.

(a) No one quite knows how Carpathian frogs were introduced into Lake Canuga but they are taking over the habitat and destroying the local species in the process. There are 10,000 Carpathian frogs there now. Baby frogs are born at the rate of 5% per month. 200 of the frogs die each month. Give a formula that will calculate how many Carpathian frogs there will be in five years if this continues.

(b) We would like to have $1,000,000 in ten years. We have $700,000 now in an account. We are withdrawing $100,000 a year from the account at the beginning of each year. What annual interest rate would we need to achieve our goal?

(c) We estimate the amount of capital needed to buy and open a very nice bed and breakfast to be $700,000 and to be increasing by 3% per year. We currently have an account with $400,000, which is earning 8% per year. How much would we need to deposit at the end of each year to be able to buy and open the bed and breakfast in seven years?

(d) You would like to have $1,000 for next Christmas to purchase presents. Your plan is to deposit a certain amount of money on the 3rd of each month in an account earning 0.25% per month. You plan to open your account on January 3 with your first deposit. You plan to make your last deposit on November 3 (11 deposits in all). You will close the account on December 2 after you receive the interest for the month. How much do you need to deposit each month?

(e) If I invest $63,000 today in a bond, the state will pay me $100,000 in seven years. My cousin says that if I loan him the money for five years he will give me double the annual compounded interest rate that the state will. He promises to pay it all off in one payment at the end of five years. How much would my cousin owe me in five years?

(f) The OhMy computer virus currently infects 250,000 computers. It is infecting 1.5% new computers per day. The only known way to destroy the virus is to wipe out the hard drive (or take a sledgehammer to the computer). 1,000 people per day are doing this. If circumstances don't change, how many computers will be infected with the virus in 180 days?

(g) Ten years ago your parents bought $10,000 worth of Trans-National Systems, Inc. stock. At the end of each year they invested another $2,000. Today the stock is worth $54,000. Give a formula that determines what annual interest rate they made on their money.

(h) There are 200,000,000 of the new dollar coins in circulation now. Each year 5% are removed from circulation for one reason or another (by collectors or are lost). The government plans to add 100,000,000 new coins at the end of each year. Give a formula that determines how many years it will be until there are 1,000,000,000 in circulation.

(i) There are 100 million traditional phones. The number is increasing by 2% per year. There are 30 million cell phones. The number is increasing by 20% per year. A number between 2010 and 2100 is in D5. Give a formula that determines whether there will be more traditional phones or cell phones in the year given in D5.

COMPUTER EXERCISES

14-4. The Friendly Mortgage Company offers your choice of 10-year, 20-year, and 30-year home mortgages all at the same interest rate. Create a worksheet that will allow you to enter the amount of the mortgage and the annual interest rate. For each type of loan the worksheet should calculate: (a) the monthly payment, (b) the total amount paid back to the mortgage company, and (c) the total amount of interest paid. That is, your worksheet should have two cells of input and nine cells of output.

14-5. As Division Manager you have $20,000,000 to invest in a new project. The Excelsior Project Team says that if you invest with them the company will receive returns of $8,000,000 after a year, $10,000,000 after two years and $12,000,000 after three years. The Indela Project Team says that if you invest with them the company will receive nothing for the first two years and then $34,000,000 at the end of the third year. Create a worksheet that determines which project team offers the better financial return on the investment. The answer "Excelsior project" or "Indela project" should appear in a cell.

14-6. Your broker suggests that you buy a zero coupon bond ("zero") with a face value of $20,000 maturing in 10 years that sells today for $6,237. That is, you pay $6,237 today and receive $20,000 10 years from now. You would like to find out the yield, the effective annual interest rate you would receive, on the zero.

(a) Create a worksheet for analyzing zeros that allows you to enter the face value, the time to maturity, and the current price. The output should be the yield. Of course, your worksheet should work for any inputs.

(b) Create a similar worksheet that allows you to enter the face value, the actual maturity date, and the current price. The output should be the yield. Use the TODAY function.

14-7. You are presented with a proposal for a project. The bottom line is that it is claimed that if you invest $20 million in a project this year, you will receive $5 million, $18 million, and $12 million over the following three years.

(a) Set up a worksheet that will tell you both the net present value of this project assuming a 12% discount rate and the internal rate of return for this project.

(b) You decide that most likely the project will cost $24 million this year and return $4 million, $14 million, and $10 million. What would be the net present value and internal rate of return?

14-8. The "Rule of 72" is a very convenient rule of thumb for performing mental calculations on the effect of compound interest. The rule indicates the approximate doubling time for money at a given interest rate or the approximate interest rate required to double your money in a certain period of time. The Rule of 72 states that to find the time required to double an investment at a given interest rate, divide the interest rate into 72. Equivalently, the Rule of 72 states that to find the interest rate required to double your money in a certain number of years, divide the number of years into 72. For example, the rule states that investments at 6% double in 12 years. Investments at 9% double in 8 years. Investments at 18% double in 4 years.

How is this helpful? What will a $20,000 investment at 14% be worth in 10 years? At 14% the doubling time is approximately 5 years. So in five years the investment will double in value to $40,000. In five more years the investment will double again to $80,000. So, $80,000 is the approximate answer.

For this exercise you are to check the validity of the Rule of 72. Create a worksheet with three columns and 72 rows plus column headings and titles. In the first column should be interest rates from 1% through 72%. In the next column should be the actual time for money to double at this interest rate as calculated using the NPER function. In the third column should be the amount of time for money to double at this interest rate predicted using the Rule of 72. Is the Rule of 72 reasonably accurate?

14-9. The Director of New Business Development has come to you with an interesting proposal. The Home Products Division of International Industries is for sale. The best estimate is that the Home Products Division will earn $4 million next year, $5 million the following year, $6 million the third year and that in the fourth year you will be able to sell it for $30 million. Your company expects to earn 20% per year on its investments.

(a) Create a worksheet that will tell you a fair price to pay today for the Home Products Division.

(b) On negotiation, International Industries says that they will accept 1/3 of the total payment today, 1/3 in a year, and 1/3 in two years. Create a worksheet that allows you to enter in a total payment and then gives you the rate of return on the investment. Have a cell at the top that tells you whether or not you achieve your goal of a 20% return.

(c) If you assume the correctness of the estimates in (a) and the results of the negotiations in (b) what would be a fair price to pay to earn 20% on your money?

(d) Suppose you can sell the Division only for $20 million instead of $30 million? Now what would be a fair price to pay?

14-10. You are considering purchasing a new car. The price would be $18,239. You would pay $2,000 now and the rest monthly in a four-year loan. The automobile dealership is offering a sales promotion where either (a) you will receive a $1,000 rebate check right now and the annual interest rate on the loan will be 11.9% or (b) the annual interest rate on the loan will be 1.9% but there is no rebate. Create a worksheet to compare the two options by calculating the present value of each of the options, assuming an 8% discount rate. Which is the better deal? Write a paragraph to justify your answer.

14-11. MobilePower is a startup company. They are out on the capital market looking for funding. They are willing to sell you 20% of the stock in their company for an investment of $500,000. According to their business plan they expect to lose money for the first two years. Then their big product will kick in and they expect to make money in the third and fourth year. These funds will be plowed back into the company for expansion. They then expect to be acquired by a major company for $10,000,000 in the fifth year. At this point you would cash out and receive 20% of the proceeds. Create a worksheet to analyze this venture in terms of the rate of return and the net present value of your investment. Since this is a very risky venture and you would buy in towards the beginning, you would expect a return of at least 30% per year on your money. Does MobilePower seem like a reasonable investment opportunity?

14-12. A loan amortization table shows the effect of each payment on the amount of principal still owed. A worksheet for constructing loan amortization tables for 48-month loans is shown below. The worksheet has two input cells: (1) the principal of the loan (the original amount borrowed) and (2) the annual interest rate. All other numbers in the worksheet are calculated. Changing either or both of these input numbers will create a new amortization table.

	File	Edit	View	Insert	Format	Tools	Data	Window	Help		

Arial ▼ 10 ▼ **B** *I* U ≡ ≡ ≡ $ % , +.0 .00

A1 ▼ *fx*

	A	B	C	D	E	F
1						
2			**Loan Amortization Table for 48 Month Loans**			
3						
4			*Principal:*		**$16,353.00**	
5			*Annual Interest rate:*		**9.90%**	
6						
7		Resulting Monthly Interest Rate:			0.825%	
8		Resulting Monthly Payment:			$413.97	
9						
10		Principal at	Monthly	Interest	Principal	Principal at
11	Month	Beginning	Payment	Payment	Payment	End of Period
12	1	$16,353.00	$413.97	$134.91	$279.06	$16,073.94
13	2	$16,073.94	$413.97	$132.61	$281.36	$15,792.58
14	3	$15,792.58	$413.97	$130.29	$283.68	$15,508.90
56	45	$1,622.28	$413.97	$13.38	$400.59	$1,221.70
57	46	$1,221.70	$413.97	$10.08	$403.89	$817.80
58	47	$817.80	$413.97	$6.75	$407.22	$410.58
59	48	$410.58	$413.97	$3.39	$410.58	$0.00
60						

⏮ ◀ ▶ ⏭ \ **48 month** / Sheet2 / Sheet3 /

Note that in the table, the amount of interest owed each month is the monthly interest rate times the amount of the principal still owed at the beginning of the month. The amount of the payment that goes to reducing the principal is the amount of the payment that is left over. If all of the calculations are correct, then the principal owed at the end of the forty-eighth month should be 0.

(a) Duplicate the worksheet. Try it on the loan indicated and then on a $53,000 loan at 12% and on a $4,000 loan at 2.9%.

(b) Construct a similar worksheet for 36-month loans. Try the worksheet on the same three sets of data.

(c) Construct a worksheet that produces an amortization table for any term loan of from one to five years (60 monthly payments). The worksheet should have three input cells: the principal of the loan, the annual interest rate, and the number of years for the loan. This is a bit tricky. While you might have 60 rows of formulas, the table should only appear to have one row for each month of payment. All rows below the final payment should appear blank.

14-13. You have been asked to analyze the proposed Skopi Project. Initial investment in the project would be $100 million, which would be spent on planning, design, and construction. This phase would take three years. It is proposed that in year 0, $10 million be spent. In year 1, $30 million be spent. In year 2, $60 million be spent.

Revenues would be generated beginning in year 3. In year 3, revenues would be $10 million. In year 4, revenues would be $30 million. In years 5 through 13, revenues would be $60 million per year. In year 14, revenues would be $30 million. At the end of year 14, the project would be scrapped. In year 15, the project would return $20 million in the scrap value of the equipment.

Expenses would be as follows. Annual operating expenses for years 3 through 14 are figured at $12.5 million for raw materials, $10 million for maintenance and repairs, $5 million for labor, and $2.5 million for other expenses.

(a) Develop a worksheet that figures out the internal rate of return of this project. You should have a separate input area with separate cells for each of the assumptions. You should have columns for each of the years from 0 through 15. You should have separate rows for each of the revenue and expense items and for the total revenues and total expenses. The bottom row should be annual cash flow. You should have a separate well-labeled cell for the rate of return. Sketch the worksheet on paper before entering it into the computer. Have your worksheet calculate the internal rate of return using the preceding assumptions.

(b) Draw a chart in Excel that shows the projected revenues, expenses, and cash flow over the life of the project.

(c) Next try some sensitivity analysis. You might want to put a copy of the full worksheet for each of these scenarios on a different sheet. Suppose revenues for years 5 through 13 are only $40 million. What would be the internal rate of return? Suppose construction costs are $100 million in year 2? Suppose labor costs are double those expected?

(d) Put together a professional report on your analysis of the project. The company expects at least a 14% rate of return on its money. What is your recommendation on this project? Include appropriate copies of worksheets and graphs in your report. To what parameters is the rate of return most susceptible?

(e) Put together a 15-minute presentation on your analysis of the Skopi Project suitable for delivery to the Executive Committee of your company. Use PowerPoint to prepare the presentation.

14-14. You have been assigned the task of comparing two sources of energy for a proposed manufacturing plant.

(a) Build a worksheet that determines the more economical of the two choices by comparing the present value of the expenses associated with each choice. A basic design for the worksheet and some projected data are given below. You may fill in whatever intermediate calculations you wish, but be sure to label these cells clearly. The bottom row of the worksheet should use an IF function to indicate whether Electricity or Fuel Oil is a more economical choice.

COMPARISON OF ENERGY SOURCES

	Electricity		Fuel Oil	
Unit Cost	$0.160	per kwh	$1.45	per gallon
Setup Cost	$15,000		$25,000	
Annual Consumption	700,000	kwh	125,000	gallons
Annual Maintenance	$3,000		$2,000	
Number of Years	8		8	
Discount Rate	0.12		0.12	

Present Value:

More Economical Energy Source:

(b) There is some uncertainty in the prices that can be negotiated in a long-term supply contract for the energy sources. Listed below are three possible scenarios. Create a new worksheet for each scenario, having your worksheet determine which choice would be more economical. To do this, you should be able to change just the values in the appropriate cells at the top of your worksheet. All other calculations should then be done automatically by the computer.

THREE UNIT COST SCENARIOS

Scenario	Electricity		Fuel Oil	
1 (original)	$0.160	per kwh	$1.45	per gallon
2	$0.195	per kwh	$1.75	per gallon
3	$0.125	per kwh	$1.15	per gallon

(c) Write a brief but professional report giving your recommendation on the energy source to select. Include appropriate copies of your worksheets.

14-15. Mary and John have been married for three years. They both work. Their salaries total $95,000 per year. They currently are paying $1,800 per month rent plus utilities. Between savings and wedding gifts they have managed to accumulate $58,000, which they have in a money market account.

Mary and John are thinking about buying a house. They have done some looking and after much dispute have settled on a suburban house that costs about $220,000. Annual real estate taxes would be about $2,800. They are asking the age-old questions: Can we afford it? Will we be better off financially 10 years from now if we buy the house instead of continuing to rent?

Your task is to design and implement a worksheet that will analyze the financial implication over the next 10 years of buying versus renting.

The issue of home ownership is a complicated one in this society. You can make some assumptions:

- Assume a fixed rate mortgage for 80% of the purchase price of the home. Mary and John will pay 20% of the price as a down payment when they purchase the home. Find out the prevailing mortgage rate by checking in the local newspaper or by calling a bank. John and Mary would use the $58,000 for the down payment, closing costs, and moving expenses.

- Assume that everything (house values, rents, real estate taxes, salaries) goes up with inflation. Have a separate cell for the inflation rate.

Of course, if they buy, Mary and John would no longer get the interest they now receive from the $58,000 in the money market account.

An important aspect of home ownership in the United States can be the income tax advantage. If Mary and John own their own home, then real estate taxes and the interest (but not the principal) they pay on their mortgage are deductible for income tax purposes. You will need to find out what income tax bracket Mary and John are in, assuming no other dependents.

From a financial point of view would Mary and John be better off buying a house or continuing to rent? Write a professional report for Mary and John. Include appropriate parts of the worksheet and a chart or two.

CHAPTER 15

RANDOM NUMBERS AND SIMULATION

OBJECTIVES

In this chapter you will learn how to:

- Use RAND to generate random numbers
- Create worksheets to simulate probabilistic situations
- Simulate situations with multiple possible outcomes using lookup tables
- Model queuing problems
- Generate random integers

One way of dealing with the complexities of the world is to build a model to simulate a situation or environment. The model then can be tested and manipulated. These results can be used to predict what will happen in the world. An airplane company wants to know how a proposed new plane will fly, so it builds a model and places the model in a wind tunnel and runs tests. Or, it creates a computer program that allows engineers to specify the plane on the screen and then mathematically simulate the plane flying under different conditions.

Of course, the effectiveness of using a model to predict what really will happen depends on how well the relevant aspects of the situation are captured in the model. One certainly can imagine an airplane whose design worked great on the computer but that crashes when it is first flown. There is a saying in the computer field, "Garbage In, Garbage Out," or "GIGO". If you put nonsense into the computer, you will get nonsense out. Don't believe everything that comes out of the computer. Just because "The computer says" something doesn't mean it is right.

People have attempted to create computer models for all kinds of situations. There are computer models of the weather. Enter in the temperature, wind velocity, and so on at many different locations on the earth. The computer predicts what the weather will be like tomorrow or next week. There are computer models of the economy. Suppose we raise the income tax rate. What will be the effect on the economy a year from now or five years from now?

We have seen how Excel can be used as a simulation tool. "What if" analysis is computer simulation. To predict the profitability of a new enterprise, create an Excel worksheet to model the projected finances and try it out under different scenarios.

Some situations are best modeled probabilistically. One third of the time this will happen; two thirds of the time something else will happen. These situations can be modeled on the computer with the use of **random numbers**. Simulations that make use of random numbers often are called **Monte Carlo simulations**. Monte Carlo is a city on the Mediterranean Sea that is the site of a well-known gambling casino.

In this chapter we will discuss random numbers in Excel and their use in simulations.

THE RAND FUNCTION

Random numbers are generated in Excel using the **RAND** function. The RAND function has no arguments. The value of the RAND function is a number between 0 and 1 (but not including 1). The user cannot predict what this number will be. An example of a worksheet with 10 random numbers is shown in Figure 15-1.

Figure 15-1. Generating ten random numbers.

The value of each call to the RAND function is calculated out to 15 digits to the right of the decimal point. Only nine decimal places of each number are displayed in each random number in Figure 15-1. To see the full numbers, select the cells and click on the Increase Decimal button.

When entering the RAND function into a formula you must include the parentheses

$$=RAND(\ )$$

even though there is nothing placed between them. If you enter =RAND with no parentheses, Excel will expect RAND to be the name of a cell so you will get a #NAME? error message.

The RAND function is a strange beast. Each time the worksheet is recalculated, the value of each RAND changes! You can force a recalculation at any time by pressing function key F9 on the keyboard.

FLIPPING COINS

Suppose we want to simulate flipping a coin in Excel. Each time we recalculate the worksheet (by pressing F9), the computer flips the coin again. The computer will say Heads or Tails, but we won't know in advance which it will be. We would like

Heads and Tails each to occur 50% of the time.

To accomplish this, we will use random numbers generated by the RAND function. We would like half the possible numbers produced by RAND to be Heads and the other half of the numbers to be Tails. Thus, we check the random number against 0.5. If the random number is less than 0.5, we call the result Heads. Otherwise, we call the result Tails. The formula is

$$=IF(RAND(\ ) < 0.5, "Heads", "Tails")$$

The worksheet is shown in Figure 15-2.

Figure 15-2. Simulating the flip of a fair coin.

Each time we press F9 a new random number between 0 and 1 is produced by RAND and hence a new coin is flipped with equal likelihood of a Heads or a Tails. We have no way of knowing before each recalculation whether the computer will say Heads or Tails.

Should we check if the random number is less than 0.5 or less than or equal to 0.5? Since 0 is a possible random number but 1 is not, it seems fairer for 0.5 to count as a Tails. Actually, there are so many possible random numbers that the probability of exactly 0.5 being generated is too small to worry about!

Suppose that we would like to rig the worksheet so that 70% of the time the flip comes out Heads and only 30% of the time the flip comes out Tails. We could change the formula, as follows

$$=IF(RAND(\ ) < 0.7, "Heads", "Tails")$$

Now 70% of the random numbers (all the numbers between 0 and 0.7) will result in Heads and only 30% of the random numbers (all the numbers from 0.7 to 1) will result in Tails.

Suppose we would like three possible outcomes. We would like Heads 49% of the time, Tails 48% of the time, and 3% of the time we would like the outcome to be Coin rolls away.

The first step is to divide up the numbers from 0 to 1 into three segments that correspond to the desired outcomes. We assign the numbers from 0 to 0.49 to correspond to Heads. (This is 49% of the numbers.) The numbers from 0.49 to 0.97 will correspond to Tails. (This is 48% of the numbers.) The numbers from 0.97 to 1 correspond to Coin rolls away. (This is 3% of the numbers.) This is illustrated in Figure 15-3.

Figure 15-3. Dividing up the number line from 0 to 1 so that 49% of the numbers correspond to Heads, 48% of the numbers correspond to Tails, and 3% of the numbers correspond to Coin rolls away.

To implement this distribution in the worksheet we might first think of writing a formula like

=IF(RAND( )<.49,"Heads",IF(RAND( )<.97,"Tails","Coin rolls away"))

This formula is the right idea but it has a subtle error. The problem is that each time the RAND function is called, it returns a different value. Thus the two calls to RAND in the preceding formula will return different random numbers and the desired probabilities will not be obeyed.

The remedy is to place the call to RAND in a different cell, for example G5, and then refer to that cell in the formula, as in

=IF(G5<.49,"Heads",IF(G5<.97,"Tails","Coin rolls away"))

This solution is shown in Figure 15-4. Now the same random number is used in both places in the formula. To flip another coin, press F9 to recalculate the worksheet. This generates another random number in G5 and another result in C5. If you would like, the actual random number can be placed in a cell off the screen or on another sheet so it does not show.

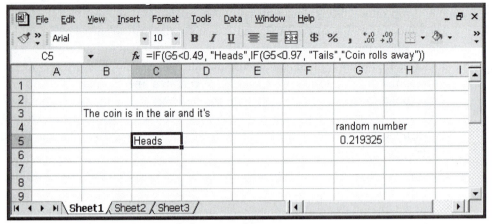

Figure 15-4. Flipping a coin with three possible outcomes.

An alternative to using the nested IF function is to use a lookup table. Lookup tables have the advantage of showing the cutoff points for the random numbers explicitly in the worksheet. An equivalent worksheet for flipping coins that uses a lookup table is shown in Figure 15-5. To determine the outcome of the coin flip, the random number in G5 is looked up in the table in G11:H13. The key formula, in C5, is

$$=VLOOKUP(G5,G11:H13,2)$$

Figure 15-5. Flipping a coin with three possibilities using a lookup table.

Recall from Chapter 12 that the VLOOKUP function takes the value of the first argument (the value in G5) and compares it against the entries in the first column of the lookup table beginning with the first entry (in G11). When it finds a value in the column that is greater than the number it is looking up, it goes up one row and over to the second column of the table and that is the value it returns. For example, if the value in G5 is 0.78, the VLOOKUP function would return Tails.

The worksheet in Figure 15-6 simulates ten coin flips. Here we use a new random number for each coin flip. Each cell in column C contains the formula =RAND( ). The formulas in the cells in column E look up the corresponding random number in the lookup table. The formula in E7 is

$$=VLOOKUP(C7,\$G\$11:\$H\$13,2)$$

Absolute addressing is used when referring to the lookup table so that the addresses do not change when the formula is filled down column E. Alternatively, we could name the table in G11:H13 Outcomes and use the formula

$$=VLOOKUP(C7,Outcomes,2)$$

It is important to use ten different random numbers in this worksheet, one for each coin flip. If we use only one random number and refer to it ten times, then all of the coin flips would come out the same.

Each time we press the recalculation key F9, ten more coin flips are simulated.

	File	Edit	View	Insert	Format	Tools	Data	Window	Help		_ ✕

	A	B	C	D	E	F	G	H	I	J
1										
2			**Ten Coin Flips**							
3										
4		*Flip*	*Random#*		*Result*					
5		1	0.5613132		Tails					
6		2	0.0424957		Heads					
7		3	0.6774087		Tails					
8		4	0.4312663		Heads			*lookup table*		
9		5	0.8930068		Tails					
10		6	0.9248225		Tails		0.00	Heads		
11		7	0.9889740		Coin rolls away		0.49	Tails		
12		8	0.6409508		Tails		0.97	Coin rolls away		
13		9	0.8088209		Tails					
14		10	0.6996841		Tails					

Cell E7: =VLOOKUP(C7,\$G\$10:\$H\$12,2)

Figure 15-6. Each flip requires a separate random number.

QUEUING PROBLEMS

A common application for Monte Carlo simulation is in queuing problems. A **queue** is a waiting line. People form a queue for a bus or when waiting to cash a check in a bank or to pay for their groceries in a supermarket. In particular, a queue is a line where the first people to arrive in the line are the first to be served. That is, a queue is what people think of as a "fair" waiting line. (A **stack** is a line where the first to arrive are the last to be served. This occurs, for example, if people are lined up for the bus and the bus stops so that the door opens at the end of the line. The last person on line would be the first on the bus.) In some situations there is one large master queue (for example, in most banks). In some situations there are multiple queues (for example, in most supermarkets).

People have studied queuing problems for years. How many tollbooths should be built at the entrance to the bridge? If too few are built, the traffic will back up too far. Widening the highway for tollbooths is expensive. If too many tollbooths are built, money will be spent unnecessarily. How many checkout registers should be built in the supermarket? At a busy intersection, for how long should the green light be on in each direction? How should tasks be divided up on an assembly line? All of these are problems involving queues.

One approach to solving queuing problems is to model the process on the computer. Once the basic model is set up, we can change some of the assumptions and see what the results would be in the model. We can do "What if" analysis with queuing models just as we can with financial models. Of course, the usefulness of the results depends on the fidelity with which the relevant portions of the world have been captured in the model.

SANTA CLAUS' AFTERNOON

It is late November and you are working as an intern in a local department store. The rival department store across town has set up Santa Claus in a big chair in their store and has invited parents to bring their children in to meet him. Their promotion seems to be working well. Your store manager has asked you to do the same in your store. To make the idea even more attractive to parents, you plan to hire a photographer to take instant photographs of the children sitting on Santa's lap.

You have limited space in the store. The department next to the area where Santa will sit is Fine Jewelry, and the manager of the department does not want a long line of screaming kids winding through the department. You decide to try a quick computer simulation to see how long the line is likely to become.

Santa Claus will be in the store from 2 PM to 5 PM each afternoon. You figure that with each kid sitting down, pulling Santa's beard, saying he or she has been good, and telling Santa what he or she wants for Christmas and then with the photographer taking a picture, that Santa can serve a child in 30 seconds, or two per minute. How many children will arrive each minute? You decide to visit the rival department store with your watch and a pad and to use their arrivals as an estimate for your store. After observing for a while you decide that in 10% of the minutes no children arrive, in 20% of the minutes 1 child arrives, in 30% of the minutes 2 children arrive, in 30% of the minutes 3 children arrive, and in 10% of the minutes 4 children arrive.

Now we need to translate this into an Excel model. Each row in the model will correspond to a different minute with Santa. We will draw a new random number each minute and use the random number to determine the number of children who arrive using the preceding distribution. For simplicity, we will assume that all children arrive right at the beginning of each minute. The number of children who see Santa each minute will depend on the number of people still waiting from the previous minute and the number of arrivals. If no children are there, then Santa has the minute off. If there is only one child there, then Santa will see the one child. If there are two or more children, then Santa will see two children that minute and any remaining children will wait on line.

The worksheet for the simulation is shown in Figure 15-7.

Figure 15-7. A minute-by-minute simulation of Santa's afternoon.

In column A the times are listed from 2:00 PM through 4:59 PM. This was accomplished by typing 2:00 PM into A6, 2:01 PM into A7, selecting A6 and A7, and then dragging the Fill Handle down to A185. The result was that AutoFill correctly filled in the minute-by-minute sequence of times.

Column B contains the random numbers. Each cell in B6:B185 contains the formula

$$=RAND(\ )$$

The number of children who arrive at the beginning of each minute is calculated in column C using the lookup table in G7:H11. The lookup table is set up so that there is a 10% chance that no children arrive, a 20% chance that 1 child arrives, a 30% chance that 2 children arrive, a 30% chance that 3 children arrive, and a 10% chance that 4 children arrive. This is illustrated in Figure 15-8.

Figure 15-8. Dividing the numbers between 0 and 1 so that 10% correspond to 0 arrivals, 20% correspond to 1 arrival, 30% correspond to 2 arrivals, 30% correspond to 3 arrivals, and 10% correspond to 4 arrivals.

The formula in C6 is

$$=VLOOKUP(B6,\$G\$7:\$H\$11,2)$$

The formula has been filled from C6 down to C185. This generates the number of children who arrive each minute.

Remember that we are estimating that Santa Claus can see at most two children per minute. In any minute the number of children available for Santa to see is the number of children already waiting in line plus the number of children who just have arrived. Thus, the formula in D6 for the number of children served is

$$=MIN(E5+C6,2)$$

This formula is then filled down to D185. This formula might require a little thought. Recall that MIN returns the smallest of its arguments. Suppose there are 4 children waiting in line and 1 child arrives. The number of children Santa can see that minute is =MIN(4+1,2), which is =MIN(5,2), which is 2.

Finally, column E contains the queue, the length of the line each minute. Here we set E5 to 0, assuming that the line would be 0 when Santa begins, though it certainly is possible that people might show up at 1:55 PM to see Santa at 2:00 PM. The length of the line each minute will be the length of the line the previous minute plus the number of arrivals minus the number of children who see Santa. So the formula in E6 is

$$=E5+C6-D6$$

This formula is filled down column E.

At the end of the day in Figure 15-7 we see that there are 23 children waiting in line and that the longest the line has been is 25 children. A total of 377 children have arrived to see Santa during the three hours.

To simulate another day we would press F9 again. A new set of random numbers would appear. For each minute a new set of arrivals would be generated, Santa would see children, the line would grow or shrink. The worksheet determines the total number of children seen and the longest length of the line during the day.

	File Edit View Insert Format Tools Data Window Help							
	Arial ▾ 10 ▾ **B** *I* U ≣ ≣ 🔳 $ % , ⁺⁰⁰ ⁰⁰⁺ 🔲 ▾ ⬧ ▾							
	D8 ▾ *fx* =MIN(E7+C8,2)							
	A	B	C	D	E	F	G	H
1								
2			Santa Claus' Afternoon					
3								
4	Time	Random#	Arrivals	Served	Queue			Number of
5	start				0			Arrivals
6	2:00 PM	0.5177	2	2	0			per Minute
7	2:01 PM	0.8030	3	2	1		0.0	0
8	2:02 PM	0.3646	2	2	1		0.1	1
9	2:03 PM	0.0578	0	1	0		0.3	2
10	2:04 PM	0.2099	1	1	0		0.6	3
11	2:05 PM	0.3487	2	2	0		0.9	4
183	4:57 PM	0.6542	3	2	33			
184	4:58 PM	0.3716	2	2	33			
185	4:59 PM	0.4908	2	2	33			
186								
187	Total arrivals		386					
188	Longest length of line:				35			
	⏮ ◀ ▶ ⏭ \ Day1 \ **Day2** / Sheet2 / Sheet3 /							

Figure 15-9. Another busy day for Santa.

We also could copy the worksheet over to a new sheet, as in Figure 15-9, and accumulate a number of different simulations. We then could compute statistics on the simulation of a month's worth of days.

What can we conclude? Under these assumptions the system is saturated. Santa would be worked at full capacity and there would be quite long lines. (Thirty children waiting in line with their parents can cause some disturbance in a small area.) The manager of the Fine Jewelry department has reason to be concerned. You should think about ways to improve the situation. Perhaps the visits with Santa could be speeded up a bit or Santa could be hired for more hours to dissipate the demand or a second Santa could be hired or you could go to a reservation system. Forewarned is forearmed.

This exercise was somewhat fanciful and simple-minded, but Monte Carlo simulation has proved useful in understanding a wide variety of queuing problems. In more sophisticated simulations we might model a probabilistic distribution for serving people as well as for arrivals. For example, some children might come with long lists of toys they want and take more time with Santa. Parents who arrive might leave if the line is too long. The probability distribution for arrivals might change as the day progresses. For example, more people might arrive right after school lets out. We might have multiple lines and multiple servers. All of these situations and more could be modeled by expanding the worksheet.

GENERATING RANDOM INTEGERS USING INT

The RAND function generates random numbers between 0 and 0.99999... (to 15 decimal places). In some situations it is useful to be able to generate a random set of integers instead. For example, we might want to simulate the rolling of a die by generating the integers 1, 2, 3, 4, 5, 6, with equal probability. We could use a nested IF function or a lookup table to accomplish this, but there is a more direct method.

First, we can expand the range of the random numbers by multiplying the RAND function by a number. For example, the formula =6*RAND( ) would produce random numbers between 0 and 5.9999... . Since the RAND function generates numbers from 0 to 0.99999... , the lowest number generated by =6*RAND( ) would be 0 and the highest would be 5.9999... . This is demonstrated in column C of Figure 15-10. Similarly, the formula =100*RAND( ) would generate random numbers from 0 to 99.999... .

Now we can convert these numbers to integers using the **INT** function. The INT function has a single argument. The INT function rounds down the argument to the nearest integer. So =INT(3.8) is 3. The formula

$$=INT(6*RAND( ))$$

Figure 15-10. Transforming random integers. Multiplying a number times RAND( ) expands the range. Taking the INT transforms the number into an integer. Adding a number shifts the range.

will generate the integers 0, 1, 2, 3, 4, 5 randomly with equal likelihood. The INT function converts the value of its argument into an integer by rounding down to the nearest integer. Any number between 0 and 0.99999... is converted to 0. Any number between 1 and 1.99999... is converted to 1, and so on. This is illustrated in column D of Figure 15-10. The random numbers in B10:B17 are multiplied by 6 in C10:C17. These numbers are then transformed into integers in D10:D17 using the INT function.

We have the random integers 0, 1, 2, 3, 4, 5. By adding 1 to the previous formula we can generate the random integers 1, 2, 3, 4, 5, 6. Hence, to simulate a die by generating the random integers 1, 2, 3, 4, 5, 6 we can use the formula

$$=INT(6*RAND( ))+1$$

This is illustrated in column E of Figure 15-10.

The general formula for generating a random integer from some sequence of integers is given by

$$=INT(N*RAND( ))+L$$

where N is the number of integers in the sequence and L is the value of the lowest integer in the sequence.

For example, if we would like to generate random integers from the sequence 40, 41, 42, ... 59 we could use the formula

$$=INT(20*RAND(\ ))+40$$

because there are 20 integers in the sequence and the lowest integer is 40.

This method works for generating integers from a sequence where we want each integer to be equally likely to occur. If we do not want the outcomes to occur with equal probabilities, then we would use nested IF functions or lookup tables as discussed earlier in the chapter. Or we can use the Random Number Generation tool in the Analysis ToolPak, which is discussed in Chapter 17.

ROLLING A PAIR OF DICE 10,000 TIMES

From playing Monopoly and other board games, and from trips to the casinos, we are interested in the probabilities of different outcomes when we roll a pair of dice. We set up the worksheet in Figure 15-11. In column A we have the number of the roll. In columns B and C we simulate rolling each die. The formula in each of the 20,000 cells in B5:C10004 is

$$=INT(6*RAND(\ ))+1$$

The worksheet uses 20,000 different random numbers. In column D we have the total that would result for the roll. In column G we summarize the 10,000 rolls using the COUNTIF function. The formula in G4 is

$$=COUNTIF(\$D\$5:\$D\$10004,F4)$$

Since F4 contains the number 2, this formula counts all of the occurrences of 2 in the range D5:D10004.

This is the first worksheet that requires enough calculations that there is a noticeable delay when pressing F9. When constructing this worksheet it is useful to turn off Automatic Calculation. This is done in the Calculation tab of the dialog box that appears after selecting *Options* in the *Tools* pull-down menu. By clicking on Manual Calculation, the worksheet will be recalculated only when F9 is pressed.

In the worksheet in Figure 15-11 we see that the most common combination is a 7 and that it occurs about one-sixth, of the time.

Figure 15-11. Simulating 10,000 rolls of a pair of dice.

PENCIL AND PAPER EXERCISE

15-1. Write out on paper how to use RAND to generate each of the following distributions. Show all formulas and tables.

(a) 50%   I win
    50%   You win

(b) 80%   I win
    20%   You win

(c) 55%   I win
    30%   You win
    15%   Tie

(d) 35%   I win
    25%   You win
    30%   Tie

10%	Rained out

(e)
32%	I win
22%	You win
25%	We both win
15%	We both lose
6%	Rained out

(f)
50%	1
50%	2

(g)
25%	7
25%	8
25%	9
25%	10

(h) the years (integers) from 2000 through 2099 with equal likelihood

(i) the (integer) temperatures from -37 through 120 degrees with equal likelihood

(j) the integers 2, 4, 6, 8 with equal likelihood

(k) the numbers 3.0, 3.1, 3.2, ... 4.9 with equal likelihood

COMPUTER EXERCISES

15-2. Create an Executive Decision Maker. The user will type in a decision that needs to be made. For example, "Should we launch a takeover bid for IBM?" or "Should I ask Pat out for dinner?" Your worksheet should respond with one of the following answers with the frequencies indicated.

60%	Go for it!
30%	No. The time is not right.
10%	Please gather more information.

15-3. The Eagles and the Warriors are playing for the championship. Each team has an equal likelihood of scoring 0, 1, 2, 3, or 4 goals. Create a worksheet to simulate the number of goals each scores and the winner of the game (Eagles, Warriors, or Tie). Each time you press F9, the recalc key, a new game should be simulated.

15-4. For each day in the month of January, the probabilities are

.19   that it will snow
.36   that it will be cloudy
.30   that it will be sunny
.15   that it will rain

Create a worksheet that uses RAND to "predict" the weather for the month of January. Each time F9 is pressed, the worksheet should show a different prediction. The worksheet should look like:

I Predict

January	1	Cloudy
January	2	Rain
January	3	Cloudy
...		
January	30	Snow
January	31	Sunny

15-5. Create a worksheet that will simulate the random selection of a single card from a deck of cards. A deck of cards has 52 cards, 13 face values in each of four suits. The face values are: 2, 3, 4, 5, 6, 7, 8, 9, 10, Jack, Queen, King, Ace. The suits are: Clubs, Diamonds, Hearts, Spades. Each time the worksheet is recalculated a new card will be selected as if from a new deck. Each of the 52 cards should have an equal chance of being selected. Print the worksheet four times: with three cards selected and with the formulas showing. Your worksheet can have more cells than show in these examples.

	A	B	C	D
1				
2		The card selected is the		
3				
4		9	of	Diamonds
5				
6				

	A	B	C	D
1				
2		The card selected is the		
3				
4		Queen	of	Clubs
5				
6				

15-6. Create an automated Fortune Teller. The user will type his or her name and the computer will tell the person's fortune. You should have at least eight possible fortunes, for example: "You will become the ruler of your country" or "You will have ten children" or "You will be the first person to land on the sun". Each time a person types in a name one of the fortunes should be displayed. If the cell with the person's name is blank, then the cell that shows the fortune should be blank. As soon as a name is entered, a fortune should appear. The fortunes themselves should not be visible on the worksheet. Put them off to the side or on another worksheet. Print the worksheet five times: with the names of three different friends and their fortunes, once with the name cell blank, and once with the full formulas showing (or handwritten if too long).

15-7. The Super Cherry slot machine has three wheels that spin independently when the handle is pulled. For each wheel the probabilities are 20% that a Cherry will appear, 30% that a Plum will appear, 25% that an Ace will appear, and 25% that a Seven will appear. For each pull of the handle you put in a bet of $1. If you get three Cherries you win your bet back plus $25. If you get any two Cherries you win your bet back plus $2. If you get one Cherry you get your bet back. Otherwise you lose your bet of $1. You start with a stake of $100. Create a worksheet to simulate a session of 100 spins. You should have 100 rows, one for each spin. You should have columns at least for the spin number (1 through 100), each of the three wheels, the amount you win or lose on the spin, and the amount of money you have at the end of the spin. Each time you press F9 (recalc) you should get a different set of spins and results according to the above probabilities.

15-8. Our soccer team has 12 games scheduled. The coach figures that for each game the probabilities are:

Our Score	Opponent's Score
10% the team scores 0 goals	35% the opponent scores 0 goals
20% the team scores 1 goal	10% the opponent scores 1 goal
40% the team scores 2 goals	10% the opponent scores 2 goals
20% the team scores 3 goals	10% the opponent scores 3 goals
10% the team scores 4 goals	35% the opponent scores 4 goals

Note that the probabilities for the team's goals are independent of the probabilities for the opponent's goals.

Create a worksheet that "predicts" the season. You should have one row in the main body of your worksheet for each game. You should have columns for at least: game number (1 through 12), random number for us, number of goals we score, random number for them, number of goals they score, result of game for us (win, lose, draw). At the bottom of the worksheet show the predicted record for the season: the number of wins, losses, and draws. Print your worksheet three times: twice with different values showing (recalculate in between) and once with all of the formulas showing.

15-9. Your stockbroker suggests you buy 1,000 shares of International Electronics. The stock currently is selling at $38.75 per share. From research on the web you discover that the stock is quite volatile and that, based on recent past data, in

21% of the weeks it goes up $1.00
17% of the weeks it goes up $0.50
10% of the weeks it remains unchanged
35% of the weeks it goes down $0.50
17% of the weeks it goes down $1.00

(a) Create a worksheet to simulate the price of the stock and the value of your portfolio for 100 weeks assuming the preceding distribution. You should have 100 rows in the main part of your worksheet, one for each week. You should have separate columns for the week number, a random number, the price change that week, the closing price of the stock that week, and the value of your portfolio. Have separate cells at the top of the worksheet for the resulting High, Low, and Close for the stock price over the 100 weeks, that is the highest price the stock reaches, the lowest price the stock reaches, and the closing price after 100 weeks. Have a separate cell that shows the amount of money you would have made (or lost) on the investment. Finally, have a cell containing either "I made money at the end of 100 weeks" or "I lost money at the end of 100 weeks" or "I was even at the end of 100 weeks". Run your simulation several times. Based on the past history data and your simulations, is this a good investment?

(b) Construct a chart with the number of the week along the X axis and the price of a share of stock along the Y axis. Press F9 repeatedly to see the result of different simulations.

(c) On telling your broker your findings she suggests that you employ the following strategy: Buy the 1,000 shares of stock now. Put in a Sell order for the stock at $43.75 or at 100 weeks, whichever comes first. That way if the stock reaches $43.75 you will sell out and achieve a profit of $5 per share. Otherwise you will sell out at the end of 100 weeks and take whatever profit or loss results. On inquiry your broker tells you that there will be a commission cost to you of $79 for purchasing the stock and another $79 for selling the stock. Create a worksheet like the worksheet in part (a) for simulating your broker's strategy. Run the simulation 10 times and record the consequences of using this investment strategy.

(d) Prepare a brief report on this investment strategy. Include copies of appropriate worksheets and charts. Would you make money or lose money on average using this strategy? How much on average? Should you invest?

15-10. The game of Rock-Paper-Scissors is played by two people. At the count of three each person puts out either a closed fist (Rock), a flat hand (Paper), or two fingers (Scissors). The winner is decided as follows: Rock breaks Scissors. Paper covers Rock. Scissors cuts Paper. If both players make the same selection, it is a tie.

(a) Create a worksheet so you can play Rock-Paper-Scissors against the computer. There will be a cell for you to enter in your choice (Rock, Paper, or Scissors). There will be another cell where the computer makes its choice. The computer should choose among the three alternatives randomly using RAND. Each choice should be equally likely. (No fair peeking at the person's choice in this formula!) A third cell should indicate the outcome: "You win", "I win", or "Tie". Test your worksheet until all nine possible combinations are tried.

(b) What happens in your worksheet if the person misspells the entry? Modify your worksheet so it says "Illegal entry." in this case.

(c) Create a workbook that allows you to play the computer 25 times. The workbook should automatically keep track of the number of times you win, it wins, and there is a tie. There are a couple of approaches to solving this problem. One approach is to have a single worksheet that automatically accumulates the results. This is a bit tricky as it will involve circular references where the cells refer to themselves in their formulas. A second approach involves having 25 sheets with the Rock-Paper-Scissors worksheet. The twenty-sixth sheet would have the summary statistics on it. You might want to set Excel to manual recalculation.

15-11. The Zing snack company is known for its high-caffeine, high-sugar snacks. Their vending machine near the computer lab has two kinds of snacks: Coffee Zings cost $1.00 each. Joltin Zings cost $1.50 each. Each morning at 10 AM the Zing delivery person stops by and fills the vending machine so it has its capacity of 150 Coffee Zings and 100 Joltin Zings.

Every ten minutes the probabilities are 35% no one buys a Coffee Zing, 30% one person buys a Coffee Zing, 25% two people buy a Coffee Zing, 10% three people buy a Coffee Zing. Every ten minutes the probabilities are 45% no one buys a Joltin Zing, 30% one person buys a Joltin Zing, and 25% two people buy a Joltin Zing. Once the machine runs out of Coffee Zings no more Coffee Zings can be purchased. Once the machine runs out of Joltin Zings no more Joltin Zings can be purchased.

Create a worksheet to simulate the operation of the vending machine over the course of one day beginning at 10 AM. For each ten-minute period show at least the number of Coffee Zings purchased, the number of Joltin Zings purchased, the number of Coffee Zings remaining in the vending machine and the number of Joltin Zings remaining in the vending machine.

For the day we would like to know: how many Coffee Zings were sold, how many Joltin Zings were sold, how many minutes the machine was out of stock of Coffee Zings, how many minutes the machine was out of stock of Joltin Zings, how much money was taken in for the day. There should be separate well-labeled cells at the top of the worksheet for each of these values.

15-12. There is 1 minute 50 seconds left to go in the championship football game. Our team is down by 5 points. We recover the ball on the opponent's 45-yard line. We have no time-outs left. There is enough time on the clock for exactly eight plays. Coach figures that on each play these are the probabilities:

20%	Gain 7 yards.
10%	Gain 15 yards.
10%	Gain 25 yards.
10%	Gain 3 yards.
10%	Sack. Lose 10 yards.
10%	Interception.
28%	Incomplete. No gain or loss.
2%	Gain 60 yards.

(a) Simulate the rest of the game. If you cross the goal line you win. If you don't make it to the goal line or there is an interception, you lose. Have a single cell at the top that gives the result of the game, either win or lose. Don't worry about first downs.

(b) Do worry about first downs. If you go four downs without a net gain of 10 yards after any down you lose.

15-13. Persistent Telemarketing, Inc. has offered you a commissioned part-time job. They will give you 500 names and telephone numbers. You are to telephone these people and sell them disposable cell phones on behalf of a well-known telephone company. The customer will receive a cell phone in the mail. The phone has a fixed number of built-in anywhere, anytime minutes. The customer pays in advance and then throws away the cell phone when the minutes run out. There are four different plans that you will be offering with different amounts of minutes allowed under each plan: $300, $400, $600, and $1000. Persistent Telemarketing will pay for all of your telephone calls and will give you a 10 percent commission on all of your sales.

You speak to a friend who has done this. She tells you that 20% of the time she reaches a person on the first call. 15% of the time she reaches a person on the second call. 10% of the time she reaches a person on the third call. She said that she never makes more than three calls to a person so 55% of the time she never reaches a person at a given number.

If she connects to the person she said that 85% of the time she doesn't make a sale. 8% of the time she connects to the person she sells the $300 plan. 4% of the time she connects to the person she sells the $400 plan. 1% of the time she connects with the person she sells the $600 plan. 2% of the time she connects with the person she sells the $1000 plan.

Assume that to make a call and not reach someone takes 15 seconds. If someone answers and the person does not buy a plan assume it takes an average of 45 seconds. If someone answers and the person does purchase a plan assume it takes an average of 5 minutes to make the sale and obtain and record all of the information.

You would like to estimate how much money you might make if you take this job, how many phone calls you will make, and how much time you will spend. Create a worksheet to simulate this job. You should have a row for each of the 500 people you'll be given. You should have a cell in each row for at least: the prospect number (1 to 500), how many calls it takes to reach the person (1, 2, 3, never), how much you sell to the person ($0, $300, $400, $600, $1000), how much you make in commission for the person, how much time you spend on each person.

On the top of the worksheet you should have well-labeled cells with: (a) the total number of calls made, (b) the total number of sales pitches (answered calls) made, (c) the total number of sales made, (d) the total amount of commission made, (e) the total time spent, and (f) the expected dollars per hour you will make.

15-14. Create a worksheet to simulate the Brady family finances for five years under the following assumptions:

Their monthly income varies. In any given month the probabilities are 10% they make no money, 25% they make $1,000, 25% they make $2,000, 25% they make $3,000, and 15% they make $4,000.

Their expenses generally (85% of the time) are $1,800 per month but in a given month there is a 10% chance their expenses are $3,000 and a 5% chance their expenses are $5,000.

All funds accumulate in their bank account. Currently they have $3,000 in the account. When the account is positive they make 0.25% per month interest on the funds. If their account goes below $0 they have to pay 1.5% per month interest on the debt. Again, this all accumulates in the account. Assume that all income and expenses occur at the end of the month.

(a) Your worksheet should have a row for each month. There should be columns at least for: month number, income, expenses, interest, balance. You can have additional cells as you wish.

(b) At the top of your worksheet please show the maximum amount in the bank account, the minimum amount in the bank account, the number of months they were in debt, and the total of the interest for the five years.

(c) Create a chart that has the month number along the X axis and dollars along the Y axis and plots the Brady family bank account over the 5 years.

Print your worksheet and chart for three different five-year simulations (one good five-year run for the Brady family, one bad five-year run, and one "average" five-year run) and also with the formulas.

15-15. Jack is taking a vacation at a tropical resort. The first evening he visits Land's End, an open-air bar, which is located on the end of a narrow pier, over the water. Unfortunately he has a bit too much to drink. Jack needs to make his way back to the hotel. The pier is 60 steps long but only eight steps wide.

In the diagram Jack is at the X. He is headed towards the hotel. Each time he takes a step, there is a 70% chance he steps forwards, towards the hotel. There is a 10% chance he stumbles a step backwards. There is a 10% chance he takes a step to his left, towards the ocean. There is a 10% chance he takes a step right, towards the ocean.

If Jack ever makes it back to the hotel the people there will look after him and see him to his room. If he ever ends up 5 steps to the right or 5 steps to the left, he will fall into the ocean. Once he is in the ocean this voyage is over. After 100 steps if Jack is still on the pier he will collapse.

Create an Excel worksheet to simulate Jack's random walk back to the hotel. There should be 100 rows in your worksheet, one for each potential step. At the top of the worksheet there should be a cell that gives Jack's final result: either "Hotel" or "Ocean" or "Collapse on pier".

Print three sets of values and also the formulas. Try your worksheet 10 times by pressing F9, the recalc key. On the first printout write down how many times each of the possible results ("Hotel", "Ocean", "Collapse") occurred in the 10 runs.

15-16. So that people feel they are getting more value for all of the taxes they pay, the United States government has decided to hold a giant national lottery. Everyone in the country automatically is entered. Once a month a Social Security number will be selected at random. Whoever has that Social Security number will be given $10,000,000 tax free.

You have been hired to create the worksheet that will generate the random Social Security number. Social Security numbers have the form 012-34-5678. Each of the billion possible Social Security numbers should be equally likely to be selected in your worksheet.

For you to receive full payment for your work the government contract officer insists that all 0's in the Social Security number selected appear in your worksheet and that the dashes appear in their usual places in the number.

15-17. The tortoise and the hare are having a race. Whoever can travel the most distance in an hour wins. For the tortoise, each minute the probabilities are 25% he rests and doesn't move, 30% he travels forward 1 foot, 35% he travels forward 2 feet, 10% he travels forward 3 feet. For the hare, each minute the probabilities are 10% he moves backward one foot, 65% he doesn't move, 25% he moves forward 5 feet.

(a) Create a worksheet to simulate the race. You should have a row for each minute. You should have columns at least for: minute number, tortoise position, hare position, who is ahead. You may use other columns and cells as you wish. At the top of the worksheet give the winner for the simulation (or possibly it's a tie). Also at the top please give the total number of minutes during which the hare is behind where he started.

(b) Create a chart that has minutes along the X axis and position in feet from the starting line along the Y axis. The chart should show the positions of the tortoise and the hare during the race. Pressing F9 to simulate a new race should cause the chart to be updated automatically.

15-18. In the game of Roulette, you bet on a number. The croupier spins the ball around the spinning Roulette wheel and the ball falls randomly in a slot with a number. If you bet on the number in which the ball falls you win 35 times your bet. If a number comes up that is different from the one on which you bet, you lose your money.

(a) Create a worksheet to simulate a session of 100 spins at the Roulette table where you bet $10 on the same number each time. The possible numbers are 0 through 36. You will enter the number on which you bet in a cell at the top of the worksheet. You will have rows for 100 spins. Each row will show at least the spin number (1 through 100), the number that comes up on the wheel (0 to 36), the amount you win or lose, and your cumulative earnings so far. At the top of your worksheet there should be a cell with the final result for your earnings for the session.

(b) Create a chart that has the number of the spin (from 1 to 100) along the X axis and dollars along the Y axis and that shows the progression of your cumulative earnings during the course of your session.

(c) In most casinos these days there is an additional number, 00 (double zero). You can bet on 00 and it is equally likely to come up on the wheel, so there are 38 possible outcomes. The payoff is still 35 to 1. Modify your worksheet to allow for 00 both in the betting and on the wheel.

(d) You begin with $300. If you ever get down to $0 you are bankrupt and cannot keep betting. If you ever reach $1,000 you walk away from the table and cash in your chips. The subsequent rows of the simulation can appear in your worksheet but the outcomes in the rows should say either "Bankrupt" or "Big Winner" if you reach either of the limits. The result also should appear at the top of your worksheet. Run the simulation 10 times. Out of the 10 times how many times did you go bankrupt? How many times did you walk away a big winner?

15-19. The game of Chuck-a-Luck is popular at carnivals and fairs and also is played in casinos. Chuck-a-Luck is played with three large dice tumbling over in a cage. You can bet on various outcomes. We will assume for a minute that each bet is for $1. Here are three of the more popular bets available:

Triple. If any number comes up on all three dice you win $30.

High. You win $1 if the total of the three dice is 11 or more, except you always lose if it is a triple.

Low. You win $1 if the total of the three dice is 10 or under, except you always lose if it is a triple.

Create a worksheet to allow a person to play Chuck-a-Luck on the computer. The person should be able to place bets for any amount on Triple, High, and Low. The worksheet should show the values of the three dice, how much the person wins or loses on each bet, and the total amount won or lost for the tumble.

You should turn off the automatic recalculation of formulas by clicking on Manual Recalculation in the Calculation tab of the *Options* selection in the *Tools* pull-down menu. Now the dice will be rolled only when F9, the recalculation key, is pressed. So you can place your bets and then tumble the dice by pressing F9.

CHAPTER 16

DATA MANAGEMENT WITH LISTS

OBJECTIVES

In this chapter you will learn how to:

- Work with large amounts of data organized as lists
- Enter new data using forms
- Find the data that match certain criteria using AutoFilters
- Sort the data into alphabetical or numerical order
- Calculate subtotals of the data
- Summarize the data using pivot tables

A major use of computers is for data management, for handling large amounts of data. Airline reservations, personnel, accounts payable and receivable, inventory, payroll all can involve large amounts of data and all profitably have been automated. A special type of software, called **database management systems**, has been developed for data management. There are database management systems for large computers and for personal computers and for all types of computers in between. Whereas a word-processor can be considered a computerized typewriter and an electronic spreadsheet can be considered a computerized calculator and ledger paper, a database management system can be considered a computerized filing cabinet.

Excel has some powerful and useful data management features. We are going to explore these capabilities in this chapter. But before we begin, it is important to point out that Excel is not considered a database management system itself. One major difference is that in a database management system most of the data is kept on the disk, thus allowing the computer to deal with millions or billions of pieces of data. In Excel the data you are working on are in the worksheets. Excel works well with dozens or hundreds or thousands of pieces of data, but not with millions or billions of pieces of data. A second major difference is that the data management facilities in Excel are designed to work with a single set of data whereas a database management system can work with multiple sets of data and their interactions.

Microsoft does provide a database management program, Access, with many versions of Office. It is possible to move sets of data back and forth between Access and Excel. It also is possible to create smaller sets of data within Excel itself. In either case, a set of data that is used in Excel usually is in the form of a **list**.

WHAT IS A LIST?

A list is a range of data that is organized so that all of the information about a single person, object, or transaction occupies a single row and so that each column contains information of the same type. The top row of the list contains the name of the data in the corresponding column.

As an example, consider the following situation. The owner of the Tri-Valley Auto Dealership decides that he would like to learn more about his customers and about which type of customers are purchasing which types of vehicles so he can segment his advertising better. He decides to keep some simple data on each of his customers and the type of vehicle each has purchased. Since setting up this worksheet, he has sold twelve vehicles, as shown in Figure 16-1.

Here, each row corresponds to the information about a different vehicle that was sold and the customer who purchased it. Column A contains the day of the sale. Column B contains the type of vehicle. The dealership offers three basic models: a family sedan, a sports utility vehicle (SUV), and a convertible. Column C shows the purchase price of the vehicle. And so on.

Figure 16-1. A database in Excel takes the form of a list.

In database terminology, in a list in Excel, a row corresponds to a **record** and a column corresponds to a **field**. The list itself is contained in A4:E16 of the worksheet. Row 4 contains the names of the columns. Note that a list can have only one row of names at the top, so officially row 3 is not part of the list. Each name in the top row of the list must be unique. None of the cells in the top row of the list should be blank.

Excel provides several capabilities for working with lists. We will explore some of those capabilities now.

USING FORMS TO ENTER NEW RECORDS

The *Data* pull-down menu contains the data management commands. If we place the active cell somewhere within the data and then select *Form...* from the *Data* pull-down menu, the dialog box in Figure 16-2 results.

To enter a new record into the list, we press the New button in the *Form...* dialog box. The field items are blanked out and we can enter them one at a time into the form. To move from one box to the next we can either click on the next box or we can press the Tab key. (See Figure 16-3.)

Figure 16-2. This dialog box results from selecting Form... in the Data pull-down menu.

Figure 16-3. Entering new data values in the form.

When we are finished with the final data item of a new record, we can click on New if we have another record to enter or Close if we are finished entering records. In either case, the new record automatically is entered at the bottom of the list in the worksheet. Of course, we could have just entered the information directly in the cells at the bottom of the list, but it wouldn't have been as snazzy or as much fun.

FINDING RECORDS WITH AUTOFILTERS

The list in our worksheet now contains 13 records. It is possible for lists to have up to 65,536 records (the number of rows in a worksheet). We might want to find records that match certain criteria. For example, we might want to find all of the sedans that were purchased by females. Or, we might want to find all the vehicles that were purchased for over $25,000 by people under 25. The easiest approach to finding records in a list is through the use of **AutoFilters**.

To activate AutoFilters, place the active cell somewhere within the list and then select *Filter* in the *Data* pull-down menu. Within the submenu in *Filter* select *AutoFilter*. Small boxes with arrows appear next to the column names in the top row of the list. These are pull-down menus! Click on the arrow and you can see the choices. (See Figure 16-4.)

Figure 16-4. AutoFilters appear as pull-down menus.

If we want to see only the records of sedans purchased by females, we filter the list in two stages. First we find the vehicles purchased by females. Then we find which of those vehicles are sedans. (We could filter in the other order.)

First we click on the *Gender* pull-down menu now located in cell E4 and select *Female*. The result is that only the records of the vehicles purchased by females are shown. Rows in the list that do not have the word Female in column E are hidden. In the worksheet in Figure 16-5 you can see that rows 5, 6, 8, 10, etc. are not shown.

| | File | Edit | View | Insert | Format | Tools | Data | Window | Help | | | | |

	A	B	C	D	E	F	G	H
1			Automobile Purchases					
2								
3				Buyer	Buyer			
4	Day	Model	Pri	A	Genc			
7	1	Sedan	$19,855	45	Female			
9	2	Sedan	$24,419	36	Female			
11	3	Convertible	$33,055	23	Female			
12	3	SUV	$24,441	33	Female			
14	4	Sedan	$20,284	68	Female			
18								
19								
20								
21								
22								
23								
24								
25								

Figure 16-5. The vehicles purchased by females.

Now to show just the sedans purchased by females, we click on the *Model* pull-down menu in cell B4 and select *Sedan*. Only the records for sedans purchased by females will be shown. All other records will be hidden.

To unhide (display) the rows, we can reverse the process. Select *All* in the *Model* pull-down menu and then *All* in the *Gender* pull-down menu. All of the records will be displayed. Or, alternatively, we can select *Filter* in the *Data* pull-down menu and then *Show All* in the submenu.

To find the vehicles that were purchased for over $25,000 by people under 25, we first make sure all of the records are displayed. Then we go into the *Price* pull-down menu in cell C4 and select *(Custom...)* in the menu. In the Custom AutoFilter dialog box we select *is greater than* in the initial menu and then type in 25,000, as in Figure 16-6.

Figure 16-6. Setting a custom AutoFilter.

When we click on OK only the records for the vehicles with price greater than $25,000 are displayed. (See Figure 16-7.)

	A	B	C	D	E	F	G	H
1			**Automobile Purchases**					
2								
3				*Buyer*	*Buyer*			
4	*Day* ▼	*Model* ▼	*Pri* ▼	*A* ▼	*Genc* ▼			
8	2	Convertible	$29,337	62	Male			
10	3	SUV	$31,720	29	Male			
11	3	Convertible	$33,055	23	Female			
13	4	Sedan	$25,962	46	Male			
18								
19								
20								
21								
22								
23								
24								
25								
26								

Figure 16-7. The vehicles that sold for over $25,000.

To display just the records of the vehicles that were purchased for over $25,000 by people under 25, we could now select *(Custom...)* in the *Age* pull-down menu in E4 and then select *is less than* and type in 25. The record for that nice convertible in row 11 will be the only record in the list displayed.

A special feature is the **Top 10** AutoFilter. This AutoFilter allows you to select, for example, the records of the 10 vehicles with the highest prices or the records of the three vehicles sold to the youngest people. The dialog box for Top 10 allows you to change the selection to Top 5 or Bottom 3 or whatever.

Notice that the Custom AutoFilter dialog box has room for two criteria for the field. This allows us to select the vehicles priced greater than 25,000 and less than 40,000. Or, we could select the vehicles with Model equal to Sedan or equal to Convertible.

AutoFilters hide rows, but the rows still are there in the worksheet. If you do calculations on a column, the hidden values will be included in the calculation. For example, if in cell C20 we put the formula =SUM(C5:C17), all vehicle prices will be included in the calculation, not just the vehicle prices of the records that are showing. To calculate, for example, the average price of the sedans that were sold, we need to use another technique.

To erase the AutoFilter pull-down menus from the worksheet select *Filter* in the *Data* pull-down menu and then select *AutoFilter* in the submenu. The AutoFilter pull-down menus will be erased and the worksheet will return to its original appearance.

SORTING

When we **sort** objects we alphabetize them or put them in numerical order. For example, you might sort the cards in your hand when you are playing gin or Go Fish.

The records in the automobile list already are sorted by day. We could sort them many other ways. To sort a list, click on a cell in the list and then select *Sort...* in the *Data* pull-down menu. The *Sort* dialog box allows us to enter the name of the column that is to serve as the main basis for the sort. This field is known as the **primary key** for the sort. In Figure 16-8 we have selected *Model* as the primary key and indicated to Excel that we would like the models listed in ascending order (A to Z). The box below in the dialog box allows us to enter a **secondary key**. The secondary key is the field that is to serve as a "tie-breaker". The question is, in what order should we put all of the vehicles of the same model type? In the dialog box in Figure 16-8 we specify that the secondary key should be *Price* and that we want all of the vehicles of each model sorted by price in descending order. (Notice that the Sort dialog box also has a box available for a **tertiary key**, a field to use to sort records that have the same values for both the primary key and the secondary key.)

We click on OK and Excel automatically sorts the records, as shown in Figure 16-9. First come all of the convertibles, then all of the sedans, then all of the SUVs. The convertibles appear in order of descending price and then the sedans appear in order of descending price and then the SUVs appear in order of descending price.

Figure 16-8. Specifying the columns to use for sorting.

	A	B	C	D	E	F	G	H
1			**Automobile Purchases**					
2								
3				Buyer	Buyer			
4	Day	Model	Price	Age	Gender			
5	3	Convertible	$33,055	23	Female			
6	2	Convertible	$29,337	62	Male			
7	4	Sedan	$25,962	46	Male			
8	2	Sedan	$24,419	36	Female			
9	1	Sedan	$22,660	35	Male			
10	5	Sedan	$21,503	42	Male			
11	4	Sedan	$20,284	68	Female			
12	1	Sedan	$19,855	45	Female			
13	5	Sedan	$19,402	34	Male			
14	3	SUV	$31,720	29	Male			
15	4	SUV	$24,747	23	Male			
16	1	SUV	$24,700	21	Male			
17	3	SUV	$24,441	33	Female			

Figure 16-9. The rows sorted by Model and within Model by Price.

SUBTOTALS

Once a list is sorted, we can have Excel add **subtotals** or similar calculations. For example, we might want to find the average price of each model of car that was sold and the average age of the purchaser. To accomplish this, we first click somewhere within the list of data so the active cell is within the list. We select *Subtotals...* in the *Data* pull-down menu. Excel displays the Subtotal dialog box, as in Figure 16-10.

Figure 16-10. Specifying Subtotal calculations.

In the Subtotal dialog box we first select *Model* as the data are sorted on Model and we want to insert a calculation for each different value of Model. Next we indicate that the function we want to calculate for the records of each type of Model is *Average*. We check off Price and Age because these are the fields for which we want to calculate the Average. We check off Summary below data because we want the calculations to appear below each set of data (rather than above). Finally we click on OK. Excel inserts the calculations in the worksheet, as shown in Figure 16-11.

The new row 7 shows us the average price of convertibles and the average age of purchasers of convertibles. These actually are "sub-average" calculations. In the new row 21 we see the Grand Average price of all vehicles and the Grand Average age of all purchasers. The range of each of the calculations is indicated at the left of the worksheet by brackets.

To remove the subtotal calculations we again select *Subtotals...* in the *Data* pull-down menu and click on the Remove All button (see Figure 16-10 again). The worksheet is returned to its prior form.

| | File | Edit | View | Insert | Format | Tools | Data | Window | Help | | | _ 🗗 × |

1 2 3		A	B	C	D	E	F	
	1			Automobile Purchases				
	2							
	3				Buyer	Buyer		
	4	Day	Model	Price	Age	Gender		
	5	3	Convertible	$33,055	23	Female		
	6	2	Convertible	$29,337	62	Male		
	7		**Convertible Average**	$31,196	42.5			
	8	4	Sedan	$25,962	46	Male		
	9	2	Sedan	$24,419	36	Female		
	10	1	Sedan	$22,660	35	Male		
	11	5	Sedan	$21,503	42	Male		
	12	4	Sedan	$20,284	68	Female		
	13	1	Sedan	$19,855	45	Female		
	14	5	Sedan	$19,402	34	Male		
	15		**Sedan Average**	$22,012	43.7			
	16	3	SUV	$31,720	29	Male		
	17	4	SUV	$24,747	23	Male		
	18	1	SUV	$24,700	21	Male		
	19	3	SUV	$24,441	33	Female		
	20		**SUV Average**	$26,402	26.5			
	21		**Grand Average**	$24,776	38.2			
	22							

Sheet1 / Sheet2 / Sheet3 /

Figure 16-11. The average purchase price and age of purchaser for each model.

PIVOT TABLES

An Excel list can have thousands of rows of data. Often it is difficult to see patterns with all of that data. What we need is a summary of the data. **A pivot table** is a summary of a list of data.

We begin again with the list of data on the vehicles sold and their purchasers. With the active cell somewhere in the list we select *PivotTable and PivotChart Report...* in the *Data* pull-down menu. This calls up the **PivotTable and PivotChart Wizard.** The first screen of the PivotTable and PivotChart Wizard is shown in Figure 16-12.

In the first step, the Wizard asks us the source of the data for the pivot table. We click that it is a *Microsoft Excel List or Database*. Here, we are informing Excel that the data is internal to the current workbook and that it is all located in one list on one worksheet. The Wizard also asks us if we want just a PivotTable or both a PivotTable and a PivotChart. To keep matters simple, we will request just a PivotTable report here.

Figure 16-12. The opening dialog box of the Wizard.

In the second step (Figure 16-13) the PivotTable and PivotChart Wizard correctly figures out the location of the list of data. If necessary, we could correct the guessed location of the list by dragging across it in the worksheet or by simply typing in the correct cell addresses for the range. It is important that the top row of the list, which contains the headings, be included in the range.

Figure 16-13. The Wizard correctly guesses the range of the list.

The third step of the PivotTable Wizard is where the work gets done. This is where we actually specify how we want the data to be summarized in the pivot table we are creating. The initial screen of the dialog box for Step 3 is shown in Figure 16-14. We decide we want the Pivot Table being created to go in its own new worksheet. The checkered flag indicates that this is the final step, but the work is still before us. We still have not specified which data we want to analyze in the Pivot Table and how it should be organized. This is most easily accomplished by clicking on the Layout... button at the bottom of the Step 3 dialog box. This brings up the key screen shown in Figure 16-15.

Figure 16-14. Click on Layout... to specify the Pivot Table.

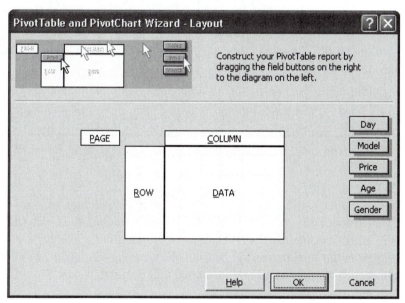

Figure 16-15. The Layout dialog box is key for setting up the Pivot Table.

The different fields or variables in our data list are shown on the right side of the Layout dialog box. The idea is to drag those variables over to the proper locations for the pivot table. For example, suppose we are interested in learning the average ages of the females who purchased convertibles, the females who purchased sedans, the females who purchased SUVs, the males who purchased convertibles, the males who purchased sedans, and the males who purchased SUVs. That is, we want the data summarized in a Model by Gender pivot table that shows the Average Age. In terms of the pivot table, we want Model to be the Rows, Gender to be the Columns, and Average Age to be the Data. To specify this in the dialog box, we drag the

Model box on the right over to the ROW box and release the mouse button. Then we drag the Gender box over to the COLUMN box and the Age box over to the DATA box. The result is the dialog box in Figure 16-16.

Figure 16-16. Informing the Wizard how we want the data summarized.

We are almost there. The PivotTable Wizard has guessed that we want to display Sum of Age. We really want to know the Average of Age. We double-click on the Sum of Age box in the middle of the dialog box to modify it. The PivotTable Wizard now displays the PivotTable Field dialog box. We click on *Average* instead of *Sum* in the Summarize by: box, as in Figure 16-17. Also, we click on Number… and specify that the values be formatted to 2 decimal places.

Figure 16-17. We want Average of Age.

Now when we click on OK the PivotTable Wizard knows we want to display the average age of the purchasers. We click on OK and then Finish, and the PivotTable Wizard produces the pivot table in Figure 16-18 for us.

Figure 16-18. The pivot table provides a very useful summary of the data.

In the pivot table we see the data summarized for us just as we requested. This is a Model by Gender analysis. Each cell in the table indicates the average age of the purchasers. For example, B6 tells us that the average age of the females who purchased sedans is 49.67. Note that the cells in the pivot table contain numbers and not formulas. If any of the values are changed or if new rows are added, we must call up the PivotTable Wizard again to generate an updated pivot table. However, we can **drill-in** to the data by double-clicking on one of the cells. For example, if we double-click on cell B6 we automatically get the table in new worksheet Sheet5 shown in Figure 16-19.

Figure 16-19. Double-clicking on B6 causes Excel to show the data that determine the cell.

With the PivotTable Wizard we could summarize the data in many different ways simply by dragging different variables over to the different locations in the Layout dialog box. In this example we have only 5 columns and 13 rows of data. We could have 50 columns and 13,000 rows of data to summarize. In this case we might want a more detailed analysis. For example, we might want to separate out the analysis of the males from the analysis of the females, so that the analysis of the males appeared in one area and the analysis of the females appeared in another. In step 3 we would drag the Gender box over to the PAGE box. We would be adding a third dimension to the pivot table.

COMPUTER EXERCISES

16-1. Enter the real estate worksheet in Figure 1-3 (in Chapter 1).

(a) Use Form to enter in a new home: 18 Elm Street, 4 bedrooms, 2 baths, 0.5 acres, Oil heat, 17 years old, on the market for $259,900.

(b) Use AutoFilters to display all of the homes with 4 or more bedrooms.

(c) Use AutoFilters to display all of the homes that heat with gas.

(d) Use AutoFilters to display all of the homes that cost between $100,000 and $200,000.

(e) Use AutoFilters to display all of the homes that are on a lot of at least 0.75 acres, heat with oil, and cost under $300,000.

(f) Sort all of the homes in descending order by price.

(g) Sort all of the homes in ascending order by heat type and within each heat type in descending order by number of bedrooms.

(h) Use Subtotals to find the average number of bedrooms, lot size, age, and price of homes of each of the different heat types.

(i) Use the PivotTable Wizard to find the total value of the homes for sale of each heat type and number of bedrooms.

(j) Use the PivotTable Wizard to find the average value of the homes for sale of each heat type and number of bedrooms.

(k) Use the PivotTable Wizard to find the average age of the homes for sale of each heat type and number of baths.

16-2. Susan is a consultant with three different clients: Allied Electronics (AE), Dynamic Solutions (DS), and International Networks (IN). She bills her clients by the hour. She is very busy and tends to switch her attention from one client to another throughout the day. Her principal activities are talking on the phone, having meetings, and working on her computer. In order to be sure that each client is billed fairly, she constantly keeps Excel open on her computer and quickly makes an entry for each period of time she spends:

Client	Minutes	Activity
DS	10	phone
IN	27	computer
DS	8	phone
DS	42	meeting
AE	12	phone
...		

(a) Enter the preceding information into a worksheet.

(b) Use a Form to make 20 more entries into the worksheet.

(c) Use AutoFilters to display only the meetings.

(d) Use AutoFilters to display all the phone calls for AE that exceeded 5 minutes.

(e) Display all of the entries sorted by activity and within each activity sorted by time.

(f) Display all of the entries sorted by client and within each client by activity and within each activity by time.

(g) Use Subtotals to display the total amount of time for each client.

(h) Find the average amount of time of a telephone call.

(i) Use the PivotTable Wizard to display a summary of the total amount of time spent on each activity for each client.

16-3. Create a data list of use to you. Some suggestions for topics: (i) companies in an industry, (ii) summer job prospects, (iii) classmates or professors or roommates or people from high school, (iv) books or video games or music or movies, (v) people you meet.

(a) Design the system. Decide what information to include. Be sure to include at least five fields (columns) total, including at least two numeric fields.

(b) Use a Form to enter at least ten records.

(c) Sort the data on one of the fields.

(d) Print the worksheet.

(e) Change the information in two of the records.

(f) Add four new records.

(g) Sort the records on a different field.

(h) Use Subtotals to display averages and totals for the numeric fields.

(i) Print the worksheet.

(j) Remove the subtotals.

(k) Use AutoFilters to display only some of the records.

(l) Enter in English the criteria used and print the worksheet.

(m) Display all of the records.

(n) Use AutoFilters to display a different set of records.

(o) Enter in English the criteria used and print the worksheet.

(p) Display all of the records.

(q) Use the PivotTable Wizard to create a pivot table. This will work best with fields with limited entries.

(r) Print the pivot table.

CHAPTER 17

ANALYZING DATA USING THE ANALYSIS TOOLPAK

OBJECTIVES

In this chapter you will learn how to:

- Use add-ins
- Access the Analysis ToolPak
- Obtain descriptive statistics on data
- Create histograms of data
- Calculate correlations
- Perform t-tests on data
- Calculate linear regressions

People use Excel to solve a wide variety of problems. One of the most popular applications of Excel is to analyze data. The **Analysis ToolPak** provides additional capabilities for analyzing data.

The Analysis ToolPak is an **add-in** program. An add-in program is a program you can add to Excel to increase its capabilities. The Analysis ToolPak is a third-party add-in, meaning it was developed by an independent company. (Microsoft is the first party; you are the second party.) Microsoft includes the Analysis ToolPak with your purchase of Excel.

GETTING ACCESS TO THE ANALYSIS TOOLPAK

If today is your lucky day then the Analysis ToolPak already will have been added into the Excel on the computer you are using. To determine if this is the case, look in the *Tools* pull-down menu and see if there is an entry toward the bottom of the menu for *Data Analysis...* You might need to wait a few seconds for all of the menu items to show. If you see *Data Analysis...* you can skip the rest of this section.

If *Data Analysis...* is not present in the *Tools* pull-down menu, then the Analysis ToolPak needs to be added in to Excel. In the *Tools* pull-down menu select *Add-Ins...* . You will see a list of the add-ins available on your disk. If you see *Analysis ToolPak* listed, this still is your lucky day. Click on the box next to *Analysis ToolPak*, as in Figure 17-1, and click on OK. The Analysis ToolPak will be added ("attached") to Excel. (Note: Be sure to use the version titled *Analysis ToolPak* rather than *Analysis ToolPak - VBA*. This latter version adds capabilities to Visual Basic in Excel.)

Figure 17-1. Adding in the Analysis ToolPak.

If you do not see *Analysis ToolPak* listed in the add-ins available, then you have a bit more work to do. You need to go back to your original CDs for Excel (or Microsoft Office) and run the Setup program again. Select the Custom option and instruct the Setup program to install the Analysis ToolPak. The reason the Analysis ToolPak might not have been included in the original installation was to save space. Once you have installed the Analysis ToolPak using the Setup program, you can reenter Excel, run the *Add-Ins* selection in the *Tools* pull-down menu as described in the previous paragraph, and you should be ready to make use of the Analysis ToolPak.

WHAT IS IN THE ANALYSIS TOOLPAK?

The Analysis ToolPak adds two types of capabilities to Excel: functions and tools.

Once you attach the Analysis ToolPak you will find some 93 new functions in Excel. These functions now will appear in the Insert Function tool integrated with the original built-in functions. These functions are of five types: Date and Time, Engineering, Financial, Information, and Math and Trig. These functions can be very useful for solving engineering and financial analysis problems.

The second type of capability added by the Analysis ToolPak is 19 statistics tools. These are not traditional built-in functions, but rather tools that analyze data in a worksheet and produce a table of output based on the analysis. It is these tools that are so useful in solving statistical problems.

THE DESCRIPTIVE STATISTICS TOOL

Consider again the real estate worksheet in Figure 17-2. This worksheet lists the homes for sale in a certain town. We are interested in calculating various statistics about the ages and prices of the homes. What is the average age? The standard deviation of the prices? We could calculate each of the statistics in a separate cell by including the appropriate formula. Or, we can use the **Descriptive Statistics tool** in the Analysis ToolPak. We select *Data Analysis...* from the *Tools* pull-down menu. Then we select Descriptive Statistics, as in Figure 17-3.

Excel displays the Descriptive Statistics dialog box (Figure 17-4). We click in the Input Range box and drag across F4:G22 to specify the location of the variables for which we wish to calculate descriptive statistics. We select Columns because the data are organized one variable per column. We notify Excel that the first row in the input range contains descriptive labels that can be used as the names of the variables. We inform Excel that we would like the output of the Descriptive Statistics tool to be placed in a new ply (worksheet). Alternatively we could have the output placed somewhere in this worksheet or in a new workbook. It is very important to check off the Summary Statistics box of the Descriptive Statistics dialog box so that Excel will calculate the full set of statistics.

ADDRESS	BDRMS	BATHS	LOT	HEAT	AGE	PRICE
		CURRENT LISTINGS				
12 Elm Street	5	3	0.4	Gas	48	$290,000
46 Hearthstone Road	5	2	1.2	Oil	3	$345,000
690 Rice Avenue	3	1	0.6	Oil	25	$109,500
90 Bay Road	2	1	0.25	Oil	33	$78,400
455 Nathan Street	2	1	0.3	Elec	16	$51,300
18 Garden Street	2	1	0.4	Elec	12	$62,700
203 Somerset Avenue	4	2	0.3	Gas	98	$159,500
34 Farley Place	7	4	2.3	Oil	52	$560,000
26 Lantern Lane	3	1	0.3	Solar	9	$104,300
11 Panama Street	3	1	0.5	Gas	38	$87,900
155 Auburn Blvd.	5	2	1.0	Oil	5	$269,600
132 Jamaica Way	4	2	0.3	Gas	67	$149,500
315 Fremont Avenue	3	1	0.4	Nuclear	8	$432,800
1322 Bellevue Road	6	3	0.3	Elec	56	$233,500
5 Pond Street	4	3	1.5	Oil	2	$275,400
349 Hill Road	2	1	1.2	Oil	34	$155,600
702 Main Street	6	2	0.3	Gas	85	$179,900
24 Golan Place	4	2	0.8	Oil	15	$189,900

Figure 17-2. The real estate worksheet.

Figure 17-3. Select Descriptive Statistics in the Data Analysis dialog box.

Figure 17-4. The Descriptive Statistics dialog box.

When we click on OK, the computer goes to work and calculates the descriptive statistics for the two columns. The results are placed beginning in A1 in a new worksheet. We widen the columns. The result is shown in Figure 17-5.

Figure 17-5. Descriptive statistics for Age and Price.

We see that the mean age of the homes for sale is 33.67 and that the median age is 29. The standard deviation of the price is $136,316.

There are two important points. First, the computer doesn't care whether or not the statistics are meaningful in this situation. It just follows its program and produces the output. It is up to you, the intelligent and knowledgeable user, to decide how to interpret the calculations and whether they make any sense. Second, notice that the cells in the output area do not contain formulas. They simply contain values, as you can see with cell D7 in Figure 17-5. The Descriptive Statistics tool deposits the numbers there once, when it is called. If you change the original data, the statistics are not recalculated automatically. Each time you want the statistics to be recalculated you must invoke the Descriptive Statistics tool all over again. This is an important difference between using tools and using formulas in cells.

USING THE HISTOGRAM TOOL

The **Histogram tool** allows us to see the distribution of values in a variable. Suppose we would like to examine the distribution of the prices of the homes. First we enter in **bin ranges** in the worksheet. That is, we inform Excel of the break points for the ranges for the histogram. We would like to see how many houses cost under $100,000, how many cost between $100,000 and $200,000 and so on. We enter $0, $100,000, $200,000, ... into cells I6:I11. We select *Data Analysis...* from the *Tools* pull-down menu. Then we select Histogram in the Data Analysis dialog box. (See Figure 17-3 again.) Excel displays the Histogram dialog box. We fill in G4:G22 for the Input Range for the Histogram tool and I6:I11 for the Bin Range, as in Figure 17-6.

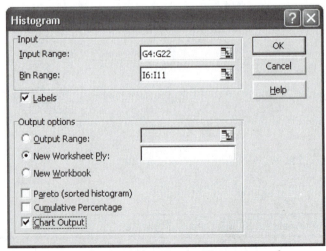

Figure 17-6. The dialog box for the Histogram tool.

In the Histogram dialog box we click on Labels because the top cell of the Input Range contains a label. We click on Chart Output at the bottom of the dialog box to request that the Histogram tool automatically chart the results.

Clicking on OK after filling in the entries as shown in Figure 17-6 automatically produces a new worksheet with the histogram and a chart. We make the chart larger by dragging on the handle in the bottom right corner. The result is shown in Figure 17-7.

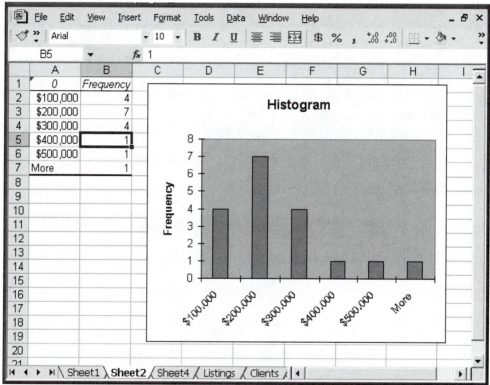

Figure 17-7. The histogram and chart of home prices produced by the Histogram tool.

The histogram in Figure 17-7 is to be understood as saying there are 4 homes with prices under $100,000, 7 homes with prices between $100,000 and $200,000, 4 homes with prices between $200,000 and $300,000, and so on. The numbers in column A of the table and along the horizontal axis of the chart are the highest values of the bins. (The bins work the opposite of the lookup tables discussed in Chapter 12.) The chart is a regular Excel chart that floats above the worksheet. We can select the chart by clicking on it and then make changes in the chart, as discussed in Chapter 10. For example, we could change the wording of a title or the maximum value of the vertical axis.

USING THE CORRELATION TOOL

The tools we have examined so far have treated each variable, each column of data, separately. Suppose we are interested in understanding the interactions between the variables. For example, we might be curious as to how the variables correlate. Do homes with many bedrooms tend to be old? Do expensive homes tend to have large lots? The **Correlation tool** will help us answer these questions.

The Correlation tool, like most of the tools in the Analysis ToolPak, works only on numeric values. With the Correlation tool all of the data must be contiguous. The Heat data in column E of the Real Estate worksheet consist of text rather than numbers. (See Figure 17-2, again.) Before we can use the Correlation tool we need to get the Heat data out of the way. So we select E4:E22 and then move it over to the blank column H by grabbing it at the top of the selected area and dragging it over. Now column E is blank. We select F4:H22 and drag it over to the left one column. The heating column now is in G4:G22 on the right of the data; all of the numeric values are contiguous (next to each other) in the range B4:F22.

In the Correlation tool dialog box in Figure 17-8 we specify that we want to correlate the five variables in columns B, C, D, E, and F. We request a new worksheet with the correlation outputs.

Figure 17-8. Specifying the correlations.

From the output of the Correlation tool in Figure 17-9 we can see that the number of bathrooms correlates very highly (0.86) with the number of bedrooms. The price of the home correlates highly with bedrooms, baths, and lot size but not at all with the age of the home.

Notice, again, that the cells in the correlation matrix contain numbers rather than formulas. Changing the original data will not cause the correlation matrix values to be changed automatically. Rather, we would need to run the Correlation tool each time we change the data.

Figure 17-9. The correlations between the variables.

USING A t-TEST TOOL

Elite athletic shoes sell for $19.99 at discount stores. The manufacturer would like to know how the Elite shoes compare with the $99 well-known brand available at upscale stores at the mall. The manufacturer decides to perform a simple test. He recruits a dozen students and gives them a pair of Elite shoes and a pair of the well-known shoes in their size. The students examine and then try out each pair of shoes. He then asks each student to rate the shoes between 1 and 5, with 5 being the best score. These scores are recorded in a worksheet (see Figure 17-10).

We would like to test the hypothesis that people rate the shoes the same. To do this we test to see if there is no difference between the means of the scores.

A **t-test** is used to determine whether the means of two sets of samples are equal. In this case we would use a paired two-sample t-test, because one person is responsible for each pair of scores. If we had a dozen people rating one type of athletic shoe and a completely different group of people rating the other brand of shoe, we would not use a paired test.

In the *Tools* pull-down menu we select *Data Analysis...* and then t-Test: Paired Two Sample for Means. We fill in the entries, as in Figure 17-11, dragging down the Variable 1 range and then the Variable 2 range.

Clicking on OK yields a new worksheet with output produced by the t-Test: Paired Two Sample for Means tool, as shown in Figure 17-12. Examining this output, we see that the mean score for the Elite shoes is 1.9 whereas the mean for the well-known brand is 3.33.

We asked only a dozen people. Is this difference in the mean statistically significant? Because we had no hypothesis before the study that one brand would score better than the other, it is appropriate to use a "two-tail" test.

Figure 17-10. The raw data for the comparison of two brands of athletic shoes.

Figure 17-11. Specifying the ranges for the t-test.

We see in cell B14 of the worksheet in Figure 17-12 that the critical value of t for a two-tail test with this number of degrees of freedom is 2.20. The value of t calculated for these scores is 3.56, which is greater than 2.20. Thus, the difference between the two sets of scores is significant at the 5% level. If these scores were drawn randomly from populations having the same means, means as different as these would occur less than 5% of the time by chance. Looking at cell B13 we see that, indeed, if these scores were drawn randomly from populations having the same means, means as different as these would occur less than 0.45% of the time by chance or less than one out of 200 times. We reject the hypothesis that the Elite athletic shoes will score the same as the well-known brand. The students do not give equal scores to the two brands. This is bad news for the manufacturer of Elite.

	A	B	C
1	t-Test: Paired Two Sample for Means		
2			
3		Elite	Brand
4	Mean	1.9166667	3.33333333
5	Variance	0.9924242	1.15151515
6	Observations	12	12
7	Pearson Correlation	0.1133868	
8	Hypothesized Mean Difference	0	
9	df	11	
10	t Stat	-3.55884	
11	P(T<=t) one-tail	0.002241	
12	t Critical one-tail	1.7958837	
13	P(T<=t) two-tail	0.004482	
14	t Critical two-tail	2.2009863	
15			
16			

Figure 17-12. The t-test result.

USING THE REGRESSION TOOL

International Financial hires recent college graduates to work on commission selling financial securities to the general public. Hiring has been a hit-and-miss affair. Some of the people hired have done very well; some have fizzled in the first year. Bringing new people on board is expensive. The VP of Sales and the Director of Hiring would like to get a handle on who succeeds and who does not. They would like to find out what factors, if any, they could use in predicting how well a person would do as a new hire. They brainstorm. They decide they like to hire athletes and students who are go-getters and report making a lot of money during the previous summer. They come up with four measures that might predict how well a person would do in the sales position: grade point average (GPA) in college, the number of sports teams a person played on in college, the amount of money the person earned in the previous summer, and how well the person did in the job interview (a number between 1 and 10, where 10 is the best, that is given by the interviewer). Last year they hired ten new people. They decide to list each of these measures for each person as well as the person's total sales in the first year. These data are given in the worksheet in Figure 17-13.

		GPA	Sports	Summer	Interview	First Year Sales
6	1	2.7	3	$0	2	$100,000
7	2	3.6	0	$1,500	5	$30,000
8	3	2.4	5	$8,500	7	$9,800,000
9	4	3.6	1	$2,000	3	$200,000
10	5	2.6	7	$6,300	9	$7,450,000
11	6	3.2	0	$3,100	6	$1,300,000
12	7	3.7	0	$0	5	$65,000
13	8	2.9	0	$1,000	7	$300,000
14	9	3.0	1	$4,000	2	$2,604,000
15	10	3.3	0	$2,900	6	$80,000

Figure 17-13. Recent hires at International Financial.

The **Regression tool** performs linear regression analysis. That is, it fits a line through a set of measures using the least squares method. Regression calculates an equation for predicting the sales performance of an employee based on the four measures given.

We call up the Regression tool by selecting *Data Analysis...* from the *Tools* pull-down menu and then selecting Regression from the list of Tools available. In the Regression dialog box we fill in the location of the Sales data for the Input Y Range and the four measures for the Input X Range. (See Figure 17-14.) The ranges either can be typed in or you can click in the box for a range in the dialog box and then drag across the appropriate cells in the worksheet. The dialog box temporarily rolls up like a window shade to get out of the way and then unrolls when you are finished.

Figure 17-14. Specifying the variables for regression analysis.

Clicking on OK yields the output in Figure 17-15. There is a lot of information here. Starting at the top, in cell B4 we see that the multiple correlation coefficient R is 0.976, which is quite high. The value of R Square is 0.953 so the four factors account for more than 95% of the variance. The Y values are sales that are in the hundreds of thousands or millions, so the sums of squares in the analysis of variance table in C12:D14 are large numbers. Because the columns are narrow and the values are large, the numbers are displayed rounded off in **E format**. The "E" stands for "exponent" or power of 10. The number 2.67E+13 in D12 is 2.67 * 10^13 or 2.67 * 10000000000000. The exact value in D12 is 26716835260031.4, which is displayed in the formula bar in Figure 17-15.

In the bottom part of the worksheet we see the effect of each of the four measures. We see from the coefficients in B17:B21 that the optimal linear formula for predicting the amount of sales that a first-year hire will make is approximately

= -522052*GPA + 460333*Sports + 825*Summer + 84704*Interview + 168836

Notice that the GPA has a negative coefficient. A recruit's Grade Point Average is associated negatively with sales. That is, the lower the GPA, the higher the sales! For each additional Sport that the person played, the formula predicts an additional $460,333 in First Year Sales. Each dollar the person made over the summer results in a predicted additional $825 in First Year Sales. Each point on the Interview is predicted to be worth an additional $84,704 in First Year Sales.

Figure 17-15. The output of the Regression tool.

When we go back and plug the linear equation into column J, we can see what the predictions would be for the existing hires. (See Figure 17-16.) Even though according to our calculations we have done extremely well in predicting the first-year sales, there is plenty of error made in the predictions. Still, the formula comes close on the big winners among the salespeople, which probably is what we are most concerned about. We'd like more $8,000,000 sellers. According to the formula, some of the recent hires are predicted to have negative sales. No one actually had negative sales, but these folks had very low actual first year sales and might do better in other jobs.

Once we have the equation, we use it in Figure 17-16 to predict the sales of new candidates. Candidate A has very low grades, played lots of sports, earned a lot of money last summer, and did very well on the interview. Candidate A is predicted to be a great salesperson. Candidate B was a straight A student, played no sports, made no money last summer, and did not do very well in the interview. According to our regression model, all four factors are the kiss of death. Candidate C is a middling prospect.

Figure 17-16. Using the regression equation to predict the sales of three new candidates.

Also listed is "null". Notice from cell B17 in Figure 17-16 and from the prediction formula that the intercept is 168836. That is, if all of the four measures are 0, the candidate is predicted to have first-year sales of $168,836. If you wish, you can force the intercept to 0 by clicking on the Constant is 0 box in the Regression dialog box. Of course, this would result in different values for the four variable coefficients.

PAPER AND PENCIL EXERCISE

17-1. How might you go about investigating each of the following situations? For each situation you should: (1) describe your general approach, (2) describe the exact data collection method you would use, (3) design an Excel workbook (on paper) for analyzing the data, (4) tell exactly which tool(s) or functions you would use in your workbook, (5) specify exactly which results, which cells, you would look at and exactly how they would help you in your analysis of the situation.

(a) An automobile manufacturer would like to know which of five different shades of red paint customers would prefer on next year's model XLT convertible.

(b) A psychologist would like to know whether there is any difference in the mathematical ability of people who are left-handed and people who are right-handed.

(c) A golf magazine would like to investigate the claim of a small manufacturer that its golf ball goes 25 yards farther than does a certain well-known golf ball.

(d) A producer of a popular TV series would like to know whether the viewers want a newly introduced character to be continued on the show or discontinued.

(e) A college admissions office would like to know whether it can predict a student's future success in its college given the information provided by each applicant.

(f) The Orange Growers' Association would like to know whether regularly drinking orange juice helps prevent people from getting colds.

(g) A finance company would like to automate the process of deciding which automobile loan applications it should approve. The finance company has access to all applications to the company for automobile loans over the past 10 years and the performance record of the loans it approved.

COMPUTER EXERCISES

17-2. A basketball coach has heard about visualization and decides it might be just what the team needs to improve its foul shooting. The idea is that in the moment before you take a foul shot you picture in your mind your successfully taking the shot and then the ball going through the hoop. Swish. Visualize success and it will be yours. To test out the idea he has the eleven members of his team shoot 20 foul shots each. Then he spends an hour describing visualization and having his team members try it. The next day at the beginning of practice he reminds them about the visualization technique and has each team member take 20 foul shots. Here are the results.

Player:	A	B	C	D	E	F	G	H	I	J	K
Day 1:	15	12	18	8	9	15	9	15	12	10	16
Day 2:	15	14	17	10	10	15	12	14	15	13	17

Summarize the data. Compare the performances without visualizing on day 1 and with visualizing on day 2. Was there an improvement? Was the improvement statistically significant? What do you conclude?

17-3. The Cranston Apperception Test was administered to 24 students majoring in Computers and 24 students majoring in English. The results were as follows:

Computer Majors
25 27 20 17 17 33 27 23 29 23 26 20 29 14 32 30 26 21 20 26 24 26 32 12

English Majors
21 29 16 7 26 23 21 18 28 18 17 29 31 25 20 32 14 32 26 24 27 23 23 17

(a) Generate descriptive statistics for both sets of data.

(b) Determine if there is any statistically significant difference in the means of the scores of the two groups at the 5% level.

17-4. A beverage company is considering a new fruit drink. To learn whether people like the drink they set up a booth at the mall. If you are willing to tell them your age and annual income, they will give you a free 8-ounce cup of the drink, which you are then asked to rate on a scale from 1 (awful) to 10 (nectar of the gods, best stuff I ever drank). You must be at least 18 years old to participate.

Here are the data they collect. The annual income is in thousands of dollars.

Person	A	B	C	D	E	F	G	H	I	J	K
Age	19	84	23	31	21	52	18	20	28	25	44
Gender	M	M	F	M	F	M	F	F	M	M	F
Income	17	12	22	27	15	34	22	6	30	18	95
Rating	3	5	6	4	7	2	5	5	5	3	7

Person	L	M	N	O	P	Q	R	S	T	U	V
Age	33	20	73	18	25	19	22	24	32	36	68
Gender	F	M	F	F	F	M	M	M	M	F	F
Income	57	19	31	15	32	13	23	26	30	55	28
Rating	9	6	5	6	6	4	5	3	4	8	5

Please enter the data into a worksheet (think about the best organization of the data). Apply the appropriate tools. What do you conclude about the new drink and to whom it appeals? Write up a professional report. Include appropriate worksheets and charts.

17-5. Consider again the real estate data in Figure 17-2. We are interested in constructing an equation to predict the price of a home based on the number of bedrooms, bathrooms, lot size, and age. Use the Regression tool to compute the coefficients of the equation. How good a fit is the equation? Enter the formula into the original worksheet and give the predicted prices for the existing homes. Now use the formula to set the prices of these homes that are about to come on the market:

15 Foxhall Road: 4 bedrooms, 2 baths, 0.6 acres, 15 years old
395 Washington Street: 3 bedrooms, 2 baths, 0.25 acres, 60 years old
24 Columbia Lane: 5 bedrooms, 3 baths, 2.1 acres, 2 years old

Write up a report. Be sure to include the formula, its predictions, and how good a job it does. Indicate how you might include the heating type in the prediction.

17-6. This problem is a little more open-ended. Many people are interested in being able to predict the price of a stock a month from now given data that are publicly available today. Examples of information that might be used include revenues, profits, price per earnings ratios, stock prices, stock volume, industry trends, market trends, and so on. For this assignment you are to come up with a formula that predicts the price of a given stock a month from now using your choice of any data available today. Try your formula by predicting historical results. Write up a report on your findings. If your formula is successful, please email your report, with your formula, to james.gips@bc.edu.

CHAPTER 18

GOAL SEEKING AND SOLVER

OBJECTIVES

In this chapter you will learn how to:

- Solve problems using Goal Seeking
- Do Goal Seeking directly from graphs
- Use the Solver tool to solve profit maximization problems
- Enter constraints into Solver
- Solve linear programming problems with Solver
- Solve transportation problems with Solver

In this final chapter we will be looking at two very powerful tools in Excel, Goal Seeking and the Solver tool.

GOAL SEEKING

Goal Seeking basically allows us to work backward in a worksheet. Suppose in our Computers course the final grade is determined 40% by homeworks and computer exercises, 15% by each of two exams, and 30% by the final exam. Our scores so far are shown in Figure 18-1.

	A	B	C	D	E	F	G	H
1								
2		**Computers Course Grades**						
3								
4					*Weighted*			
5			*Score*	*Weight*	*Score*			
6		Homeworks	95	40%	38.0			
7		Exam 1	80	15%	12.0			
8		Exam 2	78	15%	11.7			
9		Final Exam		30%	0.0			
10								
11		Course Grade			61.7			
12								

Figure 18-1. Our scores before taking the Final Exam.

With only the Final Exam to go, we would like to know what score we need to get on the Final Exam to have a final Course Grade of 90.

We could solve this problem by trial and error. That is, we could enter an initial value of, say, 90 as our score for the Final Exam. If the resulting Course Grade was below 90, we could try 100 for the Final Exam. If the resulting Course Grade was above 90, we could try 95 for the Final Exam, and so on. We could continue making closer and closer estimates of the score we need on the Final Exam for our Course Grade to be 90.

Excel automates this trial-and-error process for us. From the worksheet in Figure 18-1 we select *Goal Seek...* in the *Tools* pull-down menu. We fill in the *Goal Seek* dialog box as in Figure 18-2.

*Figure 18-2. We wish to set E11
to 90 by adjusting C9.*

We tell Excel we would like cell E11 set to 90 by changing cell C9. (Excel automatically changes addresses to absolute references in these dialog boxes.) When we click on OK Excel goes through several iterations of trial and error and then displays the results of its efforts, as shown in Figure 18-3.

	File	Edit	View	Insert	Format	Too...		
	Arial			10	B			
E11			f_x	=SUM(E6:E9				
	A	B	C					

Goal Seek Status

Goal Seeking with Cell E11 found a solution.

Target value: 90
Current value: 90

OK / Cancel / Step / Pause

	A	B	C	D	E
1					
2		Computers Course Grade			
3					
4					
5			Score		
6		Homeworks	95	40%	38.0
7		Exam 1	80	15%	12.0
8		Exam 2	78	15%	11.7
9		Final Exam	94.33333	30%	28.3
10					
11		Course Grade			90
12					

Computers / Biology / Economics / English /

Figure 18-3. The result of the Goal Seeking. We need a 94.33 on the Final Exam.

Excel has found a solution. If we receive a score of 94.333333 on the Final Exam, then our Course Grade will be 90. No problem.

Let's do another example. We would like to purchase a car. The automobile dealer requires 10% of the purchase price as a down payment. The dealer will arrange a loan for the remainder at 9% per year interest to be paid monthly over four years. We decide that the highest loan payment we can afford is $300 per month. We would like to buy this spiffy car that the dealer will let us have for a purchase price of only $17,699. We create a worksheet to help us, as shown in Figure 18-4.

	File Edit View Insert Format Tools Data Window Help					

C12 ▼ *fx* =PMT(C6/12,C7*12,C10)

	A	B	C	D	E	F
1						
2		**Loan Payment for a Car**				
3						
4		Purchase price of car	$17,699			
5		Percent down payment	10%			
6		Annual interest rate for loan	9%			
7		Number of years for loan	4			
8						
9		Down payment	$1,770			
10		Amount to be borrowed	$15,929			
11						
12		Monthly payment	($396.40)			
13						

H ◄ ► H \ **Sheet1** / Sheet2 / Sheet3 /

Figure 18-4. Calculating the monthly loan payment for a car.

The top four cells in the worksheet are input cells. The down payment is 10% of the purchase price. The amount to be borrowed is the difference between the purchase price and the down payment. The monthly payment is calculated using the PMT function, as discussed in Chapter 14.

The bad news is that the monthly payment would be $396.40. What purchase price would result in a $300 per month payment? We select *Goal Seek...* in the *Tools* pull-down menu. We fill in the *Goal Seek* dialog box to inform Excel that we would like to set cell C12 to a value of -300 by changing cell C4, as in Figure 18-5.

Figure 18-5. We can afford to pay $300 per month.

We click on OK and Excel gives us the bad news that the most we can afford is a purchase price of $13,395. (That's why people lease—so they can get a more expensive car for the monthly payment even though they will have to return the car at the end of the lease period.)

GRAPHIC GOAL SEEKING

A nice feature of Excel is the ability to do Goal Seeking graphically. Suppose we decide to open a savings account. We vow that every year, no matter what, we are going to deposit $3,000 into the account. We would like to know how much money we are going to accumulate over each of the next 10 years. We set up the worksheet in Figure 18-6.

C12		f_x =C11+C11*$C$4+$C$3
	A	B	C	D	E	F	G	H	I
1		*Savings Account*							
2									
3	Annual Deposit:		$3,000						
4	Interest Rate:		6%						
5									
6		Year	Amount						
7		start	$3,000						
8		1	$6,180						
9		2	$9,551						
10		3	$13,124						
11		4	$16,911						
12		5	$20,926						
13		6	$25,182						
14		7	$29,692						
15		8	$34,474						
16		9	$39,542						
17		10	$44,915						
18									

Figure 18-6. An account where we deposit the same amount each year.

Each year the amount in the account is the amount in the account at the end of the previous year plus the interest earned for the year plus the amount deposited at the end of the year. This is implemented in the formula displayed in Figure 18-6 for cell C12:

$$=C11 + C11*\$C\$4 + \$C\$3$$

We can graph the progress of our account using the Chart Wizard. We select B6:C17 and click on the Chart Wizard icon (see Chapter 10). We go through the ChartWizard, reset the vertical axis so the maximum value is $100,000, and end up with the chart displayed in Figure 18-7.

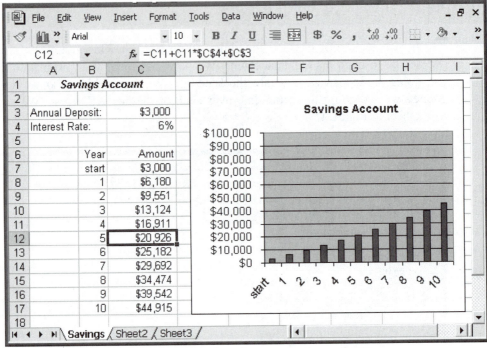

Figure 18-7. Showing the increasing value of our account as a chart.

Now we decide that we would like to have $100,000 at the end of 10 years and not a measly $44,915. We click on the chart to select it and then click on the rightmost bar to select the data series and then click again on the rightmost bar to select just that last data point. Small black squares appear around the bar to indicate it is selected. We drag the top of the rightmost bar, as indicated in Figure 18-8, upward to $100,000 where it belongs.

Figure 18-8. Select the rightmost bar and drag it up to $100,000.

Excel automatically displays the Goal Seek dialog box (see Figure 18-9).

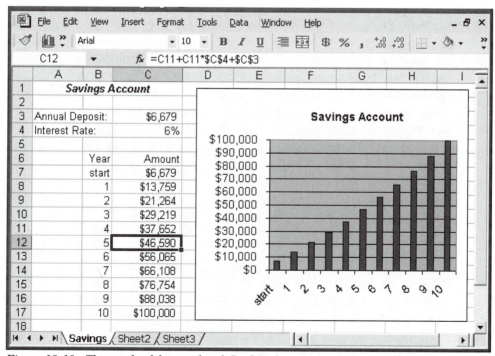

Figure 18-9. Reaching for $100,000.

We have two choices for the cell we want to change to fulfill our investment objective. Either we can change the amount we deposit or we can change the interest rate we receive. Unfortunately, the interest rate is somewhat out of our control so we enter C3, the amount deposited each year, as the cell to change. When we click OK, Excel goes through its iterative goal seeking and informs us that we will need to deposit $6,679 each year in order to reach our goal of $100,000 in 10 years. (See Figure 18-10.)

Figure 18-10. The result of the graphical Goal Seeking is that cell C3 has been changed to the amount we need to deposit each year to meet our goal of $100,000 in ten years.

SOLVER

The **Solver** tool is even more powerful and flexible than Goal Seeking. Solver can maximize or minimize the value of a cell in addition to setting a cell to a target value. Solver can change the values of several cells, not just one, to accomplish its goal. Solver can do its work subject to various constraints, or conditions, that we specify.

Solver is an add-in. As discussed at the beginning of Chapter 17 for the Analysis ToolPak, an add-in is a specialized feature of Excel that, because not everyone might want to use it and it takes up valuable space, is not automatically included when you run Excel on your computer. To see whether you have Solver ready to use, look in the *Tools* pull-down menu. About half way down in the *Tools* pull-down menu you should see *Solver...* If Solver is not present, select *Add-Ins...* in the *Tools* pull-down menu. Scroll down through the add-ins until you see *Solver Add-In*. Click on the box to the left of *Solver Add-In* so the box is selected. Solver will be added into Excel. If you do not see *Solver* in the list of add-ins, then you will have to go to the trouble of finding your original Excel or Microsoft Office CDs and custom installing Solver from there into the Excel on your computer.

USING SOLVER TO MAXIMIZE PROFITS

As a first example, let's do a simple maximization problem. We decide to publish an "Uncensored Guide to Courses and Faculty" where students give their honest opinions about specific courses and faculty, their recommendations (or warnings) to other students who are thinking about what courses to register for. We believe that if we gave the Guide away for free, we could give away 10,000 copies. For every $1.00 we charge for the Guide, we estimate that 1,000 fewer people will purchase it. So that if we charge $3.00 per copy, we figure we will sell 7,000 copies. If we charge $4.00 per copy, we figure we will sell 6,000 copies. We expect to have fixed expenses of $5,000 for manuscript preparation, delivery, promotion, and distribution. Each Guide will cost us $2.25 to print and bind. We would like to know the best price to charge for the Guide so we can make the most profit. We set up the worksheet in Figure 18-11 to help us.

Just for convenience, the formulas in the worksheet are included in text boxes to the right of the cells. We see that if we set the price at $4.00, we will sell 6,000 copies and end up with a profit of $5,500. Not bad. But we would like to find the price that will yield the maximum profits under these assumptions. We can't use Goal Seeking because we don't have a particular profit we want to achieve. We just want to find the price that results in the highest profit. We could use trial and error, changing cell D4 until we maximize D17, but that would be tedious.

Figure 18-11. Calculating the profits for our Uncensored Guide.

We select *Solver...* from the *Tools* pull-down menu. The Solver Parameters dialog box in Figure 18-12 is displayed. In the dialog box we specify that D17 is the Target cell and, on the next line, that we want to maximize the value in D17. We will allow Solver to change only D4.

Figure 18-12. Giving specifics to Solver.

When we click on the Solve button, Solver goes to work and in short order reports back its success (see Figure 18-13).

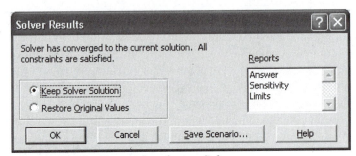

Figure 18-13. The results of using Solver.

Click on OK and we are returned to the original worksheet, but now cell D4 is changed so that the value in D17 is maximized. From Solver we learn that under these assumptions we should charge $6.12 per Guide and print up 3,875 copies. This will result in profits of $10,016. (See Figure 18-14.)

	A	B	C	D	E	F	G
1							
2			**Uncensored Guide to Courses and Faculty**				
3							
4	*Inputs*		Price per Booklet	$6.12			
5			Printing Cost per Booklet	$2.25			
6			Fixed Expenses	$5,000			
7							
8							
9	*Calculations*		Number of Booklets Sold	3,875	=10000-D4*1000		
10							
11			Revenues	$23,734	=D4*D9		
12					=D6		
13			Fixed Expenses	$5,000	=D5*D9		
14			Variable Expenses	$8,719			
15			Total Expenses	$13,719	=D13+D14		
16							
17	*Bottom Line*		Profits	$10,016	=D11-D15		
18							

Figure 18-14. Using Solver to adjust the Price per Booklet to maximize Profits.

USING SOLVER FOR A LINEAR PROGRAMMING PROBLEM

In our small manufacturing company we make grommits and widgets. Each grommit requires 4 hours of metal work and 2 hours of electrical work. Each widget requires 3 hours of metal work and 1 hour of electrical work. For each grommit we make we earn $70 of profit. For each widget we make we earn $50 of profit. This week, given our employees and equipment, we will have 240 hours of metal work available and 100 hours of electrical work. The question is, how many grommits and how many widgets should we make in order to maximize our profit?

This problem is an example of a **linear programming** problem. We have a quantity we want to maximize, in this case profits. We have **constraints**, or restrictions, on the solution. In this case we have limits on the number of hours of metal work and electrical work available. We have a range of possible solutions to the problem. The objective and constraints can all be expressed in linear equations or inequalities. There are no exponents in any of the formulas.

Linear programming has been studied for over 50 years. Linear programming techniques are applicable in many different types of problems. Solver provides a powerful and easy-to-use tool for solving many linear programming problems.

To solve this production problem we set up a worksheet that contains all of the calculations. (See Figure 18-15.)

Figure 18-15. Setting up a production problem for Solver.

In the worksheet, cells with data values that have been entered (C5:D6, G10:G11, and C13:D13) have a thin border. Cells with values that are to be determined by Solver (C8:D8) have a thick border. Cells with values that are calculated by formulas have no border, as shown in Figure 18-16.

Figure 18-16. The formulas in the production worksheet.

We want to find the best values for C8 and D8, the number of grommits and widgets to manufacture so that we maximize the value in E16, the Total Profit for the week. However, we have the added constraints that the value in F10, the hours of metal work required, must not exceed G10, the number of metal work hours available, and that the value in F11, the hours of electrical work required, must not exceed the number in G11, the hours of electrical work available.

We currently show 10 grommits and 10 widgets being made, yielding a profit of $1,200. However, we have many hours of metal work and electrical work that are not being utilized. We should increase the number of grommits and widgets we plan to make. But by how much? We could enter different numbers by hand and try to maximize the profit by trial and error. Instead, let's use Solver.

We select *Solver...* from the *Tools* pull-down menu. Excel displays the Solver Parameters dialog box, as before. (See Figure 18-17.) We fill in E16 as the cell to maximize by changing cells C8 and D8. The addresses of the cells that can be changed are separated by commas. There can be as many as 200 cells for Solver to be able to change! We have only two in this problem.

Figure 18-17. Beginning to fill in Solver parameters.

Now we have some constraints to add. We click on Add in the Constraints portion of the dialog box. We are confronted with the Add Constraint dialog box. We enter the constraint F10 <= G10, as shown in Figure 18-18.

Figure 18-18. The dialog box for adding constraints.

We click on Add. The constraint automatically is entered into the Constraints field of the Solver Parameters dialog box. We fill in the constraint F11 <= G11 and click on Add, entering the second constraint.

It may not be obvious, but we have more constraints to add. The values in C8 and D8 must be greater than or equal to 0. That is, we cannot make a negative number of grommits or widgets even if it would help maximize profits. So we add the constraints C8 >= 0 and D8 >= 0. We might also want to require that C8 and D8 be integers, that is, that we do not make 3.25 grommits in a week. We could do this by clicking on C8 for the first field of the Add Constraint dialog box (or by typing C8) and then using the arrow in the operator pull-down menu in the middle of the dialog box to select *int*, as shown in Figure 18-19. We are allowed to specify up to 100 different constraints for Solver.

Figure 18-19. Specifying that C8 must be an integer.

After a constraint is specified in the Add Constraint dialog box, a click on Add will enter the constraint and keep you in the Add Constraint dialog box to enter another constraint. A click on OK will enter the constraint and bring you back to the Solver Parameter dialog box, as in Figure 18-20. Note again that Excel automatically adds $ signs so that all of the addresses are absolute references.

Figure 18-20. The final set of parameters for the production problem.

We click on Solve and Solver goes to work. In short order Solver reports back its success. (See Figure 18-21.)

Figure 18-21. Solver has found an optimal solution.

If we would like, Solver will give us three reports on its work: an Answer report, a Sensitivity report, and a Limits report. We can select the reports we want to see by clicking on the report names in the field in the right side of the dialog box in Figure 18-21. If we want more than one report, we hold down the Ctrl or Control key while clicking. The reports will be inserted into new sheets immediately before the worksheet that contains the data. We select the Answer report and click on OK. The original worksheet is displayed with Solver's solutions entered into C8 and D8. (See Figure 18-22.)

| | File | Edit | View | Insert | Format | Tools | Data | Window | Help | | | _ ◻ × |

E16 ▼ *fx* =C15+D15

	A	B	C	D	E	F	G
1	A production problem -- How many grommits and widgets should we make to maximize profit?						
2							
3			Grommits	Widgets			
4							
5		Hours metal work per unit	4	3			
6		Hours electrical work per unit	2	1			
7						Total	Total
8		Units to make	30	40		Hours	Hours
9						Required	Available
10		Total hours metal work	120	120		240	240
11		Total hours electrical work	60	40		100	100
12							
13		Profit per unit	$70	$50			
14							
15		Profit	$2,100	$2,000			
16		Total Profit			$4,100		
17							

Answer Report 1 \ **Sheet1** / Sheet2 / Sheet3

Figure 18-22. Solver's solution.

Solver has found that if we make 30 Grommits and 40 Widgets this week, we will produce a maximal Total Profit of $4,100. With this solution, we utilize all of the metal work and electrical work capacity available, namely 240 hours of metal work and 100 hours of electrical work.

Clicking on the sheet tab for Answer Report 1 shows the worksheet in Figure 18-23. This worksheet summarizes the results of solving the linear programming problem. As you can see in Figure 18-23, cell E8 contains the final optimal Total Profit found. The cell contains a number, 4100, rather than a formula. If we want to change some of the data values in the original worksheet in Figure 18-16, we would need to run Solver again to produce a new optimal solution.

Figure 18-23. The Answer Report from Solver.

USING SOLVER ON A TRANSPORTATION PROBLEM

We have three warehouses: in San Diego, Dubai, and Dublin. We have orders from customers in London, Delhi, Lagos, Seoul, and Auckland that need to be filled. Which customers should we ship to from which warehouse? The situation is summarized in the worksheet in Figure 18-24.

In the top half of the worksheet we see the cost of shipping from each warehouse to each customer. For example, it costs $50 per unit to ship from our warehouse in Dubai to the customer in Delhi.

In the bottom half of the worksheet we have quantity information. At the very bottom, in row 17, is the total number of units needed by each customer. We can see that the customer in Delhi ordered 400 units. On the right, in H12:H14 we see the number of units in each warehouse. We currently have 1400 units in Dublin. The cells in B12:F14 currently contain 1's. These are the values we need to fill in, or rather that Solver will be filling in. These are the values that dictate how many units will be shipped from each warehouse to each customer.

Figure 18-24. A transportation problem. How many units should be shipped from each warehouse to each destination?

The key cell is H5. This cell calculates the total cost of all the shipping, the value we want to minimize. The formula in H5 could be

$$= B12*B5 + C12*C5 + D12*D5 + E12*E5 + F12*F5 + B13*B6 + C13*C6 + D13*D6 + E13*E6 + F13*F6 + B14*B7 + C14*C7 + D14*D7 + E14*E7 + F14*F7$$

Alternatively, the formula in H14 can use the **SUMPRODUCT** function

$$=SUMPRODUCT(B12:F14,B5:F7)$$

This formula calculates the sum of B12*B5 plus C12*C5 and so on, just as in the preceding formula.

There are 15 cells to be filled in (B12:F14) so that the value in H5 is minimized. Plus there are various constraints that must be satisfied. This is a problem for Solver.

The key in setting up any worksheet for Solver is to be sure all of the input values are included in separate cells and that all of the formulas needed are included, especially the formula for calculating the value that is to be minimized or maximized.

We select *Solver...* in the *Tools* pull-down menu. In the Solver Parameters dialog box, we indicate that the target cell is H5 and that we want the value in the cell to be minimized by changing the cells in B12:F14. Excel allows us to use ranges in both the By Changing Cells: entry and also in the constraints. The first constraint is

$$\$B\$12:\$F\$14 = Integer$$

All the values set from B12 through F14 must be integers. We can't ship fractions of units. The second constraint is

$$\$B\$12:\$F\$14 >= 0$$

We can only ship positive numbers of units. The third constraint is

$$\$B\$15:\$F\$15 = \$B\$17:\$F17$$

This constraint specifies that B15 must equal B17, C15 must equal C17, and so on. That is, that the number of units shipped to each customer must be the same as the number ordered by the customer. The final constraint is

$$\$G\$12:\$G\$14 <= \$H\$12:\$H\$14$$

That is, from each warehouse we can ship at most the number of units in the warehouse. The final Solver Parameters dialog box is shown in Figure 18-25.

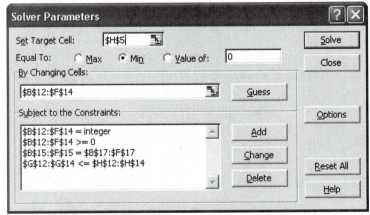

Figure 18-25. The Solver Parameters dialog box for the transportation problem.

We click on Solve and in a short time we obtain the solution shown in Figure 18-26.

Figure 18-26. The optimal solution found by Solver.

Note that Lagos is to receive units from all three warehouses.

Excel contains many powerful features. The key is to use them wisely.

COMPUTER EXERCISES

18-1. (From Exercise 2-21) The Body Mass Index (BMI) often is used by scientists and physicians to determine whether a person is underweight or overweight. The BMI is calculated as follows:

Step 1.   Multiply your body weight in pounds by 0.45.
Step 2.   Multiply your height in inches by 0.025.
Step 3.   Square the answer from Step 2.
Step 4.   Divide the answer from Step 1 by the answer from Step 3.

A healthy BMI is between 19 and 25. The BMI is said to work equally well for both men and women. Create a worksheet to calculate a person's BMI. There should be four values entered into the worksheet: the person's name, the person's weight in pounds, and the person's height in feet and inches. The worksheet should calculate the total height in inches, the values for each of the steps, and then prominently show the resulting BMI. The worksheet should display "Healthy weight", "Underweight", or "Overweight" in a separate cell based on the value of the BMI.

(a) Try your worksheet on the following people: (i) Jan, 115 pounds, 5 feet 8 inches; (ii) Fran, 325 pounds, 5 feet 1 inch; (iii) Dana, 240 pounds, 6 feet 4 inches; and (iv) Slim, 104 pounds, 5 feet 6 inches.

(b) Use Goal Seeking to determine (i) the weight that would result in a person who is 6 feet 4 inches having a BMI of 22, (ii) the lowest healthy weight for a person who is 5 feet 8 inches (BMI of 19), and (iii) the highest healthy weight for a person who is 5 feet 8 inches (BMI of 25).

18-2. United Manufacturing is planning on spending up to $4,000,000 on new automated assembly machinery. They have decided to purchase two different models of equipment and are trying to decide how many of each model they should purchase. The F300 model costs $350,000 each. The S250 model costs $220,000 each. The F300 has some extra features so at least one third of the models purchased should be the F300. The annual maintenance budget for the new equipment is set at $120,000. The annual maintenance cost of each F300 is $12,000. The annual maintenance cost of each S250 is $7,500. Each F300 will produce 125 units per day. Each S250 will produce 81 units per day. Set up a worksheet and then use Solver to determine how many of each model to purchase so that the daily production is maximized as long as the other constraints are met.

18-3. Seven new projects are being proposed for our division. Each would require investments over the next three years, but each ultimately would result in a positive return on our investment.

Project	Year 1	Year 2	Year 3	Return in $ Millions
A	5	1	8	20
B	4	7	9	36
C	3	8	4	28
D	3	9	2	20
E	7	4	1	18
F	3	2	3	12
G	6	8	9	40

Expenditures in $ Millions

The CEO has decided that we have a maximum of $25 million each year to invest. Just on the basis of the numbers, which combination of projects should we invest in so that the sum of the returns is maximized? Set up a worksheet and use Solver to come up with a solution. You should set up the worksheet so there is a cell for each project that contains either a 1 (meaning we invest in the project) or a 0 (meaning we do not invest in the project). Solver should find the combination of 1's and 0's that maximizes the sum of the returns subject to the constraints.

18-4. The Always Open Restaurant is, as the name implies, open 24 hours a day. It is always reasonably busy, but it is busier at some times than at others. Waiters work 8-hour shifts beginning at Midnight, 4 AM, 8 AM, Noon, 4 PM, or 8 PM. Management has decided that the minimal number of waiters required for each 4-hour period during the day is as follows:

Midnight to 4 AM	3
4 AM to 8 AM	10
8 AM to Noon	8
Noon to 4 PM	16
4 PM to 8 PM	14
8 PM to Midnight	8

Management would like to know how many waiters should begin their 8-hour shifts at each of the possible times, so that there is at least the minimum required waiters for each shift yet the fewest waiters possible hired.

18-5. The Greentree Financial Management Group manages funds for institutional clients. A pension fund has placed $100,000,000 with the Group. The Research Department at the Group identifies eight types of investments and rates them as follows:

	Expected Annual Yield	Risk Factor
Common stocks - aggressive	12%	2
Common stocks - growth	9%	1.5
Common stocks - conservative	7%	1
Corporate bonds	6%	0.5
Commodities	15%	3
Government bonds	4%	0
Real estate	15%	2.5
Venture capital	40%	5

The pension fund management would like the risk factor for the portfolio as a whole to be less than or equal to 1. Of course, given that constraint, they would like to maximize the yield for the entire portfolio.

Use Solver to find the best allocation of funds among the eight types of investments assuming the validity of the analyses supplied by Research. What is the expected annual yield of the entire portfolio?

18-6. We have three factories (A, B, C) and five distributors (P, Q, R, S, T) of our products. The products are shipped by truck from factory to distributor. At most 180 units of our product fit in a truck. The shipping cost is $1 per unit to load the truck and $1 per unit to unload the truck plus the mileage cost. The mileage cost is based on the mileage the truck must travel between the factory and the distributor. The mileage cost is independent of how many units are in the truck. The mileage cost is the same whether there are five units in the truck or 180 units, namely $15 per mile. The maximum monthly productions of the factories are: A 4000 units, B 2000 units, and C 1500 units. The monthly demands by the distributors are: P 1000 units, Q 1600 units, R 1500 units, S 2000 units, and T 1400 units. The mileage chart of the distances between factories and distributors is:

			Distributors		
Factories	P	Q	R	S	T
A	100	140	200	150	35
B	50	65	60	70	80
C	40	150	100	90	130

Use Solver to determine the number of units to send each month from each factory to each distributor so as to minimize the total shipping costs. Your worksheet also should show the number of trucks to send from each factory to each distributor and the total shipping cost.

INDEX